Jesus, Son of God, Son of Mary, Immanuel

Donald J. Goergen, O.P.

A Michael Glazier Book
THE LITURGICAL PRESS
Collegeville, Minnesota

A THEOLOGY OF JESUS
Volume 4

A Michael Glazier Book published by The Liturgical Press

Cover design by Mary Jo Pauly

The Scripture quotations contained herein are from the Revised Standard Version Bible, Catholic edition, © 1957 by the Division of Christian Education of the National Council of Churches of Christ in the USA. Used by permission. All rights reserved.

1   2   3   4   5   6   7   8

Library of Congress Cataloging-in-Publication Data

Goergen, Donald.
    Jesus, Son of God, Son of Mary, Immanuel / Donald J. Goergen.
        p.   cm. — (A theology of Jesus ; v. 4)
    "A Michael Glazier book."
    Includes bibliographical references.
    ISBN 0-8146-5520-3
    1. Jesus Christ—Person and offices. I. Title. II. Series:
Goergen, Donald. Theology of Jesus ; v. 4.
BT202.G566   1995
232'.8—dc20
                                    95-20357
                                      CIP

To Stan, Ann, and Francine

Contents

Preface

In the preface to the first volume of this series, I raised Jesus' question: "Who do you say that I am?" (Mark 8:29). A response to that question requires historical, theological, and personal reflection. The first two volumes in this series were an interpretation of the earthly Jesus, or more precisely, the Jesus of historiography. The third volume was an interpretation of the Christian tradition's understanding of Jesus—the Jesus of faith or the Jesus of Christian history.

This fourth and final volume presupposes the previous volumes and relies upon them. In the light of both historiographical research and faith, who do we say that Jesus is? We have indicated in the previous volumes both the importance and necessity of historiography and its insufficiency. Ultimately Jesus is meta-historiographical. He requires theology in order to be understood. And this reveals that ultimately history is also meta-historiographical. It, too, requires theology for its interpretation. Historiography and theology must be partners in the quest for Jesus if we desire the truth about him.

Originally I had projected five volumes for this series. However, with this volume the series comes to a close. Nevertheless, the quest for Jesus continues. It is never ending, since it takes us into the very heart of God and the depths of ourselves and the human community.

We will see Jesus in this volume as the risen Christ, the incarnate Word, the prophet and sage from Galilee, the crucified Savior, Son of God, son of Mary, Immanuel—and we could go on and on. As I said in volume 1, Christology is an invitation to an encounter.

This volume represents a constructive or creative moment in doing Christology. In volume 1 I referred to this as the third task in doing Christology, namely, hermeneutical reconstruction. It represents personal conviction. Who do I say that Jesus is? "His name shall be Immanu-el" (Isa 7:14).

The projected fifth volume was to concern itself with the social and political implications of Christology. Some of these are evident from the preceding volumes. Further exploration into the issues of class, gender, race, religion, and spirituality require more attention than one volume can give and also a different methodology, namely, that of contextual theology. Thus the search for Christ does not come to a close, but simply opens up new vistas, sets us off on new journeys, and invites new approaches and dialogues. I still hope to pursue these issues further with other formats. Christology in the end must be socially as well as professionally and ecclesially responsible. Christology is also an invitation to a way of life, the path of discipleship. To know Jesus in truth is to follow him.

There are many to whom I am indebted. My intellectual pursuit of the truth about Jesus Christ as well as my personal experience of him both have long histories. I thank God for the many who have helped me and been with me in my life journey with Jesus. I thank in particular Stan Drongowski for his constant and faithful friendship, Ann Willits for her compassionate and unsurpassable encouragement, and Frances Plass for her years of generosity and service.

1

Christology Reconsidered

Biblical, critical, and historiographical research have given us various interpretations of the historical Jesus of Nazareth. This same research has invited us or forced us to make some decision vis-à-vis the resurrection of Jesus. Research can bring us face-to-face with the question of the resurrection of Jesus, but it cannot make the affirmation of faith that Jesus was in fact raised from the dead. Eventually critical research and faith confront us with the same questions: Was Jesus raised from the dead? Is he the Christ? What is being stated in these proclamations of faith?

On the one hand, Christology can begin with an interpretation of the earthly Jesus (see volumes 1 and 2 of this series). On the other hand, it can begin with the eternal Word or divine Son (see the Christologies in volume 3 of this series). But the most proper starting point for Christology today is that of the resurrection of Jesus.

With the resurrection, both as historical fact and as invitation to faith, we begin to see Jesus in a new light—as the Christ. With the resurrection, Jesus is revealed as the Christ of God. What that means must be further unveiled.

In one of the earliest Christological statements preserved for us, Luke professes the faith of the early Christians: "God has made this Jesus whom we crucified both Lord and Christ" (Acts 2:36). The resurrection was a turning point, or starting point. This does not mean that Jesus was not the Christ prior to his resurrection from the dead. Rather, the resurrection is the point at which it is most clearly revealed who Jesus is. The resurrection forces

1

us to think about Jesus in Christological terms in a way that the pre-Easter Jesus does not.

For Paul, it seems as if Jesus became the Messiah (or Christ) only as of his resurrection from the dead: "God's Son was descended from David according to the flesh and designated Son of God in power according to the Spirit of holiness by his resurrection from the dead" (Rom 1:4). Mark's Gospel suggests that Jesus was designated to be the Messiah as of his baptism: "Thou art my beloved Son; with thee I am well pleased" (Mark 1:11). For Matthew and Luke, Jesus was the Messiah, from the moment of his conception (Matt 1–2, Luke 1–2). In the Gospel of John, Jesus had a pre-history that is essential to understanding who he truly is, namely, the Word incarnate (John 1:1-18). Whether Jesus was Messiah-designate before he was ever conceived or born, or became the Messiah on account of his death and resurrection from the dead, is not our immediate concern. It it still the resurrection of Jesus that historically revealed most clearly that Jesus is the Christ. Thus a theology of Jesus is a theology of the Christ, a Christology. What does it mean to say that Jesus is the Christ? Who is this Jesus Christ? The resurrection is where we begin.

The Resurrection of Jesus

There have been many approaches to Jesus Christ throughout Christian history and in our own times. Each approach can have value and each contains insights, whether the medieval Christology of Thomas Aquinas or the contemporary Christology of a Latin American liberation theologian. No one method should be absolutized to the exclusion of others. Each Christology by itself alone is inadequate to the mystery of Jesus Christ. Each Christology reflects particular cultural, historical, and social concerns. Its perspective is valid but partial. Ultimately its value will be judged in terms of its effectiveness for Christian life.

Nevertheless, one may speak of the most appropriate starting point for Christology proper, and that seems to be the resurrection of Jesus Christ, the Risen Christ, Jesus raised from the dead.[1]

---

[1]Two Catholic authors who emphasize the resurrection as the most appropriate starting point for Christology are Gerald O'Collins, *Jesus Risen* (New York: Paulist Press, 1987); and Franz Jozef van Beeck, *Christ Proclaimed, Christology As Rhetoric* (New York: Paulist Press, 1979).

We already discussed the historicity and theology of the resurrection in the second volume of this series,[2] but we now return to several aspects of that discussion.

Christology proper begins with the resurrection of Jesus because the resurrection (1) reveals Jesus as the Christ, (2) requires the act of faith necessary for Christology, and (3) urges us toward a decision about our own discipleship. These are prerequisites before we can go any further.

1. The resurrection reveals Jesus as the Christ, and opens the door for further exploration of the kind of Christ he is. The resurrection reveals that there is more to Jesus than what appears on the surface. Although it became clear to some of Jesus' disciples after the resurrection that he had already been the Messiah prior to the resurrection, it was nevertheless the resurrection which made them aware of his uniqueness as Messiah. Jesus was proclaimed as the Christ (Acts 2:36).

For Paul, Jesus became the Christ, or Son of God in power, as of the resurrection (Rom 1:1-4).[3] It was the resurrection that necessitated a deeper understanding of the kind of Son of God that Jesus was. This deeper probing revealed him both as exalted Lord and as God's unique Son in the full Johannine sense of the term (John 20:28).[4]

Thus the question asked by Jesus himself, "Who do you say that I am?" (Mark 8:27), took on new meaning due to the experiences of the Risen Jesus. Jesus was a prophet, sage, and servant-martyr, but also more than those words can convey. Jesus was also Messiah, Lord, and Son, and in ways not previously understood. He was the Messiah, but not the kind of Messiah the disciples had been expecting. He was their lord and teacher, but now Lord in an utterly unique and exalted way. He was God's son, but now his unique sonship needed clarification. The resur-

[2]Donald J. Goergen, *The Death and Resurrection of Jesus,* vol. 2 of *A Theology of Jesus* (Wilmington, Del.: Michael Glazier, 1988) esp. 141-59, 160-79, 183-203.

[3]James D. G. Dunn, *Christology in the Making* (Philadelphia: The Westminster Press, 1980) 33-46.

[4]See Goergen, *The Death and Resurrection of Jesus,* 160-79; and *The Jesus of Christian History,* vol. 3 of *A Theology of Jesus* (Collegeville, Minn.: The Liturgical Press, 1992) 9-35.

rection required and continues to require Christological reflection if Jesus is to be more adequately understood.

2. The resurrection of Jesus also requires faith. Although it was an historical event (i.e., it actually happened to Jesus himself in the course of history), it was not the kind of event sufficiently accessible to historical research to be historiographically demonstrable. This does not imply that faith in the resurrection of Jesus is not a reasonable, probable, and intelligible assertion. It only means that faith in the resurrection is precisely that: faith. The resurrection is a historical but meta-historiographical event apprehended by faith. It ultimately pertains more to personal, experiential, faith knowledge than to objective, demonstrable, historiographical knowledge. While historiography and faith both have roles to play, in the end affirming the resurrection of Jesus is an act of faith.[5] This in no way diminishes the reality of the resurrection as an event that personally happened to Jesus in history: one simply cannot limit reality to the historiographically accessible.

Christology cannot therefore begin with some neutral, faithless stance, but only with faith in Jesus as raised from the dead, as the Christ of God, and as a unique act of God. Christology does not seek to demonstrate objectively or scientifically that Jesus is the Christ but rather to explicate what it means to say by personal faith that Jesus is the Christ. For the purposes of Christology, priority is not given to the historiographical verification of Jesus' resurrection, although Christian apologetics or fundamental theology may have that concern.

Two biblical traditions give witness to the reality of the resurrection of Jesus (i.e., testifying to the disciples' faith that Jesus has been raised from the dead).[6] There are the appearance narratives, elaborating the appearance-experiences of the disciples, associated more with the experiences of the men, Peter and the Eleven, and perhaps the basis for a Galilean tradition. Then there are the tomb narratives, associated more with the women, particularly Mary Magdalene, the basis for a Jerusalem tradition which may have had its origins not only in the empty tomb but

[5]See Goergen, *The Death and Resurrection of Jesus*, 155–59, 188–203.

[6]Ibid., 118–39. Also see Gerald O'Collins, "Mary Magdalene as Major Witness to Jesus' Resurrection," in *Interpreting the Resurrection* (New York: Paulist Press, 1988) 22–38, originally in *Theological Studies* 48 (1987) 631–46.

also in the appearance-experience of Mary Magdalene or of the women in the vicinity of the tomb.

The appearances of the risen Jesus and the concomitant experiences of the disciples were the way in which the disciples, women and men, came to a personal knowledge of Jesus as alive, as raised from the dead. Whatever the nature of the appearances and experiences may have been, they were the source of the disciples' faith in Jesus as still with them. The appearance narratives are of two sorts and describe two types of appearance-experiences or two aspects of them.[7] In some of the narratives, the appearance-experiences lead to recognition and thus the resumption of discipleship (Matt 28:9-10; Luke 24:13-35; John 20:24-29). In others they lead to mission (Matt 28:16-20; Luke 24:36-49; John 20:19-23). Thus, theologically, and perhaps historically, the experience of the Risen Christ involves recognition, vocation, and mission.

Although it is historiographically probable that Jesus' tomb was empty, even the empty tomb narratives themselves do not associate the experience of the empty grave with the awareness that Jesus had been raised from the dead. Only the appearances or experiences of the Risen Jesus himself led to faith.

We are all destined to be raised from the dead. Yet the empty grave and the particular character of the appearances of Jesus put his resurrection in a class by itself. Only Jesus became Lord and was exalted to the right hand of the Father.[8] Thus the resurrection of Jesus revealed the unique character of his relationship to the Father. The resurrection of Jesus was a unique, meta-historiographical event. Thus we come to see that Jesus' uniqueness is meta-historiographical. It is something which will be theologically pursued because of faith, but not something for which there necessarily will be historiographical proof.[9]

3. The resurrection is the crucial event for Christianity and for Christian theology. It forces us to make a decision: either we accept Jesus Christ as the unique Son of God or we do not. If we do not, if we do not appropriate the resurrection of Jesus in some personal way, if we are not open to experiencing the presence of

[7]Goergen, *The Death and Resurrection of Jesus,* 118-33.

[8]Ibid., 167-70.

[9]Van Beeck, *Christ Proclaimed,* 255-57.

the Risen Christ, we can still have great respect and admiration for Jesus as a historically significant prophet, sage, and martyr. On the other hand, if we do accept Jesus as raised by God from the dead, as the vindicated and validated crucified Messiah, as God's unique Son, the historiographical categories remain valid but incomplete. The resurrection makes Christian theology necessary.

Critical historical research gives us certain portraits of Jesus, the Jesus of historiography. But this research cannot give us the whole of Jesus, not even the whole of the earthly Jesus. Historical research leads us right to the door of the resurrection but can take us no further. Like Dante's Virgil, it has to hand us over to Beatrice.[10] The resurrection confronts us with a decision— whether to believe in it or not. Do you believe in Jesus raised from the dead? Yes or no? You must decide before going further. Or you must decide whether to go further. This is the meta-historiographical significance of the empty tomb. This is the question with which it confronts us. To believe in Jesus raised from the dead is to become his disciple, or to take up one's discipleship at a new level. Those Jews who believed in Jesus raised from the dead and in Jesus as the Christ became Christian Jews. The other Jews did not. The resurrection required a response. It still does.

To recognize Jesus is to follow him. After the resurrection the appearance-experiences for the first disciples were opportunities for recognition, renewed discipleship, another call, and mission. To know Jesus as he truly is means becoming his disciple. This is the message of the Fourth Gospel. Not to follow Jesus means not to know Jesus in truth, not to know who Jesus truly is. The resurrection confronts us with the truth about Jesus.

The basic fact that Christology confronts, and attempts feebly to explain, is the central role of Easter in history, theology, liturgy, and Christian life. And just as historically the resurrection of Jesus cannot be separated from the gift of the Spirit, whether that gift was given on the occasion of the post-resurrection appearances or on the feast of Pentecost, so likewise for Christians, Easter is inseparable from Pentecost. Easter and Pentecost *together* are the starting point for Christology. Theology takes its

---

[10]Dante, *Purgatorio* canto 30.

cue here from liturgy. Easter and Pentecost are one liturgical season: the paschal mystery which seeks to be unveiled in Christian life, Christian worship, and Christian theology.[11] There is no Christology without pneumatology. The paschal mystery is the point of entry into God's love affair with humanity as it is revealed to us in the mystery of Jesus Christ.

Thus Christology starts with the Risen Christ, hence the presence of Christ, the present Christ: not a past Christ, or dead Christ, or historical Christ, but Christ present now through the Spirit. Christology is a response to that presence of Christ, an act of faith seeking to explicate itself, an act of faith that at some point finds itself in the grip of what it thought it could grasp.

The Risen Christ is present to us in the Eucharist and one could well ask whether Christology ought not begin with a theology of the Eucharist. We certainly need to raise the question of where it is that we encounter the risen Christ among us today. Another facet of the resurrection is hope. Perhaps Christology ought to be placed within the theology and history of hope. We slowly begin to see that Christology, the mystery of Jesus Christ, the story of the life, death, and resurrection of Jesus Christ is the starting point or key to all of Christian theology: our theology of God, anthropology, eschatology, soteriology, our theology of the Church, of the sacraments, and of Christian life.

From Resurrection to Incarnation

In volumes 1 and 2 of this series, we began with the human, earthly Jesus. We spoke about Jesus as being one of us, called by God, for our sake, who became Lord. That way of speaking reflects an approach to Jesus "from below," from within history. There is nothing false about that way of speaking. It follows upon the humanity of Jesus, which is affirmed both biblically and dogmatically. It provides a two-stage Christology, an understanding of the story of Jesus in two parts—the pre-resurrection, earthly history and the post-resurrection, exalted activity of Jesus.

Most of the Christologies described in the third volume, including that of the Fourth Gospel, began with the theology of the Logos, not with the man Jesus. Even among the Antiochenes,

---

[11] Cf. O'Collins, *Jesus Risen,* 202-06.

whose starting point was the humanity of Jesus, the two natures of Jesus, the reality of the Logos in his history, were taken for granted. They could not understand Jesus apart from the Logos. His divinity, fully affirmed, was the divinity of the Logos. This classical Christological language reflects Christology "from above," Christology based upon the prior existence of the eternal Word, and it is into the Word's history that we are drawn by a study of Jesus. Some variation of this approach to Christology can be considered as the traditional Christian faith. There is more to Jesus than his being one of us, although this "more" can never exclude the fact that he was also truly and fully one of us. Such Christologies had three stages: the pre-existence of the Word; the enfleshment of the Word and its conception, development, life, and mission on earth as part of our history; and the resurrection and exalted lordship of the incarnate Word.

While the resurrection is pivotal in Pauline Christology to an understanding of who Jesus truly is, the incarnation is pivotal in Johannine Christology. Paul's theology is a Christology of the Risen Jesus. Synoptic Christologies give centrality not only to the death and resurrection of Jesus but also to his life and ministry. The Fourth Gospel pushes the understanding of Jesus further or deeper: Jesus ultimately *is* the Word. Is a Christology grounded in the resurrection compatible with a Christology grounded in the incarnation? What is the effect of a theology of the incarnation on a theology of the resurrection? on the significance of the earthly ministry and mission of Jesus? on our understanding of the death of Jesus? Does the Christology of the Fourth Gospel manifest the fullest understanding of who Jesus is as a result of the resurrection, the appearance-experiences of the disciples, the gift of the Spirit of the risen Lord to his followers, and the comprehension of Jesus to which this paschal and pentecostal event led? In this volume, problems raised by the Christology of the Fourth Gospel will become central. What is the effect of a three-stage Christology on our theology of Jesus? Can Jesus be both "Jesus" and "incarnate Word"?

The challenge that faces us now is whether these two approaches to Christology (two-stage and three-stage, from below and from above) are irreconcilable or not. Can they complement each other or do they inevitably work at cross purposes with each other? Of course, in some sense, this is the same challenge that all traditional Christologies faced: whether Jesus could be both human and divine. But the problem has been posed anew with the rise of a critical exegesis of the Scriptures. We cannot facilely assume that the results of Jesus research and the dogmatic tradition of the Churches do not contradict each other. They have different biases and different objectives. They arrive at seemingly different results based upon contrasting methodologies. Thus it is not simply a question of whether humanity and divinity can be reconciled in one Jesus, but whether the biblical, historical Jesus looks anything like the traditional, dogmatic Christ. Must we choose between the Jesus of biblical historiographical research and the Jesus Christ of the traditional historical faith? Such an either/or is an implicit assumption of much modern theology. If choose we must, then we will. But we must first ask whether these two contrasting approaches to Christology are ultimately irreconcilable—whether the convictions and insights of "objective science" and "the traditional, historical faith" are contradictory or complementary.

Any Christology that assumes that both Christology from above and Christology from below have a role to play in the future of Christology begins by being a three-stage Christology: the Logos, or God, is not to be left out of the picture. Thus the question facing us is whether a Logos-grounded Christology is compatible with the Jesus of Nazareth to whom the Scriptures give witness (and to some degree whether Synoptic and Johannine Christologies present a contrast or a contradiction). It is a question of whether a theology of incarnation affirms or destroys the humanness of the man we call Jesus, of whether talk of an incarnation is incompatible with the earthly Jesus of history. It is interesting that, at a popular level, "liberal theology" often wants to be incarnational without an incarnation, and "conservative theology" insists upon an incarnation without being incarnational. Thus it is nothing other than a proper understanding of the incarnation that challenges us here. What does "incarnation" mean for us today?

There are at least two closely related issues that function as obstacles to belief in the incarnation. First, are divinity and humanity incompatible? Does being divine necessarily make one less than or other than human? In other words, are they diametrically opposed? And second, does it necessarily follow that an incarnation would mean that Jesus' humanity, although real in some sense, was not like ours? that he perhaps shared in some common, abstract human nature but not our common, existential human condition? that he was not human in the way that we are human, so that Jesus' humanness, existentially speaking, is almost an equivocation? We will turn to these questions in the next two chapters.

There are many challenges to faith today, and many challenges to faith in an incarnation of the eternal Word, but the challenge which faces us in this volume is a viable theology of the incarnation. A theology of the incarnation presupposes two things. (1) God is not *totally* Other. This is not to say that the distinction between Creator and creature is to be blurred, or that estrangement between God and us is not real, but rather that there is neither an existential nor a metaphysically unbridgeable gulf between God and us. In fact, to be God is to be in relationship. Relationality is of the very nature of God, as is God's otherness. Incarnation presupposes that God is relational. Incarnation says something about our theology of God. (2) The reality of God is a mystery to us. This does not mean complete unintelligibility, but rather incomprehensibility. If the incarnation presupposes a certain theology of God, any theology of God presupposes mystery, the *mysterium,* that which we can only contemplate, not grasp, that face-to-face with which we stand in awe. This *mysterium* is at the starting point of Christology. The *mysterium Christi* underlies and undergirds even the earthly Jesus of history.

One Christ, Many Christologies

Although there was but one Jesus Christ, one Jesus of Nazareth, the efforts to understand or interpret him have been many and diverse. Such diversity was manifest in the New Testament period itself (as we saw in volume 2), as well as in the history of Christian theology (as we saw in volume 3), and it continues to our own day. Different communities, different individuals, different experiences of the faith, different cultures, different languages, different socio-political milieux, different periods of history, different concerns—different Christologies. The different Christologies can manifest varied approaches or methods or models or types, and no one method or model is "right," or definitive. This is not to deny that some may or may not be orthodox, acceptable as expressing the catholic faith, or that some are more adequate than others, although criteria for adequacy are not universally agreed upon. Yet no one Christology in and of itself is absolute. Such a claim would turn Christology into ideology and idolatry. No single Christology by itself is adequate for all places and all times simply because of the mystery that Jesus Christ is. The *mysterium Christi* can never be so confined. In the New Testament documents and since, the fate of some Christologies has been rejection. But we cannot predict the fate of a Christology ahead of time. Some are judged to be unfaithful to the tradition. Others fail to respond to the signs of the times. Still others achieve a degree of balance between tradition and modernity; they have something to say. The ages-old mystery of Jesus is handed on afresh.

Christology takes many shapes and forms. It may be primarily a theology of the incarnation, or of the cross, or of the resurrection. Or it may be simply a theology of Jesus, not one event in his life, but his life and ministry as a whole. We can talk about approaching Christology from above (a theology of the incarnation) or from below (a theology of the man Jesus). Christology may focus on the history of Jesus or the history of the Logos. It may be a two-stage or a three-stage Christology. It may be more functional or more ontological. It may be more of a two-nature Christology conceived less historically than a stage-by-stage Christology. If so, the two natures may be approached more in terms of metaphysics or in terms of paradox. It may be judged as "unitive" or as "divisive," as "Alexandrian" or "Antiochene," as "Logos-sarx" or "Logos-anthropos," as Johannine or Synoptic. All of these great testimonies to the faith give witness to the apostolic, evangelical, kerygmatic, intellectual challenge posed by the life and death of this one man.

For Karl Rahner Christology and Christological statements comprise two basic types: the saving history type, a Christology viewed from below, and the metaphysical type, a Christology developing from above.[12] While they are not capable of being ef-

---

[12]Karl Rahner, "The Two Basic Types of Christology," in *Theological Investigations* 13 (New York: Seabury Press, 1975) 213–23.

fectively united in a higher synthesis, they are interrelated. Each of them can be expressed in an orthodox or a heterodox way.

John Knox, in his study of patterns in Christology, delineated three distinct patterns in the New Testament which manifest the development of Christology in the New Testament period.[13] The earliest New Testament Christology was "adoptionist," though it should not be identified with later adoptionist monarchianism or with the thought of Paul of Samosata. This early "adoptionist" pattern can be found in Acts 2:36. The second phase in the development of Christology was kenoticism. The notion of preexistence became a prologue to the story of Christ. The primary biblical example of kenotic Christology for Knox was Philippians 2:5-11. The third stage of development was that of an incarnationism, with pre-existence prominently affecting the Christology. Its roots are in the Johannine prologue. Incarnationism is on the path of development toward Docetism. Yet, according to Knox, Docetism was a pattern or stage to which neither the New Testament nor the Church was willing to go. Adoptionist, kenotic, and incarnational Christologies, on the other hand, were within the acceptable limits of the New Testament.

Walter Kuenneth also identified three typical forms of Christology, but used as his starting point the multiplicity within the history of dogma and theology.[14] Kuenneth's three types were Logos Christology, Spirit Christology, and paradox Christology. He then suggested a fourth along the lines he himself pursued: a resurrection Christology. For Kuenneth, the fundamental question of all Christian theology was the Christological question. His starting point for Christology was not the Jesus of history but the faith of the Church. "Christology is that teaching about Christ which is gained by thinking through in a dogmatic way the believing knowledge which speaks of the encounter with God in Jesus Christ."[15] The task of Christology is to clarify the relation of Jesus to God. In Christian history, this was primarily done in three ways. A Logos Christology is essentially a metaphysical Christol-

[13] John Knox, *The Humanity and Divinity of Christ* (Cambridge: Cambridge University Press, 1967) esp. 1-18.

[14] Walter Kuenneth, *The Theology of the Resurrection* (St. Louis: Concordia Publishing House, 1965) esp. 111-17.

[15] Ibid., 111.

ogy and it can readily become ahistoric and abstract. A Spirit Christology gives attention to human psychology and human history in the story of Jesus, as well as his union with God through perfect obedience. But the difference between the presence of God in Christ and in the Christian often becomes one of degree rather than kind. Paradox Christology (and one can see both Luther and Kierkegaard in the background here) does not attempt to resolve the tension between the divinity and humanity of Jesus by any metaphysical or psychological or historical explanation. It simply proclaims the paradox. For Kuenneth, a Logos Christology does not do justice to the dynamic action of God in Christ, a Spirit Christology alters the true meaning of the divinity of Christ, and a paradox Christology dispenses with grounding the divinity of Christ at all. Thus he proposed a Christology which takes as its basic starting point the resurrection of Jesus. Wolfhart Pannenberg also argues for resurrection Christology, yet his theology and Kuenneth's are quite distinguishable.[16] Pannenberg comes at the resurrection from below and from the perspective of historical criticism; Kuenneth considers the historical approach to the resurrection untenable. Any general type of Christology comprises similarly significant individual variations.

Michael Cook, Avery Dulles, and John O'Grady, three contemporary Catholic theologians, also exemplify the tendency to group varied Christologies into manageable but diverse approaches or models. Cook does not attempt a system of classification or typology into which all or most Christologies could fit.[17] Rather he selects four contemporary approaches to Christology that he has found personally significant. Although distinct from one another, all begin Christology from below, from the concrete and historical existence of Jesus. They manifest four dimensions or ingredients that must be integrated into any adequate Christology. These Christologies and their starting points are: (1) the incarnation and the Christology of Piet Schoonenberg,[18] (2) the

---

[16]See Wolfhart Pannenberg, *Jesus—God and Man,* trans. Duane Priebe and Lewis Wilkins (Philadelphia: The Westminster Press, 1968). Also see van Beeck, *Christ Proclaimed.*

[17]Michael Cook, *The Jesus of Faith* (New York: Paulist Press, 1981) 133-208.

[18]See esp. Piet Schoonenberg, *The Christ,* trans. Della Couling (New York: Herder and Herder, 1971). See also ch. 4 of this volume.

resurrection and the Christology of Wolfhart Pannenberg,[19] (3) the crucifixion and the Christology of Jürgen Moltmann,[20] and (4) the concrete historical Word and the Christology of Peter Hodgson.[21]

Dulles's typology groups the contemporary proliferation of Christologies into five basic approaches, each having a distinctive point of departure and a distinctive goal.[22] In ten theses he suggests the strength and the weakness of each approach. (1) The dogmatic approach, the most traditional of the five, takes its point of departure from official Church teaching and the early Christological councils (to some degree these are traditional Christologies from above). (2) The historical approach focuses on the quest for the historical Jesus, including the nineteenth-century quest as well as the new twentieth-century, post-Bultmannian quest (to some degree this is a category comprising Jesus research which does not always have a specific Christological purpose). (3) The biblical-kerygmatic approach takes as its point of departure neither Church dogma nor the Jesus of history but the kergyma or proclamation of the early Church, and thus focuses on the death and resurrection of Jesus. (4) The liturgical-sacramental approach has its point of departure in the experience of Christ in worship and the theology of Christ as sacrament (here Dulles lists the early Edward Schillebeeckx of *Christ the Sacrament of the Encounter With God* as the chief example although Dulles would have to re-classify Schillebeeckx after his more recent Jesus work). (5) The secular-dialogic approach takes its point of departure in the dialogue between traditional faith and the contemporary world (Dulles places here thinkers as diverse as Paul Tillich and Pierre Teilhard de Chardin).

O'Grady's analysis[23] of contemporary Christology leads him to select six models: (1) an incarnational model, Jesus as Second

[19]See esp. Pannenberg, *Jesus—God and Man.*

[20]See esp. Jürgen Moltmann, *The Crucified God,* trans. R. A. Wilson and John Bowden (New York: Harper and Row, 1974).

[21]Peter Hodgson, *Jesus—Word and Presence* (Philadelphia: Fortress Press, 1971).

[22]Avery Dulles, "Contemporary Approaches to Christology: Analysis and Reflections," in *Living Light* 13 (1976) 119–44.

[23]John F. O'Grady, *Models of Jesus* (Garden City, N.Y.: Doubleday Image, 1982).

Person of the Blessed Trinity, (2) a mythological model, Jesus as a "mythical" figure, (3) Jesus as ethical liberator, particularly exemplified in contemporary Latin American Christology, (4) Jesus as the human face of God, (5) Jesus as the man for others, and (6) Jesus as personal savior.

Other examples of the effort to give some shape to contemporary Christology could also be mentioned.[24] All give witness, however, to the diversity and variety of Christologies today which manifest different starting points, methodologies, and goals. This pluralism is not a mark of the contemporary period alone but was already manifest in the New Testament period and throughout the history of the Christian Church. There has never been only one Christology. This is not to say, of course, that all are of equal value. Yet the many faces of Christ thus revealed do help to put us in contact with the reality and mystery that Jesus Christ was and is.

Besides a consciousness of methodology, starting points, goals, and objectives, the study of diverse Christologies makes us conscious of language and the character of Christological language, Jesus-talk and Christ-talk. The limits of language, as well as the different kinds of language and statements, is not a new problem for Christology, but one that has accompanied it throughout history (as we saw in volume 3 of this series).[25] The early Christological disputes were conscious of the importance of language; they were not about "mere semantics." The development of the doctrine of the *communicatio idiomatum* was always concerned with the proper expression of the faith of Christians.[26] Language itself is a theological concern, and a concern of Christology both because of the mystery that the Christ is and because of the character of human cognition and speech. Every expression *about* Christ is a human expression, and thus time-conditioned, never completely adequate to express the mystery. This does not mean that we are doomed to ignorance or vacuous speech. On the contrary, our speech becomes intelligent only if we are aware of its limits.

[24]E.g., one ought to mention the study of John McIntyre, *The Shape of Christology* (Philadelphia: The Westminster Press, 1966), for its discussion on method and models in Christology and its consideration of three models in particular: the two-nature model, the psychological model, and the revelation model.

[25]See Goergen, *The Jesus of Christian History,* esp. 206–56.

[26]Ibid., 233–37, 49–50.

To claim more for Christological language than it can bear is to turn Christology into ideology and idolatry.

A danger in any Christology from above (metaphysical) is to turn the mystery of Christ into a philosophical problem, to reduce Christology to metaphysics. Christological language is not primarily metaphysical language, though metaphysics can be put at the service of the faith.

A danger in any Christology from below (historical) is to turn the mystery of Christ into a historiographical problem, to reduce Christology to history. Christological language is not primarily historiographical language, though historiography can be put at the service of the faith.

Christological language is rather theological language, religious discourse, metaphorical speech. It is neither "literal" nor "figurative," but analogical. It can say what we want to say, what needs to be said, *but not quite.* Christological language is primarily the language of proclamation. Its ultimate function is not objective precision but proclamation. Christology exists primarily for the sake of preaching. For that reason, no one Christology is ever totally adequate. No one model is sufficient. The preaching event requires an openness to the whole of Christ and to the mystery of Christ. Christology is a creative reappropriation of the mystery of Jesus Christ for the sake of its proclamation here and now.

We could continue endlessly to delineate criteria for doing Christology. Yet we must eventually set criteria for ourselves. The following are six such criteria to guide me here in my own project of reconstruction.

1. Christology must do justice to Jesus, the earthly and historical Jesus, but also all of Jesus. Christology must be sensitive to Jesus research but not limit itself to Jesus' historiographical availability. Christology seeks to understand Jesus of Nazareth.

2. Christology must ground itself in Scripture, not just part but all of Scripture. The New Testament is a trustworthy access to Jesus, the earliest witness to the faith, and the starting point for Christology. Christology seeks to illuminate the biblical faith.

3. Christology must seek to identify itself with Christian tradition, its history of the interpretation of Scripture, and its understanding of Jesus Christ. One can have a theology of Jesus which is not Christian in the sense of the historical Christian faith. Christology is not simply Jesus research. It is the articulation of

Christian faith. Christology is not simply private. It is ecclesial. It is done in relationship to a community of believers.

4. At the service of the community, Christology seeks to remain faithful to tradition, Scripture, and Jesus of Nazareth. But it also sees itself as called into ministry and fidelity to the contemporary community. Christology is not only historically and biblically conscious; it is pastorally conscious. It is sensitive to the hurts and needs, hungers and cries, pains and joys of this moment of history. Christology exists above all for the people just as Jesus did; it belongs to the people and, in being so, remains faithful to the consciousness of Jesus Christ. Christology is conscious of the political and personal, spiritual and material well-being of those to whom the Christ has been sent.

5. In being pastorally sensitive, Christology is also conscious that it is "in a world." It is socially conscious of the secular and religiously pluralistic world which is not necessarily an enemy. The selfsame God that one has found at work in Jesus is found to be still at work in *our* world. Christology knows that it is related to this world, will have an effect on this world, for good or for ill, and will likewise be affected by this world.

6. The Christological task is always unfinished, never done once and for all, never fully adequate, always open ended. It is conscious of its limitations both because it is culturally and historically situated and because of the mystery before which it stands. Christology cannot be separated from prayer or from pain, from humor or from hope. Thus it needs to be continually reexamined.

In my effort to think through the mystery of Christ and understand who Jesus is, I attempt to speak to our world with its peoples the word to which Scripture and tradition have struggled to remain faithful, the word *Jesus* as a symbol of faith, hope, and love. At the service of this word we must be critical, faithful, and humble.

A Strong No to Adoptionism

In chapter 1 of the first volume of this series I spoke of the need for a strong no to Docetism.[27] Now is the time to utter an equally strong no to Adoptionism. These two are the Scylla and

[27]Donald J. Goergen, *The Mission and Ministry of Jesus,* vol. 1 of *A Theology of Jesus* (Wilmington, Del.: Michael Glazier, 1986) 32–37.

Charybdis of Christology. *Adoptionism* can be used either strictly or loosely. In general it connotes that Jesus was an adopted son of God rather than the natural Son of God. The moment of such adoption may have been Jesus' resurrection, or baptism, or even some earlier point in his life. An Adoptionist Christology is in general a contrast to an incarnational Christology in which God becomes human in and through the incarnation. In Adoptionism the divine element in Christ is more likely to be described in terms of a human being becoming God rather than God becoming human.

Strictly speaking, Adoptionism refers to the eighth-century heresy espoused in Spain by Elipandus, archbishop of Toledo, and Felix, bishop of Urgel. It was condemned by Pope Adrian I as well as by a council in Frankfurt in 794 (see Denziger, 610–15). Elipandus and Felix taught a double sonship in Christ, linking sonship with the two natures rather than the one person. Thus the eternal Logos was the natural Son, who assumed the son of Mary, God's adopted son. Opponents understood this Adoptionism to be a form of Nestorianism. There was a form or revival of Adoptionism in the twelfth century among some who held that the union between the Logos and the human nature was accidental rather than substantial and thus held that Jesus as human was an adopted son of God (Abelard, Gilbert de la Porrée).

Elipandus's formula ("Christus adoptivus filius Altissimi humanitate, et nequaquam adoptivus divinitate") can be interpreted as referring to the distinction between the two natures in Christ and, as such, orthodox. It could, however, be easily misunderstood and was even likely to be misunderstood. Thus, although Elipandus spoke of Christ as both *filius adoptivus* (humanity) and *filius proprius* (divinity), it was nevertheless judged that Jesus' sonship was in no way an adoption. Jesus was the natural Son of God.

In a looser fashion, Adoptionism has come to be applied to the dynamic Monarchians and the thought of Paul of Samosata in the second and third centuries. Whereas the preservation of the humanity of Christ was a concern for the eighth-century Adoptionists, and in that they were of a kindred spirit with the ancient Antiochenes, the concern of the Monarchians was the preservation of the unity or oneness of God: monotheism. Their history is a part of the development of Trinitarian thought.

The Monarchians (whose name was coined by Tertullian) saw Trinitarian thought as tritheistic. They comprised two types: dynamic or "adoptionist," and modalist. The modalists, called Patripassians by Cyprian, held that there was one God and that the Father, Son, and Spirit were not really distinct but only modes of expression. These were three names for the one God who is made manifest in different ways at different times. Noetus and Sabellius were noteworthy modalists.

The dynamic Monarchians, also concerned with maintaining and expressing the unity of God, interpreted Jesus not so much as divine but as a human being possessed of the divine spirit in a unique way, and thus adopted by God. The first prominent dynamic Monarchian was Theodotus of Byzantium who came to Rome about 190 and taught that Jesus was a holy man upon whom the Spirit descended at his baptism. Some of his followers maintained that Jesus became in some sense divine at his resurrection. A similar view was held by Paul of Samosata, bishop of Antioch ca. 260, for whom Jesus was a man filled with the power of God by the indwelling Logos, by which he was inseparably and morally one with God. The dynamic Monarchians denied the true divinity of Christ and have come to be called Adoptionists as well.

By way of extension, *Adoptionist* is also used to refer to the heterodox Jewish-Christians who developed along with the orthodox Jewish Christians of the Jerusalem community. The Jewish-Christian Christology of Cerinthus and the heterodox Ebionites saw Jesus as only human. Jesus was a prophet, supplied on the day of his baptism with divine power, and given the rank of Messiah.

The word *Adoptionism* is further used, as we saw above with John Knox, to describe the biblical Christology suggested in Acts 2:36. Knox's use of the word, however, is even looser and more accommodated, for the text is not talking about the divinity or sonship of Christ. It expresses instead a resurrection-exaltation Christology, part of the early apostolic preaching which proclaims Jesus as raised from the dead and made Lord and Christ. The notions of pre-existence and incarnation were not yet Christological issues.

Thus we see that *Adoptionism* is a widely and loosely used expression. In that sense it is like *Docetism,* referring not so much to a specific heresy but to a heterodox tendency that tends to manifest itself fairly frequently. One can say that Adoptionism and Docetism represent the two extremes between which a Christology or theology of Jesus must be worked out. Just as a Christology from above, or "Alexandrianism," can readily fall prey to an incipient Docetism, so Christology from below, or "Antiochianism," can easily be distorted into Adoptionism. One denies or fails to do justice to the genuine humanity of Christ. The other denies or fails to do justice to the divinity of Christ. Adoptionism in this sense must be rejected as strongly as Docetism. Even if a particular biblical image of Christ can be interpreted along these lines, Adoptionism does not do justice to the historical Christian faith nor to the whole of the biblical testimony.

By Adoptionism I mean an interpretation of Jesus that denies his true divinity, that dismisses the notion of pre-existence and sees Jesus as human only, albeit called or even divinized by God at some stage of his life or ministry. Adoptionism is a rejection of Jesus as the Word incarnate. In this sense it does not apply to Antiochene theology, Theodore, or Nestorius. Adoptionism maintains that Jesus can only properly be called God at some moment or time in his life and not from the beginning. Any adequate Christology, however, must hold that Jesus was who he was from the moment of his conception, although his life, development, and mission lay ahead of him. The category or image of "adoption" is inadequate for Christology or for understanding Jesus' divinity. We can describe Jesus as an "adopted" son only in an accommodated way which obscures the truth of his real identity. We must look elsewhere than to the language of adoption for an adequate and contemporary theology of Jesus.

In Conclusion

Jesus was God's prophet, sage, and servant, the victim martyred on the cross. God raised him from the dead, exalted him, made him Lord of heaven and earth, and revealed that he was the Christ or Messiah. This Christ, God's uniquely beloved son on earth, made Son of God in power through the Spirit in the resurrection, *was* God's very own eternal Word, the Son of God uniquely begotten from all eternity. The Christ of God was God's Word incarnate. This Word was embodied in the earthly mission and ministry of Jesus and was raised from the dead. This resurrection is the starting point of Christology proper—the self-presentation of the Risen Christ, whether historical, liturgical, pastoral, or theological. It requires a response of faith in Jesus as uniquely God's Son. We shall return later in this volume to the earthly, incarnate mission and ministry of the Word and of the Risen Christ, but first we shall have to explore the meaning of the incarnation itself.

2

Jesus' Divinity and Ours

One of the primary concerns of Christology today is the humanness of Jesus. If we undermine this, Jesus has little to say to us. Thus the first thing to be said about Jesus in any Christology is that he is human like us.

A major contemporary obstacle to traditional faith in Jesus is the conscious or unconscious presumption that his divinity, at least as popularly understood, gets in the way of his humanity. If Jesus is truly one of us, he cannot also be truly divine; or, if Jesus is divine by nature, then he is not human in ways that we are human. A strong affirmation of his humanity diminishes his divinity or vice versa.

But is the question best formulated as an either/or? Certainly the divinity of Jesus Christ *seems* to place something in the way of his full identity with us. It is sometimes easier for us to place Jesus in another world and make him a different kind of being. We are then justified in dismissing the challenge to which his life calls us. We cannot be expected to be like him. Thus it is often easier to believe more in the divinity of Jesus than in his humanity. If he were truly human, his humanity would have real implications for us.

Part of the problem is the way in which we tend to define divinity and humanity over against each other as if they were incompatible. Does being divine mean being less human, unhuman, inhuman, other than human? Does being human have no relationship to being divine? To what realities do these words refer?

Faith in the incarnation forces us to rethink our preconceptions about both divinity and humanity. The question is not how someone could be both human and divine but rather how someone could not be. The answer to the latter question is sin. Apart from sin, to be human is to partake in some fashion in the divine nature. We think of Jesus as being divine and think of ourselves as not being divine. The real difference between Jesus and us, however, is that we are sinners and he is not. We will return to the issue of Jesus' sinlessness later. Our present purpose is to realize that divinity does not make anyone less genuinely human. If anything, it makes one more genuinely human. To be fully human is to be in some way also divine. Our only purpose here is to try to remove that obstacle which almost immediately arises and makes us choose between the two realities of humanity and divinity that we ourselves are or in which we at least participate.

We can think back to a methodological point made in volume 1 of this series when we discussed the priesthood of Christ in the Letter to the Hebrews.[1] We cautioned against bringing preconceptions to Jesus and letting these define too facilely who he is. Rather we must allow Jesus to challenge and help us redefine our preconceptions. At that point one of our concerns was the humanity of Jesus, and we cautioned against assuming that we know what humanness is prior to Jesus. We must allow Jesus to disclose or reveal the meaning of humanness to us.

So with divinity. This is not to say that all our preconceptions are false, whether they are derived from the history of religions, or philosophy, or Judaism, or our own upbringing and experience. But when we encounter the mystery of Jesus, we want to allow him to reveal to us what it means to be divine. At this point we must place our preconceptions aside.

In other words, deductive theology will not do for Christology. Christology is the foundation of Christian theology and must be revelatory. It must help us to open up the mystery that the life and death of Jesus poses for our self-understanding as well as for our understanding of God. We may make no deductions of this sort: God is all-knowing; Jesus is God; therefore Jesus is all-knowing. Or, God is all-powerful; Jesus is God; therefore Jesus is all-powerful. This only forces Jesus into preconceptions

---

[1] Goergen, *The Mission and Ministry of Jesus,* 26–31.

formed apart from him and robs him of his revelatory power. We come to God through Christ and not the other way around. Christology precedes the theology of God. In fact, it was the encounter with Jesus that led the Christian movement to its theology of God as triune, and not vice versa. We come to Jesus by longing to know the divine, and we open ourselves to what Jesus has to teach us. And we learn that the divine reality or substance is not incompatible with true humanness.

The difference between Jesus and us is not that he is divine and we are not. Jesus' uniqueness does not lie as such in his twofold nature. We too are truly divine, albeit not by nature but by grace. The issue then is not Jesus' divinity, but our own, and the need to recognize that we too are divine.

Our concern is not merely an abstract or theoretical one: it pertains to the very essence of what it means to be human. We can quote here from Nikos Kazantzakis to whom we referred in volume 1.[2]

> The dual substance of Christ—the yearning, so human, so super-human, to attain to God or, more exactly, to return to God and identify with God—has always been a deep inscrutable mystery to me. This nostalgia for God, at once so mysterious and so real, has opened in me large wounds and also large flowing springs.
>
> My principal anguish and the source of all my joys and sorrows from my youth onward has been the incessant, merciless battle between the spirit and the flesh.
>
> Within me are the dark immemorial forces of the Evil One, human and pre-human; within me too are the luminous forces, human and pre-human, of God—and my soul is the arena where these two armies have clashed and met.
>
> The anguish has been intense. I loved my body and did not want it to perish; I loved my soul and did not want it to decay. I have fought to reconcile these two primordial forces which are so contrary to each other, to make them realize that they are not enemies but, rather, fellow workers, so that they might rejoice in their harmony—and so that I might rejoice in them.
>
> All human beings partake of the divine nature in both their spirit and their flesh. That is why the mystery of Christ is not

[2]Ibid., 25–26.

simply a mystery for a particular creed: it is universal. The struggle between God and the human breaks out in everyone, together with the longing for reconciliation. Most often this struggle is unconscious and short-lived. A weak soul does not have the endurance to resist the flesh for very long. It grows heavy, becomes flesh itself, and the contest ends. But among responsible people, people who keep their eyes riveted day and night upon the Supreme Duty, the conflict between flesh and spirit breaks out mercilessly and may last until death.

The stronger the soul and the flesh, the more fruitful the struggle and the richer the final harmony. God does not love weak souls and flabby flesh. The Spirit wants to have to wrestle with flesh which is strong and full of resistance. It is a carnivorous bird which is incessantly hungry; it eats flesh and, by assimilating it, makes it disappear.

Struggle between the flesh and the spirit, rebellion and resistance, reconciliation and submission, and finally—the supreme purpose of the struggle—union with God: this was the ascent taken by Christ, the ascent which he invites us to take as well, following in his bloody tracks.

This is the Supreme Duty of the person who struggles—to set out for the lofty peak which Christ, the first-born son of salvation, attained. How can we begin?

If we are to be able to follow him we must have a profound knowledge of his conflict, we must relive his anguish: his victory over the blossoming snares of the earth, his sacrifice of the great and small joys and his ascent from sacrifice to sacrifice, exploit to exploit, to martyrdom's summit, the Cross.[3]

We may or may not agree with Kazantzakis's formulation of the question, but the question of God is intimately tied to the question of what it means to be human, and the question of humanity is equally tied to what it means to be divine.

Grace and Sanctification

In one sense all of Christian theology is Christology. In another sense it is the theology of grace. The doctrines are intrinsically

[3]Nikos Kazantzakis, *The Last Temptation of Christ,* trans. P. A. Bien (New York: Simon and Schuster, 1960) 1–2. Edited for inclusive language.

related. The doctrine of grace is at the heart of Christian life and experience, the horizon within which Christian theology is done. Grace is God; and God's free gift of himself to the human person, if accepted, sanctifies the person. The expression "sanctifying grace" is in itself a late expression; the Fathers did not use it. Medieval theology spoke of *gratia gratum faciens,* the grace that makes one pleasing to God. Thomas Aquinas spoke of habitual grace rather than of sanctifying grace. Yet grace does sanctify. Grace and sanctification go together in our human effort to understand the relationship between God and ourselves.

Our purpose here is not to survey grace from biblical, historical, or theological perspectives, but rather to heighten our attention to the reality to which the doctrine of grace points us and to see in grace a union with God analogous to the union between God and the human nature in Jesus Christ.

Grace or its effects have been variously described in both traditional and contemporary theology: participation in the divine life, a supernatural principle of life and activity, the seed of glory, partaking of the divine nature, a metaphysical solidarity with God, the presence of God in the human person, an habitual union with God, divine self-communication, friendship with God, becoming children of God, becoming co-heirs with Christ, the divine indwelling, and intimacy with the triune God. Jesus Christ himself is seen by Christians as the supreme exemplification of grace both in his hypostatic unity with the Godhead, called the grace of union, and in the human fullness of his own life of sanctifying grace.

Through the life of habitual or sanctifying grace and the concomitant gift of the Holy Spirit every Christian truly becomes a child of God. An all-loving, infinitely caring God does not see me or treat me as a stranger in the divine household, but rather as truly God's very own child. Although we may speak of being God's child as the grace of adoption (Rom 8:14-17; Gal 4:6), the human category of adoption does not convey the fullness of the reality. In this adoption I am truly begotten by God, born again, recreated. This second birth, however, is one of grace rather than of nature (John 1:12; 3:5; 1 John 3:1; 5:1). We can see how real our sonship or daughtership of God is. We are truly God's very own children. What Jesus was by nature (Son of God), we become through grace (sons and daughters of God). The distinction between Jesus' divinity or way of being divine or mode of union with God and ours is also real. He is Son of God by nature. We are daughters and sons by grace. His is the grace of a hypostatic unity. Ours is a union of sanctifying grace. The question is what is the difference between these two kinds of union.

Jesus cannot not be united to God, for God is his very *ousia* or *hypostasis,* whereas our union with God can be lost, through sin. Yet the life of sanctifying grace means a real sharing in the divine nature itself. By this grace I am what I am most deeply called to be, a child of God. For Thomas Aquinas the difference could be stated thus: Jesus' very own act of being is the Word of God, he *is* the Word of God. I am not God. My act of existence is a created act, but I *become* one with God through grace. Jesus' union, the hypostatic union, also falls in the order of grace, but it is a different kind of union, a particular grace. Jesus *is* an incarnation of God. Through sanctifying grace we *become* what Jesus was from the moment of conception.

Our being children of God is purely a gift of God. Nothing within human nature in the abstract requires that God share with us in this way. Existentially, of course, we have been created or structured for union with God: it is our destiny and our completion. Our adopted status is not merely a metaphor. It points to the reality that we have been begotten again by water and the Holy Spirit. The divine nature itself is shared with us. Our sonship or daughtership is analogous to that of Jesus. In fact, our sonship or daughtership is a participation in that of the eternal and incarnate Word. Yet our union with God and with the Word is not a substantial union (not according to *ousia* or *hypostasis*). Rather, medieval theology described the union of sanctifying grace as an accidental union which is nevertheless a real modification (deification) of our human nature.

We are accustomed to thinking of the grace of hypostatic unity as being an incarnation of God. We are not so accustomed, however, to considering the union of sanctifying grace as being equally real and profound, that through this grace we *are* daughters and sons, that we *become* what God wants us to be, that our deepest selves *are* actualized. Through the graciousness of God, human persons are truly sanctified, and God comes to make a home in those persons who then dwell in God and God in them. A circuminsession takes place and we are given a new capacity for knowing and loving God. Sanctifying grace is not some thing with independent existence. It is rather a way of being both human and divine, the way of a human being in union with God.

Karl Rahner has spoken of this grace as a quasi-formal cause. Classically it was seen as an entitative habit, for it tended to be habitual *(gratia habitualis)* and also affected the very being of a person: the person becomes a new creature. Created grace is analogous to a formal cause: it makes us what we are at a level even deeper than that of nature. A human person in an ungraced mode of existence is like a body without its soul. Sanctifying grace and the Holy Spirit are the soul of our souls, or the form of our forms. Through this grace we are brought into unity with the Godhead, even if not hypostatically.

We see in our lives of union with God two important consequences of this grace: (1) the healing or "medicinal" character, which is related to our being sinners, and (2) the elevating or "deifying" character by which human nature itself is deepened to a level of fuller life. The basis for appreciating the former—which is strongly emphasized in the Western theology of grace, especially in its Augustinian and Pauline forms—is our sinfulness. The focus of the latter, emphasized in Eastern theology and having Johannine roots, is the gift of the Holy Spirit, the divine indwelling, and participation in the divine life. These two sides of the mystery of grace cannot be separated. Both East and West contribute much to a truly catholic theology of grace. Because of their particular histories, the West came to discuss what later was called *actual grace* whereas the East developed the theology of deification to which we must turn. Our brief look at the theology of grace, of God as Uncreated Grace itself, and of created, sanctifying grace by which God comes to live with us and within our very selves, helps us to see the way in which we speak about our divinity in traditional terms. Through grace we are both human and divine.

Deification in Eastern Theology

For many, the word *deification* may be strong, especially in the West and particularly within Protestantism. The theologies that lie behind words like *deification, sanctification,* and *justification* can hardly all be reconciled or synthesized. They continue to be the object of Christian ecumenical reflection. Our concern here is not to insist upon the doctrine of deification but, rather, to make some effort to understand a major tenet in the theology of Eastern Christianity. We shall begin by looking at its biblical basis.

The theology of the *imago Dei* ("Then God said, 'Let us make humankind in our image, after our likeness . . . ,' " Gen 1:26-27; also 5:1; 9:6) is closely related to the theology of deification. The human person or race is in some sense the image *(eikon)* of God, or a likeness *(homoiosis)* of God, the icon or mirror of God. This is not a prominent theme within the Hebrew Scriptures,[4] but one which did serve the Church as it explored the basis for the incarnation: one could pursue this theology in Irenaeus, Clement, Origen, Athanasius, and Gregory of Nyssa. The doctrine of the image of God was undoubtedly elaborated in conjunction with Christianity's encounter with Hellenism. Although it is not as such a biblical doctrine, nevertheless it has a biblical basis. The Genesis text was open to new meaning and further elaboration in the light of Jesus Christ.

Paul calls the Son "the image of the invisible God" (Col 1:15) and speaks of Christ as "the likeness of God" (2 Cor 4:4). This is a significant Christological expression central to the theology of the *imago Dei*. The supreme exemplification of the *imago* is Jesus Christ. In the perspective of Johannine theology, this is the incarnate Word. The theologies of the *imago* and of the incarnation are related to each other.

Within a Trinitarian context, the Logos/Son is the consubstantial image of the Father (he who knows the Son, knows the Father: Matt 11:27; John 14:9). Some would likewise say that the Holy Spirit is the image of the Son. Vladimir Lossky, following John Damascene, writes, "So it is in the Holy Spirit that we know Christ as Son of God and God, and it is by the Son that we see the Father."[5] Yet the supreme visible exemplification of the image of God remains the incarnation. Thus a less prominent biblical text became prominent in the Christian tradition. Christologically the human person is an image of the Image. We are im-

[4] R. H. Charles, *Eschatology, The Doctrine of a Future Life* (New York: Schocken Books, 1963) 54–55.

[5] Vladimir Lossky, "The Theology of the Image," in *In the Image and Likeness of God* (New York: St. Vladimir's Seminary Press, 1974) 135.

ages of God or like unto God by grace. The human person, however, is never consubstantial *(homoousios)* with God.

As in other areas of Christian understanding there is no one theology of the image of God. The Fathers of the Church hold various theories as to what it is in human nature that constitutes the basis for our being the image and likeness of God. Some regard the image and likeness as having two different referents (Irenaeus, and in a different way Clement).[6] Others recognize no such distinction (Gregory of Nyssa).[7] Ordinarily it is thought that the human individual person is in the image and likeness of God, with this being variously associated with human reason, or freedom, or immortality, or the whole individual person. But sometimes the image is seen corporately as residing in humankind as a whole (Gregory of Nyssa).[8] This latter emphasis brings us back to the relationship between the incarnation and the theology of the *imago Dei.* Gregory did not teach that the Word was hypostatically united to all humankind. But given the solidarity of all humankind, the Word could not unite itself to a specific human nature without having an effect beyond that on humanity as a whole.

There are two New Testament texts pertinent to the doctrine of deification that go further than Genesis 1:26-27: 2 Peter 1:4 and John 10:31-39 with its basis in Psalm 82:6.

Most scholars do not accept the Petrine authorship of 2 Peter. The epistle is a late writing, probably early second century, and many scholars see it as the latest of all the New Testament writings. Its lateness does not negate its value as a source for early Christian theology. The author unambiguously affirms that as Christians we become "partakers of the divine nature" (1:4): a bold way of speaking, probably Hellenistic. This particular expression occurs nowhere else in the Scriptures, although one could contrast its meaning with that of John 1:3; 3:2, 9; 15:4; 17:22-23.

A more significant text for us is that of John 10:31-39.

---

[6] Jean Danielou, *Gospel Message and Hellenistic Culture,* trans. John Austin Baker (Philadelphia: The Westminster Press, 1973) 399, 408-09.

[7] Jean Danielou, *From Glory to Glory,* trans. Herbert Musurillo (New York: St. Vladimir's Seminary Press, 1979) 10-11.

[8] Ibid., 17-18.

> The Jews took up stones again to stone him. Jesus answered them, "I have shown you many good works from the Father; for which of these do you stone me?"
>
> The Jews answered him, "It is not for a good work that we stone you but for blasphemy; because you being human, make yourself God."
>
> Jesus answered them, "Is it not written in your law, 'I said you are gods'? If he called them gods to whom the word of God came (and scripture cannot be broken), do you say to him whom the Father consecrated and sent into the world, 'You are blaspheming,' because I said, 'I am the Son of God'? If I am not doing the works of my Father, then do not believe me; but if I do them, even though you do not believe me, believe the works, that you may know and understand that the Father is in me and I am in the Father." Again they tried to arrest him, but he escaped from their hands.

The Johannine Jesus' response to the charge of blasphemy is an exemplification of Johannine theology in general. Jesus had just said, "I and the Father are one" (10:30). For this, some of the people, deeply offended, were about to stone him for blasphemy. The text interprets the Johannine understanding of what is at stake: Jesus, who is a human being, had made himself in some way God. The Johannine Jesus did not say, "No, you misunderstand me." He did not refute the charge. Rather he defended it and defended himself, moderating it by referring to himself as the Son of God, which is the wording of the psalm from which he quotes as well. He concluded by saying in a slightly different way that he and the Father are one: "The Father is in me and I am in the Father."

It is Jesus' defense which most interests us. It was based upon Jesus' (John's) interpretation of the Scriptures or of Psalm 82: "I say, 'You are gods, sons of the Most High, all of you; nevertheless, you shall die like human beings, and fall like any prince'" (Ps 82:6-7). Jesus defended his divinity on the grounds that we too are divine. And he did so by cleverly basing his argument on the Scriptures.

Jesus quoted to the people from their Scriptures, from one of the psalms they would frequently have recited, on which Jesus himself would have often meditated, which perhaps was signifi-

cant in the Johannine community setting: "I said, you are gods."
If the inspired psalmist calls all those to whom the psalm is addressed gods, if the people are in some sense gods, then what is
wrong with Jesus speaking about himself as being a god or the
Son of God? Has he not given witness to the fact that he is from
the Father? In other words, Jesus' defense rested upon his interpretation of the Scriptures as teaching that we too are divine.
The Johannine Jesus defended his divinity on the grounds that
he was one of the people, or one of us. If we are divine (as Scripture says), what is so blasphemous about Jesus' acknowledging
this divinity, which he has come to understand in his personal
and experiential relationship with the Father?

We are not saying that the Johannine Jesus' exegesis or interpretation of the psalm is correct. We are not saying what it meant
to the psalmist or to the Hebrew people.[9] Perhaps here we simply
have a Johannine interpretation of Scripture within Scripture.
Nevertheless, Psalm 82 led to an insight in the light of Jesus Christ,
an insight into who Jesus is and into who we are as hearers of
the word.

Although this way of speaking is not prominent in the New
Testament as a whole, these two texts (2 Peter, John 10), as well
as the whole of the Gospel of John, modeled a way of speaking
which later became prominent in the language and doctrine of
deification.

The classic statement of the doctrine of deification is that of
Athanasius: "God became one of us that we might become God"
(*De incarnatione verbi Dei* 54). We find the same theology already
in Irenaeus (*Adversus haereses* 5, preface), although Irenaeus does
not use the words *theopoiesis* or *theosis*. This same teaching is
consistently found in some form after Justin Martyr (*Dialogue
with Trypho* 124), among the Alexandrians (Clement, Origen,
Athanasius) and Cappadocians (the two Gregorys), as well as in
pseudo-Dionysius, Maximus the Confessor, John of Damascus,
and Gregory Palamas. It is the Eastern understanding of redemption. According to Vladimir Lossky, "The Fathers and Orthodox theologians have repeated them [the words of Athanasius
above] in every century with the same emphasis, wishing to sum

[9]For an interpretation of this psalm as Hebrew Scripture, see Mitchell Dahood,
Psalms II, Anchor Bible, vol. 17 (Garden City, N.Y.: Doubleday and Co., 1968)
268–71.

up in this striking sentence the very essence of Christianity: an ineffable descent of God to the ultimate limit of our fallen human condition, even unto death—a descent of God which opens to men a path of ascent, the unlimited vistas of the union of created beings with the Divinity.''[10] All of creation exists through participation in the being of God, but the human person participates in God to a different degree and in a different way, freely and consciously.

In Byzantine theology, the doctrine of salvation as deification is a unifying thread running through all of theology. John Meyendorff writes,

> If one keeps in mind the Greek patristic notion that the true nature of man means life in God, realized once and for all, through the Holy Spirit, in the hypostatic union of the man Jesus with the Logos and made accessible to all men, through the same Holy Spirit, in the humanity of Christ, in His body, the Church, Christology acquires a new and universal dimension. It cannot be isolated any longer from either the doctrine of the Holy Spirit or the doctrine of man, and it becomes a key for the understanding of the Gospel as a whole.[11]

Deification is integrally related to Christian anthropology, for it is the goal for which we were created. The human person is by nature a creature, existing outside of God, and yet in our very nature we are created for union with God. The perfection of our nature consists in becoming this likeness of God. In and through the process of deification, we recover the spiritual principle of life which had become obscured by the Fall—the *nous,* or divine spark, or image of God within—and we realize the destiny for which we were created. Our very nature was created for this deification.

Deification in Eastern thought is integrally related to its doctrine of God. In addition to the three hypostases that God is, Eastern theology, particularly since Gregory Palamas, makes a real

---

[10]Vladimir Lossky, "Redemption and Deification," in *In the Image and Likeness of God,* 97.

[11]John Meyendorff, *Byzantine Theology: Historical Trends and Doctrinal Themes* (New York: Fordham University Press, 1974) 32. See also John Meyendorff, "New Life in Christ: Salvation in Orthodox Theology," in *Theological Studies* 50 (1989) 481-99.

distinction between the divine "essence" and the divine "energy"
or "energies." God is utterly transcendent in essence but immanent by reason of the energies. God's essence is completely incomprehensible and humanly unknowable. It is not by reason of
God's essence that God is related to creation. God is rather related and present to creation *ad extra* by virtue of the uncreated
energies that God is. When one says that the human person knows,
experiences, or partakes of God, it is the divine energies (and not
essence) to which one is referring. The distinction is the basis for
preserving both the transcendence of God and at the same time
the doctrine of deification. The human person does not become
or partake of the divine essence—a necessary distinction for understanding deification.

Deification is integrally related to Christology. Not only is
Christ hypostatically united to the Word, but in and through the
hypostatic union, the very humanity of Jesus itself is deified. The
communication of properties is not simply verbal fiction. In the
union, Christ's humanity itself is penetrated with the divine
energy. Christ's humanity is a deified humanity—which does not
mean that it is any less human than ours. Thus, in Christ, human
nature has already experienced deification. The human nature of
Jesus Christ, due to its *koinonia* with the divine nature through
the hypostatic union, *becomes* divine. Therefore we, through our
koinonia with Christ, can also become divine through grace.
Christ is not only the Word made flesh, but also the supreme exemplification or prototype of a human being made God. Thus
the incarnation is not an exception, but rather a sacrament of that
which is elsewhere possible: deification. The theology and language of deification, which can sometimes appear so strange or
bold to the West, is simply the other side of a true understanding
of the doctrine of incarnation. In and through incarnation and
deification, Christology and anthropology are wed.

Deification is integrally related to pneumatology as well. For
the Word became flesh through the power of the Spirit, and it
is through the gift of the selfsame Spirit that we too can become
divine, not hypostatically but by grace. Deification, therefore, is
a work of both the Son and the Spirit. It was through the incarnation of the Word that Christ's humanity became deified, and
it is through the power of the Spirit that we are what we are *in
Christ*. In Christ we become what we were created to be.

Deification is never seen as a work humanly accomplished. It is rather a work of the Holy Spirit, a gift, accomplished by grace. We become gods only by grace. The theology of deification depends upon the Eastern theology of grace and the Holy Spirit. The descent *(katabasis)* of the Word is the inseparable counterpart and antecedent of the ascent *(anabasis)* and *theosis* of created, fallen human beings in the Holy Spirit. The Son has become like us by incarnation. We become like him by deification. The deifying work of the Spirit is to communicate the divine life to each of us. From the point of view of our fallenness, we have been redeemed. From the point of view of our destiny as creatures, we have been deified. We have become the images and likenesses of God that we were intended to be.

Deification, becoming the likeness of God and sharing in the divine energies, never means becoming less than or something other than fully human. A fundamental presupposition of any theology of grace or deification, Eastern or Western, is that grace does not diminish or destroy humanity but rather perfects it. Deification makes us more fully and authentically human. In fact, apart from grace and the gift of the Spirit, we are not human or at least not fully human. We become human or fully human in and through our sharing in the divine life. This awareness has come to be realized in the modern West as well. Pierre Teilhard de Chardin wrote persuasively about the correlative character of humanization and divinization.[12] And Edward Schillebeeckx has written, more recently: "The Greek patristic *theopoiesis* or divinization at the same time denotes the full extent of humanity. To be human is in the last resort a grace."[13]

The incarnation is the Christological basis of the anthropological and pneumatological doctrine of deification. Christ's deification is communicated to us who are in Christ. Yet we are different from Christ. We are human *hypostases* united to God by grace, deified by the divine energy and gifts of the Spirit. We are not united to the Godhead hypostatically.

---

[12]Pierre Teilhard de Chardin, *The Divine Milieu* (New York: Harper and Row, 1960).

[13]Edward Schillebeeckx, *Christ: The Experience of Jesus as Lord,* trans. John Bowden (New York: Seabury Press, 1980) 896 n. 139a.

Contained within the Eastern theology of deification is the basis for a way of speaking which makes sense of both Christ's divinity and our own without confusing the two. Deification is no more of a scandal nor more bold than the doctrine of incarnation itself. The incarnation points to that which is elsewhere true. It does not *confine* God's relationship to humankind but does *define* that relationship.[14]

Deification in Western Mysticism

The theology of the Christian life in Western thought has been more reserved about the doctrine of deification. Catholicism has been more inclined to speak of sanctifying grace than deifying grace. Yet Catholic liturgy recognizes the call to share in the divine life. During the Eucharistic liturgy, at the preparation of the gifts and the altar, the deacon or priest says the prayer, ordinarily inaudibly: "By the mystery of this water and wine may we come to share in the divinity of Christ, who humbled himself to share in our humanity."

Although doctrinal theology in the West has focused more on the language of sanctification and justification, mystical theology and Western mysticism have spoken very boldly about deification. John G. Arintero (1860–1928), a relatively unknown writer on the spiritual life, a Spanish Dominican priest, scientist, and theologian, presents the doctrine of deification in a bold and orthodox fashion, especially developed in *The Mystical Evolution in the Development and Vitality of the Church*. In the introduction, he writes:

> The apologetic method most universal, most efficacious, most facile, and most in harmony with the systems of present-day thought is a positive exposition, vital and pulsating with the mysteries of the Christian life and the whole process of the deification of souls. Such a method will demonstrate in a practical way that the supernatural does not come to us as an exterior and violent imposition, oppressing us and depriving us of our nature, but as an increase of life, freely accepted, liberating and

[14]Cf. Norman Pittenger, *Christology Reconsidered* (London: SCM Press, 1970) esp. 81–87.

> ennobling us. It does not destroy our humanity; it makes us
> superhuman, sons of God, gods by participation.[15]

Arintero continues later, "This deification, so well known to the
Fathers but unfortunately forgotten today, is the primary purpose of the Christian Life."[16] "We are created gods, whereas He
alone is the living and eternal Yahweh who, being God by nature, can make us gods by participation. He is the deifying God;
we are deified gods."[17]

In developing his theology of the spiritual life, Arintero treats
all those themes which are integral to the doctrine of deification:
grace, divine adoption, the divine indwelling, the Holy Spirit,
union with God. He quotes abundantly from the history of spirituality: from Augustine ("He calls people gods because they are
deified by His grace and not because they are born of His substance," *On Psalm 48,* no. 2) to Eadmer, an unknown disciple
of Anselm ("God makes other gods, but in such a fashion that
He alone is the God who deifies and we are the gods who are
deified," *Liber de similit,* 66).[18] Arintero is systematically re-
capitulating a prominent theme of spiritual theology which found
some of its boldest exponents among the Rhineland mystics and
the Friends of God movement of the fourteenth century.[19] A danger of spiritual theology in the West has been to assume that the
mystical life is for others, an extraordinary path to perfection and
not the ordinary life for all Christians. Arintero's theology repu-
diates this distinction between the ordinary and extraordinary.

[15]John G. Arintero, *The Mystical Evolution in the Development and Vitality
of the Church,* 2 vols., trans. Jordan Aumann (St. Louis: B. Herder Book Co.,
1949) 1:7. Particularly significant for the present theme are chs. 1 and 2 of vol.
1 and the sections on divine adoption and indwelling. Also by Arintero, *Stages
in Prayer,* trans. Kathleen Pond (London: Blackfriars Publications, 1957), which
gives special attention to the thought of St. Teresa. A systematic treatment of
traditional theology on the spiritual life can also be found in Jordan Aumann,
Spiritual Theology (Huntington, Ind.: Our Sunday Visitor, 1980).

[16]J. G. Arintero, *The Mystical Evolution,* 1:23.

[17]Ibid., 89–90.

[18]Ibid., 90 nn. 14 and 15. Arintero's footnotes are a rich source of further
references.

[19]Rufus M. Jones, *The Flowering of Mysticism: The Friends of God in the Fourteenth Century* (New York, 1939). Anna Groh Seesholtz, *Friends of God: Practical Mystics of the Fourteenth Century* (New York: AMS Press, 1934/1970).

Although someone may experience spiritual phenomena that are out of the ordinary, the divine indwelling, gifts of the Spirit, adoption, and deification are not for "mystics" in contrast to other Christians. For Arintero all baptized Christians are called to the mystical life.[20] This tendency in the West to think of the mystic as a Christian apart is not a danger in Eastern thought where theology and spirituality are closely tied together. The saints simply exemplify for us the life of grace in which we all share.

A prominent theme in Meister Eckhart[21] is the birth of the Word in the soul, the third birth of Christ (the first two being the eternal birth of the Word from the Unbegotten One and the historical birth of the Word as incarnate in Bethlehem). "God's chief aim is giving birth. He is never content till He begets His Son in us. And the soul, too, is in no way content until the Son of God is born in her."[22] "May the God who has been born again as man assist us to this birth, eternally helping us, weak men, to be born in him again as God."[23] "Why did God become man? That I might be born God Himself."[24]

---

[20]Cf. Arintero, *Stages in Prayer,* esp. preface to second Spanish edition, vii, and 1–4. Also, *The Mystical Evolution,* 1:19–20. The supernatural life is the ordinary way of life for a Christian.

[21]A translation of the German sermons of Eckhart can be found in *Meister Eckhart, Sermons and Treatises,* 2 vols. (London: Watkins Publishing, 1979 and 1981) ed. and trans. M. O'C. Walshe. Selections from both the Latin works and the German works can be found in *Meister Eckhart,* ed. and trans. Edmund Colledge and Bernard McGinn, Classics of Western Spirituality (New York: Paulist Press, 1981) and *Meister Eckhart, Teacher and Preacher,* Classics of Western Spirituality (New York: Paulist Press, 1986). In addition to the introductions to Eckhart in both of the above, see Jeanne Ancelet-Hustache, *Master Eckhart and the Rhineland Mystics* (New York: Harper Torchbooks, 1957); Cyprian Smith, *Spiritual Life as Taught by Meister Eckhart, The Way of Paradox* (New York: Paulist Press, 1987); and Richard Woods, *Eckhart's Way* (Wilmington, Del.: Michael Glazier, 1986). More advanced works on Eckhart include C. F. Kelley, *Meister Eckhart on Divine Knowledge* (New Haven: Yale University Press, 1977); and Vladimir Lossky, *Théologie négative et connaissance de Dieu chez Maître Eckhart* (Paris: J. Vrin, 1973). An extensive Eckhart bibliography can be found in *The Thomist* 42 (1978) 313–36.

[22]Eckhart, *Sermon 68,* Walshe edition, 2:157.

[23]Ibid., *Sermon 1,* 1:12.

[24]Ibid., *Sermon 16,* 1:138. For further pertinent references, see the Colledge and McGinn edition, *Sermon 6,* 185–89; and the *Book of Divine Consolation,* 209–39.

John Tauler[25] continues the Eckhartian theme of the birth of the Word as well as the psychology of the soul in which the ground *(Grund)* of the soul and the abyss *(Abgrund)* that God is become one. "The first and most sublime of these three births which we celebrate today is the birth, within the Godhead, of the only Son of the Heavenly Father, divinely begotten by Him and distinct from Him in person only. The second is His human birth, when Mary became His mother without any loss of her virgin purity. The third is the spiritual birth; and every hour God is born into the souls of all just men, through grace and love."[26] "We are drawn out of human activities into a divine life, out of all sorrow into a divine peace, in which man is so deified that everything which he is and does, God is and does in him. He is so far above his natural self that he truly becomes, by grace, what God in His being is by nature."[27]

Within the same mystical tradition Henry Suso writes, "Essential reward lies in the contemplative union of the soul with the naked Godhead, for it will never rest until it is led above all its powers and strength, and brought into the essential nature of the Persons, and into the simple purity of the Being . . . the deeper the penetration into the wild desert and the profound abyss of the pathless Godhead, into which it [the soul] sinks, is swept away, and united, in such a way that it cannot will anything but what God wills; and that is to be the same as God is; that is, that they are blessed by grace, as He is blessed by nature."[28]

[25]An English translation of some of the sermons of Tauler can be found in *Spiritual Conferences by Johann Tauler* (Rockford, Ill.: Tan Books and Publishers, 1961) ed. and trans. Colledge and Sister M. Jane; and Johannes Tauler, *Sermons,* trans. Maria Shrady, Classics of Western Spirituality (New York: Paulist Press, 1985). All the authentic sermons can be found in a French edition, *Sermons de Tauler,* 3 vols. (Paris: Librairie Desclée, 1927–1935) ed. and trans. E. Hugueney, G. Thery, and A. L. Corin. An introduction to Tauler is contained in James M. Clark, *The Great German Mystics: Eckhart, Tauler, and Suso* (Oxford, 1949).

[26]*Spiritual Conferences by Johann Tauler,* 153, from sermon 1 for the Nativity, sermon 1 in vol. 1 of the Hugeney et al. edition.

[27]Ibid., 199, sermon 40 in vol. 2 in the Hugeney et al. edition. For further references to the image and likeness of God, the divine spark in the soul, the divine abyss, and deification, see *Spiritual Conferences by Johann Tauler,* 40, 75, 76, 94, 99, 119–24, 141–47, 157, 166–67, 186–87, 195, 212, 227.

[28]Henry Suso, *Little Book of Eternal Wisdom* and *Little Book of Truth,* trans. James M. Clark (London: Faber and Faber, 1953) 92. For an English translation

The classic representatives of the Western mystical tradition are today often seen to be the Spanish mystics of the sixteenth century. John of the Cross[29] writes as boldly as the Rhineland mystics. "Although the substance of this soul is not the substance of God, since it cannot undergo a substantial conversion into Him, it has become God through participation in God, being united to and absorbed in Him, as it is in this state."[30] Chapter 5 of *The Ascent of Mount Carmel* gives a succinct explanation of the nature of the union of the soul with God. John of the Cross writes, "When God grants this supernatural favor to the soul, so great a union is caused that all the things of both God and the soul become one in participant transformation, and the soul appears to be God more than a soul. Indeed, it is God by participation. Yet truly, its being (even though transformed) is naturally as distinct from God's as it was before, just as the window although illumed by the ray [a ray of sunlight], has an existence distinct from the ray."[31]

In the history of theology we find individual differences within any school or tradition. Among the Alexandrians, for example, Athanasius is not Origen. So likewise here. No two schools of Western mysticism expound exactly the same doctrine, nor do their representative authors. John and Teresa are distinctive as well as closely related. So with Eckhart and Tauler. Nevertheless, it is clear that the West offers witness to the fact that we too are divine. This divinity is effected by grace.

The Theology of Divine Presence

Whether we talk about grace or deification, we are talking about God's presence to God's people. Peter Fransen writes, "In unraveling the mystery of grace, we find a most appropriate scheme

---

of the works of Suso, see *The Exemplar,* trans. Frank Tobin, Classics of Western Spirituality (New York: Paulist Press, 1989).

[29]An excellent introductory biography is Richard P. Hardy, *Search for Nothing, The Life of John of the Cross* (New York: Crossroad, 1982). For the works of John, see *The Collected Works of St. John of the Cross,* trans. Kieran Kavanaugh and Otilio Rodriguez (Washington, D.C.: Institute of Carmelite Studies, 1973).

[30]From *The Living Flame of Love,* stanza 2, par. 34, in *Collected Works,* 608.

[31]From *The Ascent of Mount Carmel,* book 2, ch. 5, in *Collected Works,* 117–18.

of thought in personalistic philosophy, especially in the description of the *presence* of one person to another. Grace in general can be described as the secret of God's presence in our lives. . . . Grace is the mystery of God's intense, living presence in us."[32] A theology of divine presence links God's presence in us and to us with the great acts of God by which God became present in history as well. God's presence to us is an historical presence. God's presence with us is in continuity with the history of the divine presence. Placing God's presence in Christ in the wider context of God's presence by grace helps us to understand God's relationship to Jesus better and also gives a historical character to the Christ-event that is often lacking in an approach to Jesus through the doctrine of two natures. The hypostatic union is one particular and unique instance in the history of God's presence among people. Jesus' divinity, as well as our own, must be placed in the context of the history of salvation, and even a history wider than what we may ordinarily think of as salvific history.

The theme of God's presence as a way of situating Jesus of Nazareth is developed by Yves Congar in his *Mystery of the Temple* (1958), subtitled "The Manner of God's Presence to His Creatures from Genesis to the Apocalypse," and later is offered as the basis for a biblical theology of both the Hebrew and Christian Bibles by Samuel Terrien in *The Elusive Presence* (1978). Divine presence is another way of talking about God's actions *ad extra,* of which the incarnation is a supreme exemplification. For the God of Jesus of Nazareth is the God of his ancestors, the God of Abraham and Sarah, Isaac and Rebekah, Jacob and Rachel. Jesus' God was already the God of Isaiah, namely *ēl imānū* (God-is-with-us).

Biblical revelation is a revelation of God's self-disclosure, of God as being with us and for us, of the divine nearness, of God as coming to us. The biblical God comes to be with people, and they become a people because God has come to be with them. Yet, as Terrien points out, the biblical understanding of the presence of God has incorporated the awareness of the absence of God as well. The prophets, psalmists, and Job are aware of how elusive the divine presence is, how unpredictable and uncontrollable. Terrien describes it as "elusive, intangible, unpredictable,

[32]Peter Fransen, *The New Life of Grace,* trans. Georges Dupont (New York: Seabury Press, 1973) 24–25.

untamed, inaccessible to empirical verification, outwardly invisible but inwardly irresistible.''[33] God is surprising and elusive as well as close and caring. God will be who God will be. God need not conform to human definitions. Yet God is a real presence, whether to Moses in the presence of the burning bush, in Jesus as the Word made flesh, or in the Eucharistic presence of Christ to a Christian community. All are a part of the story of God's presence to God's people, of which Jesus is a supreme but not exclusive exemplification.

In the patriarchal narratives of the Hebrew Scriptures, God is a God who visits people like Abraham, who is called upon to leave Haran and go to an unknown land (Gen 12:1-9), or is paid a surprising visit by the Lord in the guise of three strangers at the oaks of Mamre (Gen 18). Jacob had acute experiences of God in a dream at Bethel (Gen 28:10-22) and in his fight with God at Penuel (Gen 32:23-32). In the former, Jacob saw a ladder joining heaven to earth. And the Lord spoke words which run as a continuous theme throughout Scripture, "Behold, I am with you" (28:15). Jacob awakened and was aware of the proximity of God, and said, "Surely the Lord is in this place" (28:16), and so he named the place *Bethel* (28:19), which means "house of God" *(bēt-ēl)*. Later when God spoke to Jacob, God was identified as the God whom Jacob met at Bethel (31:13).

In the experience Jacob had of God at the Jabbok ford he saw another side of God and was left with a permanent limp to remember the experience. Jacob asked for God's name, but God only responded, "Why is it that you ask my name?" (32:29). God was not to be pinned down or controlled: God will be who God will be. Jacob described the encounter, "I have seen God face to face" (32:30) and thus named the place Penuel (*pānīm el-pānīm,* face to face; *penē-ēl,* face of God). What is astounding is that Jacob had wrestled with God and survived (32:30). Yet Jacob came through the ordeal maimed (32:25, 31). He found out that the presence of God can sometimes be a disturbing presence, one of judgment as one wrestles with guilt. Both transcendence (or freedom or elusiveness) and immanence were part of Jacob's God. The "face of God" is sometimes inaccessible, God's innermost

[33]Samuel Terrien, *The Elusive Presence* (New York: Harper and Row Publishers, 1978) 457.

self, and sometimes present, as to Jacob. Yet God promises continuing companionship (to Isaac, Gen 26:24; to Jacob, Gen 28:15).

The great theophanies of God to Moses, although different from the divine visitations described in the patriarchal narratives, are a part of the ongoing revelation of God as near to people. In the narrative of the burning bush (Exod 3:1–4:14), the text conveys the awesomeness of being in the presence of God: Moses removed his shoes (3:5). God was identified as the God of Abraham, Isaac, and Jacob (3:6). Moses was afraid to look at God (3:6) and the text distinguishes between God's word and God's glory, between ear and eye.[34] God was really present to Moses but invisible. The eye cannot attain to God. God was revealed or spoke to Moses as one who had sympathy for the afflicted and oppressed (3:7-10). And again the divine reassurance: "I will be with you" (3:12). Moses inquired, as had Jacob, concerning God's name (3:13), and God's response was both elusive and revelatory, and has been so ever since: "I am who I am" (3:14). Moses encountered a personal but elusive "I will be who I will be" (33:19). God was revealed as both "I Am" and as I-am-One-who-is-with-you.

The covenant theophany at Sinai (Exod 19:1–24:18) and the ongoing encounters of Moses with "I am who I am" in the wilderness were formative of a people who will be God's people. The Lord spoke to Moses (19:3-6). It was the voice of the Lord whom the people were to obey (19:5). God told Moses of the divine presence in a cloud so that others might hear God as well (19:9). The cloud, linked as it was to a manifestation of God, both veiled and manifested God's presence. The Lord finally came in the midst of a storm and descended on the mountain in the form of fire. God spoke to Moses (14:21-22; 20:1-17). Moses, Aaron, Nadab, and Abihu are described as "seeing" and "gazing on" God (24:9-11). The "glory of God" settled on the mountain. It seemed like a devouring fire. Moses entered the cloud and stayed with the Lord for forty days and forty nights (24:12-18). His intimacy with God continued. The two met in the tent of meeting with the pillar of cloud at the entrance. "The Lord used to speak to Moses face

---

[34] This distinction is consistently given attention by Terrien, *The Elusive Presence,* in his discussion of the modes of divine presence in the biblical narratives. According to Terrien, the theology of the name and of hearing relate more to the northern, Elohist, Horeb traditions, whereas the southern, Yahwist, Sinai traditions bring out visual aspects and a theology of the glory. See esp. 106–52.

to face, as a person speaks to a friend" (33:11). Moses wanted
to know the ways of God and the hours of the journey ahead.
But God's reassurance was: "My presence will go with you"
(33:14). Moses was not completely reassured (33:15-17). He prayed
to *see* God's glory. But God replied, "You cannot see my face,
for a human being shall not see me and live" (33:20). A human
being cannot behold the brightness of God. Yet a human can hear
God's voice. For God is both near and unapproachable, elusive
and present. God said to Moses, "While my glory passes by I will
put you in a cleft of the rock, and I will cover you with my hand
until I have passed by; then I will take away my hand, and you
shall see my back; but my face shall not be seen" (33:22-23). What
was revealed to Moses was the name but not the glory of the Lord.

This nearness of God continued during the reigns of David and
Solomon and with the theology of the Temple and the promise
made to David. Prior to the construction of the Temple there had
been no fixed dwelling for God. As the Lord said to David through
the prophet Nathan, "I have not dwelt in a house since the day
I brought up the people of Israel from Egypt to this day, but I
have been moving about in a tent for my dwelling" (2 Sam 7:6).
Although there had been no fixed space in which the divine presence dwelled, God's presence had been associated with both "the
ark of the covenant" and "the tent of meeting." The tent of meeting had its origin in the wilderness as the place where God met
with the people, especially Moses (Exod 33:7-11; Num 12:1-8).
The ark contained the two stone tablets on which the Lord had
written for Moses (1 Kgs 8:9; Exod 25:10-22; Deut 10:1-5) and
it played an important role in the history of Israel as a sign of
the covenant and of God's presence to people (Josh 6:4-16; 1 Sam
4-6; 2 Sam 6; 1 Kgs 8:1-9). After the conquest of Canaan, the
ark rested first in Shiloh; later it was brought by David to Jerusalem where it contributed to the growing significance of Zion. Neither the ark nor the tent of meeting were fixed abodes for the
presence of the Lord. The Lord came and went from the tent,
and the ark moved and accompanied the Israelites.

A significant understanding of God's presence is contained in
Nathan's prophecy to David, an important prophecy for later messianism.

> The king said to Nathan the prophet, "See now, I dwell in
> a house of cedar, but the ark of God dwells in a tent." And

Nathan said to the king, "Go, do all that is in your heart; for
the Lord is with you."

But that same night the word of the Lord came to Nathan,
"Go and tell my servant David, 'Thus says the Lord: Would
you build me a house to dwell in? I have not dwelt in a house
since the day I brought up the people of Israel from Egypt to
this day, but I have been moving about in a tent for my dwelling. In all places where I have moved with all the people of Israel, did I speak a word with any of the judges of Israel, whom
I commanded to shepherd my people Israel, saying: Why have
you not built me a house of cedar?' Now therefore thus you
shall say to my servant David, 'Thus says the Lord of hosts,
I took you from the pasture, from following the sheep, that
you should be prince over my people Israel; and I have been
with you wherever you went, and have cut off all your enemies
from before you; and I will make for you a great name, like
the name of the great ones of the earth. And I will appoint a
place for my people Israel, and will plant them, that they may
dwell in their own place, and be disturbed no more; and vio-
lent men shall afflict them no more, as formerly, from the time
that I appointed judges over my people Israel; and I will give
you rest from all your enemies. Moreover the Lord declares to
you that the Lord will make you a house. When your days are
fulfilled and you lie down with your fathers, I will raise up your
offspring after you, who shall come forth from your body, and
I will establish his kingdom.

" 'He shall build a house for my name, and I will establish
the throne of his kingdom forever. I will be his father, and he
shall be my son. When he commits iniquity, I will chasten him
with the rod of men, with the stripes of the sons of men; but
I will not take my steadfast love from him, as I took it from
Saul, whom I put away before you. And your house and your
kingdom shall be made sure forever before me; your throne shall
be established forever.' " In accordance with all these words,
and in accordance with all this vision, Nathan spoke to David
(2 Sam 7:1-16).

The intent of the prophecy involves a play on the word *house
(bayit)*. David was intent upon building a house for the Lord (7:2).
But the Lord never had need for a house in order to be with the
people (7:5-7). In fact, it was the Lord who would provide a house

for David (7:11-12), but a house of a different sort, one that has a temporal rather than a spatial character: David's offspring. This would be the sign of God's abiding presence. The Lord needed no house of cedar. Yet David's son would build the house for the Lord that David wanted, and David's son would be like a son to the Lord as well. God would not be one who would dwell in any one particular place. Rather God would be the One-who-is-with-us.[35]

David's son Solomon was the one who constructed the Temple. Solomon's prayer at the completion of the Temple reflected the long history behind the theology of God's presence (1 Kgs 8:22-53). For the heavens cannot contain the Lord (8:27) and the heavens are God's proper dwelling place (vv. 34, 36, 39, 43, 49). It is only the name of the Lord that dwells in the Temple (vv. 29, 43, 48). Yet for centuries the Temple of Solomon would be the supreme sign of God's nearness and presence. It would play an increasingly significant role in the history of Israel and Judah.

God's continuing and elusive presence to people during the time of the monarchy is the story of the great prophetic tradition. Moses had been a prophet, and David was seen as a prophet-king. But in the ninth century Elijah's encounter with God in the cave at Mount Horeb manifested a new mode of presence (1 Kgs 19:9-18). God was not in the wind or the earthquake or the fire. God's presence had been accompanied by these in the Mosaic theophanies (wind, earthquake) and in Elijah's victory on Mount Carmel (fire) (1 Kgs 18:20-40). At Horeb, however, Elijah experienced the presence of God in the stillness: "But the Lord was not in the fire, and after the fire a still small voice" (1 Kgs 19:12). Elijah was not another Moses, but another kind of prophet, more reflective of the great eighth-century prophets to come, with their intensely personal experiences of God. Their experiences were not characterized by the nature miracles in which God's presence was previously situated. God will be who God will be. God's presence would be real but unpredictable. Terrien writes, "The God who is coming is altogether different from the one that man expects. He is not the God whom memory, reason, or imagination

---

[35]Cf. Yves M.-J. Congar, *The Mystery of the Temple,* trans. Reginald F. Trevett (Westminster, Md.: The Newman Press, 1962) 20–53.

anticipates, however marvelous and comforting the traditions may have been."[36]

The prophets experienced unexpected calls which they did not initiate. They found themselves quite abruptly in the presence of God (Amos 7:14-15; Hos 1:2; 2:1-3; Isa 6:1-13; Jer 1:4-10; Ezek 1:1-3:15). They did respect the Temple and its cult: Isaiah's vision and call involved the presence of the Lord in the Temple; much of Jeremiah's activity was in the vicinity of the Temple. Yet their critique extended to and included the priesthood and Temple sacrifice, for their concern was always true worship, true religion, a true relationship with God (Amos 6:21-27; Hos 8:13; 6:6; Isa 1:10-17; 2:9-19; 29:13, quoted by Jesus in Matt 15:7-8; Jer 4:20; 7:21-28; and many others). The prophets were not opposed in principle to the Temple or sacrifice, but recognized that these can too easily become efforts to manipulate God. "The Presence of which the prophets have the most vivid experience and to which they give priority is not the Presence to be worshipped in a place (Zion), it is the active Presence of the sovereign will by which God demands obedience and intervenes in history."[37]

The Exile was a dramatic, critical experience of the absence of God or abandonment by God. But the prophetic voice continued to speak. The Temple was no more, but God had never been confined to the Temple. God was and would continue to be with the people. As the Exile was interpreted, a hope for restoration was promised and a new Temple envisioned: this was the message of Jeremiah, Ezekiel, and Isaiah of Babylon. God's presence was in the hearts of those who love God.

> For thus says the high and lofty One
> who inhabits eternity, whose name is Holy:
> "I dwell in the high and holy place,
> and also with him who is of a contrite and humble spirit,
> to revive the spirit of the humble,
> and to revive the heart of the contrite" (Isa 57:15).

The God of the prophets was always the One-who-brought-you-out-of-Egypt (Exod 20:2; Deut 5:6; Num 23:22; Amos 3:1; Hos 12:4; Mic 6:4; Jer 2:6; 16:14; 23:7; 34:13; Ezek 20:1-10). And this

---

[36]Terrien, *The Elusive Presence,* 234.

[37]Congar, *The Mystery of the Temple,* 60.

belief was particularly intense for the prophets of the Exile. The first Exodus was the basis for understanding the Exile as a second Exodus (Jer 16:14-15). The One-who-is also was the One-who-brought-you-out-of-Egypt: both phrases functioned as proper names for the God of Israel. The Isaian prophecy (7:14) named the God whose presence has been with the people. The Lord is God-is-with-you. This was the pervasive religious intuition of Israel and the prophets and the basis for the prophetic hope of restoration during the Exile. God was present in the ark and the Temple. God's most basic presence, however, was with the people.

The Temple and its worship increased in significance during the Second Temple period and the emergence of early Judaism. Although prophetic activity died out, the people never lost faith in God as the One-who-is-with-you. The One whom they celebrated in the Shema was the strength of the Maccabean martyrs. The Lord would vindicate them for the Lord was the One-who-was-with-them. Yet Zion was the Lord's own city, and after the Exile a supreme sign of another of the mighty acts of God on behalf of the people. The Lord was the One-who-brought-you-out-of-the-land-of-captivity. These were the acts of God celebrated in the holy city during the great pilgrimage festivals.

The utterly transcendent and yet intimate presence of God to the people was acknowledged by the psalmists whose hymns covered the history of Israel from the time of David through the post-Exilic restoration. The divine presence was compared to a rock (Ps 18:1-2, 31-32, 46). The Lord was shepherd (Ps 23).

> The Lord is my light and my salvation; whom shall I fear?
> The Lord is the stronghold of my life; of whom shall I be afraid?
> When evildoers assail me, uttering slanders against me,
> my adversaries and foes, they shall stumble and fall.
> Though a host encamp against me, my heart shall not fear;
> though war arise against me, yet I will be confident.
> One thing have I asked of the Lord, that will I seek after;
> that I may dwell in the house of the Lord all the days of my life,
> to behold the beauty of the Lord, and to inquire in his temple.
> For he will hide me in his shelter in the day of trouble;
> he will conceal me under the cover of his tent,
> he will set me high upon a rock.

> And now my head shall be lifted up above my enemies round
>   about me;
> and I will offer in his tent sacrifices with shouts of joy;
> I will sing and make melody to the Lord.
> Hear, O Lord, when I cry aloud, be gracious to me and answer
>   me!
> Thou hast said, "Seek ye my face." My heart says to thee,
> "Thy face, Lord, do I seek." Hide not thy face from me.
> Turn not thy servant away in anger, thou who hast been my
>   help.
> Cast me not off, forsake me not, O God of my salvation!
> For my father and my mother have forsaken me, but the Lord
>   will take me up.
> Teach me the way, O Lord; and lead me on a level path be-
>   cause of my enemies.
> Give me not up to the will of my adversaries; for false witnesses
> have risen against me, and they breathe out violence.
> I believe that I shall see the goodness of the Lord in the land
>   of the living!
> Wait for the Lord; be strong, and let your heart take courage;
>   yea, wait for the Lord! (Ps 27).

The repentant one prays not to be removed from the divine presence: "Cast me not away from thy presence; and take not thy holy Spirit from me" (Ps 51:11). And Israel celebrates the Lord's love which lasts forever (Ps 89).

Whether we turn to the patriarchs or kings, to prophecy or psalmody, to narratives of distress or triumph, to cult or wisdom, the sense of the elusive divine nearness is there. If we cannot always speak of God coming to earth, it is then God's word or spirit or wisdom that comes. For wisdom is both transcendent and immanent, the first born of all creatures, setting up a dwelling place among us, a playful delight to God.

> It was Yahweh who begot me, first fruit of his power,
> prelude to his masterpieces of old,
> From all times I was consecrated,
>   from the beginning, from the first days of the earth.
> I was conceived when the abysses were not yet,
>   even before the fountains of the deep came to exist.

> Before the mountains had been planted in their bases,
>   ahead of the hills, I was brought forth.
> [It was] at a time when he had not yet made the earth or space,
>   or even the first of the cosmic dust.
>
> I was there when he prepared the heavens,
>   when he drew a circle on the face of the abyss,
> When he condensed the clouds for the waters of above,
>   and the springs of the abyss gushed forth,
> When he assigned an engraved limit to the sea
>   that its waters should not trespass [the word of] his mouth,
>   and when he traced the foundations of the earth.
> Then I was at his side, [his] darling child!
>   then I was [his] delight day after day,
> Playing and dancing in the whole span of the earth!
>   and [now] my delight is with the sons of men!
> Thus, my sons, listen to me!
>   Happy are those who keep my ways! (Prov 8:22-31).[38]

Although with God from the beginning, wisdom also dwelled on earth.

> Does not wisdom call,
>   does not understanding raise her voice?
> On the heights beside the way,
>   in the paths she takes her stand;
> beside the gates in front of the town,
>   at the entrance of the portals
>   she cries aloud (Prov 8:1-3).

Even Job's dramatic experience of the divine absence, or elusiveness, was an experience of God as *mysterium tremendum*.

> Then Job answered the Lord:
> "I know that thou canst do all things,
>   and that no purpose of thine can be thwarted.
> 'Who is this that hides counsel without knowledge?'
> Therefore I have uttered what I did not understand,
>   things too wonderful for me, which I did not know.

---

[38]According to the translation in Terrien, *The Elusive Presence,* 355–56.

> I had heard of thee by the hearing of the ear,
> but now my eye sees thee;
> therefore I despise myself,
> and repent in dust and ashes" (Job 42:1-3, 5-6).

In Congar's *The Mystery of the Temple,* this history of God's coming to the people, as the One-who-is-with-you, is the context for understanding Jesus Christ. This *Heilsgeschichte* must precede any understanding of Jesus in terms of two natures, for the first fact about Jesus is that he takes his place in history. To abstract Jesus out of history is to present a docetic Christ. Jesus was the historical presence of God as well as a hypostatic presence of God. Jesus is the hypostatic presence of God *in history.*

With the emergence of Johannine theology, it was understood that the true temple, the locus of God's presence, is Jesus Christ (John 2:19-22). Yet Jesus becomes the true temple only in and through the process of dying and rising. It is in the "humiliation" and "exaltation" of Jesus that the old Temple has been replaced. In the prologue to the Fourth Gospel, Jesus is God dwelling among us, God's house on earth. In the Fourth Gospel, it is Jesus' body as destined for destruction that inaugurates the new era (John 12:23-28; cf. Heb 10:10).

For Congar,[39] God's temple, that is to say God's presence, is a mystery in a threefold sense: first in the theological sense of its incomprehensibility, second in the Pauline and patristic sense of an unfolding of the divine plan or economy of salvation, and third in the liturgical sense of a re-enactment and commemoration of the great acts of God. The incarnation is another stage in the story of God as present to people. Jesus is God's presence in history, that is, God present in history.

Thomas Aquinas distinguished three ways in which God is present to creation, three degrees of ever-greater intensification of God's presence (*Sentences* I, 37, 1, 2; *Colossians* c. 2, lect. 2; *ST* III, 43, 1). The first is that by which God is cosmically present to all creation simply in order that things may exist. The second is God's presence in rational creatures through grace. This mode of presence is an indwelling. The third is God's hypostatic presence in Jesus Christ. This mode of presence is incarnation. Through Jesus God dwells bodily in the world. Congar identifies

---

[39] See Congar, *The Mystery of the Temple,* 236–48.

these three modes or degrees of presence in Thomas with the three parts of his *Summa:* creation, the human person, Jesus Christ.[40]

The history of God's presence does not end with Jesus Christ, however, nor with the close of the apostolic age. It is ongoing, everlasting, universal, yet always elusive and unpredictable. The history of God's real presence, of God as the One-who-is-with-us, includes God's ongoing presence in Word and Eucharist, in the assembly of the faithful, and in the individual Christian.[41] The new temple, God's dwelling with people, is the body of Christ. But the Eucharist is the body of Christ, as is the Church. These are Christ really present and God-in-Christ as still the One-who-is-with-us. And through the uncontainable indwelling of the Spirit, the Christian (and not only the Christian) becomes a temple of the living God. Yet, for the Christian, Christ remains the supreme exemplification of God's presence to people. And, at the same time, the true "house of God" is the "people of God," as the Lord early revealed to David through Nathan the prophet.

The biblical theme of the immanent presence of the transcendent God is reflected in the post-biblical, targumic, and rabbinic teaching on the *shekinah* (from the Hebrew verb *shakan,* "to dwell").[42] *Shekinah* is a reverent circumlocution for God that expresses God's nearness to people. Its circumlocutional character suggests respect for the transcendence of God while the word itself indicates the presence of God. As we have seen, in the Hebrew Scriptures this sense of presence had been expressed particularly through the name, glory, spirit, word, or wisdom of God. *Shekinah* denoted God as active or dwelling on earth. The Targum of Onkelos (ca. 100–130 C.E.) substituted *shekinah* for *name* in Deuteronomy 12:5, and identified the shekinah with the angel in Genesis 16:13, and with the face of the Lord in Numbers 6:25 and Deuteronomy 31:18. In Exodus 34:6 it is the shekinah

---

[40]Ibid., 238–39 n. 3.

[41]Ibid., 151–203.

[42]Cf. J. Abelson, *The Immanence of God in Rabbinical Literature* (New York: Hermon Press, 1912/1969) 77–149. Eric Burrows, "The Doctrine of the Shekinah and the Theology of the Incarnation," in *The Gospel of the Infancy and Other Biblical Essays* (London: Burns, Oates, and Washbourne, 1940) 101–10. George Foot Moore, *Judaism in the First Centuries of the Christian Era* (New York: Schocken Books, 1971) 1:423–42; and "Intermediaries in Jewish Theology, Memra, Schechinah, Metraton," in *Harvard Theological Review* 15 (1922) 41–85.

that passes before Moses. Although the Talmud contains many references to the shekinah, the Mishnah itself contains only two. The second, from the tractate *Aboth,* is an interesting parallel to Matthew 18:20. "If two sit together and no words of the Law [are spoken] between them, there is the seat of the scornful. . . . But if two sit together and words of the Law [are spoken] between them, the Divine Presence [the shekinah] rests between them."[43]

For Christians, Jesus of Nazareth was and remains the supreme exemplification of the divine nearness. Jesus, even as hypostatically united to the eternal Word of God, cannot be abstracted from the history of God's dwelling with people. For Christians, Jesus is the One-who-is-with-us, *immānū Ēl.*

Two Modes of Union, Hypostatic and Indwelling

It is time to return to the central concern of this chapter, namely that Jesus' divinity is not an obstacle to full identity with us, that Jesus' divine nature does not make him a different kind of being than we are, and that this is true to some degree because we too are divine, or at least structured to share in the divine nature. When we do so we are not less than human or other than human. Rather we are more profoundly and genuinely human, being who we are intended to be, images or icons of God. In both Eastern and Western theology, the human person in some sense becomes divine by grace. In the theology of divine presence and the history of salvation, we see Jesus as an exemplification of a general reality: God coming to be with people. Jesus is not an isolated unique phenomenon in that sense. Whatever his uniqueness consists in, it is not that he is the only instance of the presence of God in history, nor the only instance of a human being in union with the divine.

Thus the apparent gap between Jesus and us is not unbridgeable. Jesus is indeed one of us, and Christology is simply the anthropology of the man Jesus, the "special anthropology"[44] or the

[43]*Aboth* 3.1; from the translation of Herbert Danby, *The Mishnah* (Oxford University Press, 1933/1980) 450. The second mishnaic reference to *shekinah* is from *Sanhedrin* 6.5, but see Danby's notes on this reference, 390 nn. 8 and 9.

[44]See Karl Barth, *Christ and Adam: Man and Humanity in Romans 5,* trans. T. A. Smail (New York: The Macmillan Co., 1968).

"transcendental anthropology"[45] of Jesus Christ. The history and theology of Jesus affect anthropology. Because of this man, Christian anthropology is never philosophical anthropology alone. For this particular *adam* (human being) gives us insight into every other *adam*.

Thus also the apparent gap between God and humankind is not unbridgeable. God can indeed come to be with people. God *is* the One-who-is-with-us. The infinite qualitative difference between God and us must be understood in the context of the incarnation, which reveals that God and humankind can be at one with each other and that this is precisely God's intention for humankind. The incarnation radically qualifies the gap, reveals to us that the God of Jesus Christ is not and never has been a God "out there," that Deism presents us with a false god and not the living God, and that all the divine immanence in the whole world does not deny, exhaust, or negate the infinite transcendence that God is. God's infinity does not limit him to remoteness but is rather the basis for his intense intimacy with us, to the degree that we are capable of experiencing it.

Just as a theology of grace, no matter how articulate it may be, does not remove the mystery that God is in relationship with us, and perhaps only helps us to situate or pronounce that mystery more clearly, so a theology of the hypostatic union does not solve a problem. It too only reveals the *mysterium* that Christ Jesus is. It does not, cannot, remove Jesus from our midst. It only helps to disclose the unfathomable mystery of humankind in relationship with its God. Thus no theology of the hypostatic union is ever final. The Council of Chalcedon defined *that* Jesus was hypostatically one, but never tried to and never could explain the depth of mystery of any union with God. And so, recognizing the distinctiveness of Jesus' union with God as its hypostatic character, how does this union in the concrete course of existential and historical life differ from our union with God in grace? What does Jesus' natural sonship do for his human nature or history that adopted sonship or daughtership cannot do for us? Although we Christians recognize Jesus as Lord, and are thus careful

---

⁴⁵See Karl Rahner, "Christology within an Evolutionary View of the World," in *Theological Investigations* 5, trans. Karl H. Kruger (Baltimore: Helican Press, 1966) 157–92.

to distinguish the language by which we articulate Jesus' divinity and our own (hypostatic union, union of sanctifying grace; son of God by nature, children of God by adoption; God by nature, gods by grace), when we go beyond the language to the realities and truth they long to express, there is no biblical or dogmatic statement that makes Jesus less human or other than one of us. "Except for sin" is both the biblical and the traditional way of expressing Jesus' uniqueness: Jesus is unique in his relationship to sin, *not* in his oneness with God.

Karl Rahner's Christology raises the question of the relationship between the hypostatic union and the union of grace.[46] From the perspective of theological anthropology, the human person is open to self-transcendence. And from the perspective of the theology of revelation, God communicates God's very own self to humanity. "Becoming," for Rahner, is not a question of becoming other. It is rather, in its truest sense, a becoming *more,* a real self-transcendence which takes place by a power other than that which is constitutive of the essence of a finite being, but a power nevertheless deeply interior to the being. God does not simply create creatures who are other, God gives God's self to them, communicates God's self, and even becomes the innermost life of some creatures who are existentially structured for this life with God. There is then an interrelationship between the human being's openness to self-transcendence and God's goal of self-communication. The human person transcends his- or herself in and through God's self-communication through grace. And God's self-communication, as our self-transcendence, takes place historically.

Jesus Christ is then an instance in this history of God's self-communication to creatures. Creation and incarnation are not two disparate, unrelated acts of God, but two phases in the process of God's self-communication. The incarnation means that God has truly entered the cosmos and history. God has become material. As Rahner writes, "The divine Logos himself both really creates and accepts this corporeality—which is part of the world—*as his* own reality; he brings it into existence as something other than himself in such a way, therefore, that this very materiality ex-

---

[46]Ibid. This particular essay of Rahner's is very significant for this discussion.

presses *him,* the Logos himself, and lets him be present in his world.''[47]

How then does God's self-communication in grace and glory to all human beings relate to God's self-communication to this one particular human being, Jesus? As Rahner puts the question:

> How then does the doctrine of the Hypostatic Union of a determined *single* human nature with God's Logos fit into this basic conception? Is this to be conceived merely as a *proper,* still higher stage of an essentially newer and higher kind of divine self-communication to the creature, which this time is given only in one single "case"? Or is it possible to conceive that, even though this Hypostatic Union is given only once in its essential characteristics, it is nevertheless precisely the way in which the divinization of the spiritual creature is and *must* be carried out if it is to happen at all?[48]

The implication of course is that Rahner wants to situate the hypostatic union in a wider context, namely, that of the whole history of God's self-communication.

> The Incarnation itself is to be made intelligible *in* its uniqueness and *in* the degree of reality given by it . . . as an intrinsic and necessary element in the process of God's giving himself in grace to the world as a whole. . . . The Hypostatic Union takes effect interiorly *for* the human nature of the Logos precisely in what, and really only in what, the same theology prescribes for *all* men as their goal and consummation.[49]

Thus, for Rahner, grace and hypostatic unity can only be thought of together, in their interrelatedness. Both realities manifest God's freely chosen self-communication. "Hence the thesis toward which we are working purports to show that, even though the Hypostatic Union is in its proper nature a unique event and—when seen in itself—is certainly the highest conceivable event, it is nevertheless an intrinsic factor of the whole process of the bestowal of grace on the spiritual creature in general."[50]

[47]Ibid., 177.
[48]Ibid., 179.
[49]Ibid., 180–81.
[50]Ibid., 191.

We can see why there has been a shift in contemporary Christology away from the theology of the hypostatic union as such to the question of the uniqueness of Jesus Christ. The latter question does not necessarily deny the former reality, nor does the former reality necessarily answer the latter question. We can also see how easy it is for the question of the difference between Jesus and us (given the fact that he is one of us) to be posed in terms of whether it is a difference of degree or a difference of kind. We shall return later to the questions of Jesus' uniqueness. All we are saying now is that his uniqueness does not consist in his sharing in the divine nature as such, although his particular mode of unity with the divine nature is unique.

When we come to the question of whether the difference between Jesus and ourselves is one of degree or one of kind, we can only answer that it is both. The kind of union by means of which Jesus is God's Son, namely, hypostatic, is different than that by means of which we are God's daughters and sons by sanctifying grace. This is the traditional understanding, whether Chalcedonian with its hypostatic union, or Johannine, in which Jesus is born from above whereas we are re-born from above, or even Matthean and Lucan, in which Jesus' conception effects his sonship in a way that our conceptions do not. But as we assert this distinctiveness, we must also assert that the hypostatic union only makes Jesus other than us to a degree. It certainly does not make him a different kind of being than you and I are, for he is human by nature. He is not a different kind of being, even though a unique being. Even his divinity is not a different kind of divinity than ours. Indeed, there is only one kind of divinity, only one God, and that is God's very own life. Thus the difference between Jesus and us is both one of degree and one of kind. But that understanding only confronts us once again with the mystery that Christ is. Christians believe God's presence in Christ and God's union with Christ to be unique, but defining this uniqueness is not a problem to be solved. All the theologies of the hypostatic union themselves do not solve the mystery. They only make us confront the mystery of an unsurpassed event in the story of God's presence to God's people.

In his own Christology, Louis Bouyer raises two important questions for us. The first is the question on which we have reflected in this chapter: "How can we stop thinking about the divinity and humanity of Christ as two 'natures' that are estranged from one another and often in opposition to one another?''[51] The humanity of Jesus is not negated by affirming his divinity, nor vice versa. Christologies that place divinity and humanity in such opposition to each other are rooted in a false image of God as "the sublime stranger.''[52] Rather than being the antithesis of God, the human being is created as an image of God. The eternal Word is the perfect Image of God, the incarnate Word is this Image made visible through the humanity of Christ, and we ourselves are images of this Image.

To use language which I used in volume 1 of this series, Jesus *is* solidarity with God. Jesus also *is* solidarity with us, or consubstantial with us. Bouyer's second question makes this point equally strongly. How can Jesus as the Word incarnate be of concern to us, all of us, in such a way that he has salvific significance for us?[53] This is the soteriological question. Is Jesus' solidarity with us as real and as profound as his solidarity with God? Bouyer makes the point that our intimacy with Christ is no less unique than Christ's intimacy with God.[54] Christ's consubstantiality or solidarity with us is also unique. Soteriology is related to this unique bond between Christ and us. Jesus may be uniquely human and uniquely divine, but not unique in being both human and divine.

In Conclusion

The thesis of this chapter has just been stated. The incarnation is not a contradiction in terms but rather the supreme exemplification of a general reality. It is a revelation of who we ourselves ultimately are or are intended to be. Jesus Christ is a sacrament of humanity because he is an icon of God. The divine "nature" and human "nature," or Godhead and humanity, are not irreconcilable opposites, at least not by nature, but complementary realities, even if existentially estranged due to sin. Neither Jesus' divinity nor ours makes us anything other than more truly human.

[51]Louis Bouyer, *The Eternal Son,* trans. Simone Inkel and John F. Laughlin (Huntington, Ind.: Our Sunday Visitor, Inc., 1978) 385.

[52]Ibid., 399.

[53]Ibid., 393–96.

[54]Ibid., 391.

3

Jesus' Humanity and Ours

The only Jesus we experience today is the risen Jesus, the risen Christ. Our affirmation that Jesus is the Christ is itself a profession of faith that Jesus has been raised from the dead and lives. This living, risen Jesus, however, is that same earthly Jesus who lived and died as a Galilean Jew in the first century of the common era, that same Jesus transformed, raised, and exalted. This Jesus, however, as the Fourth Gospel so clearly presents him, is God's Word incarnate. Jesus *is* the Word as incarnate, and the Word *is* God as self-revealing. The Christian tradition holds to two unyielding convictions about Jesus. First, he is thoroughly human, one of us, a full participant in our history and historical existence. Second, he cannot be understood apart from God. His definition includes God.

These two convictions have been theologically explored and emphasized, sometimes one at the expense of the other, but always in an effort to hold them together in balance. The Alexandrian theology of the Logos made Jesus' divinity the starting point for interpreting or understanding him. The Antiochene theological anthropology, or theology of the human, led to a starting point in Jesus' humanity, which God indwelled. The Council of Chalcedon insisted that Jesus, the Christ, was ontologically only one *hypostasis* but was nevertheless both fully human and truly divine.

Insofar as the Christ of God, both when risen and while on earth, was and is the Word of God incarnate, we cannot escape the two poles within which Jesus has been traditionally understood. Tradition has set limits within which one must remain in order to do justice to Jesus. Docetism and Adoptionism, or Apollinarianism and "Nestorianism," represent these outer limits. Jesus is fully human, but not only human, truly divine, but not only divine.

In the last chapter I explained why Jesus' divinity need not lessen his humanity. There is nothing irreconcilable or contradictory about an individual being both divine and human. We too are divine, or at least destined to be so, indeed must be so if we are to be fully human. And there is nothing inappropriate or inconceivable about God's wanting to be totally one with us. That is simply an affirmation of who our God is: the One-who-is-with-us. God is with us and we are in God: this is the mystery of salvation disclosed in the doctrine of the incarnation.

Yet even if we grant all this, we are still left with the need to explore the humanity of Jesus further. This has been called "the special anthropology of Jesus." Both the Letter to the Hebrews (4:15) and the Council of Chalcedon affirm that Jesus was like us in all ways except for sin. Jesus' sinlessness we shall consider later. Now we must give attention to whether Jesus' humanity is indeed like ours, granting the one exception.

Our starting point for understanding Jesus is the resurrection, which we have considered in the first chapter and even more fully in volume 2 of this series. The resurrection of Jesus calls for a decision of faith. In the light of that faith, we are forced to look backwards from the resurrection to "see" Jesus more clearly. Faith in the risen Jesus led Johannine Christian Jews and later Christians to "see" God's Word in Jesus. Throughout most of this volume we will be struggling with the theology of this incarnation. The incarnation is not the starting point for a contemporary Christology, but it is still a reality or affirmation of faith that cannot be ignored. What are we saying when we say that Jesus *is* God's Word? And what do we mean when we say that Jesus *is* one of us, consubstantial with us?

In this chapter we will look at the Christological hymn in Philippians, reflect upon the meaning of Jesus' pre-existence, and explore further Thomas Aquinas's theology of the humanity of Jesus. In the next chapter we will look at two contemporary approaches to the humanity of Jesus: those of kenotic Christologies and that of Piet Schoonenberg. All this is by way of preparation for my own conclusions.

The Humble and Obedient One
Philippians 2:6-11

Paul visited Philippi for the first time during his second missionary journey, ca. 48–49 C.E. While in Troas, he had had a vision of a man from Macedonia who invited him to Macedonia to preach (Acts 16:6-12). Paul landed at Neapolis, present-day Kavalla, and then went on to Philippi. He established there his first Christian community outside of Asia. His personal love for this community is reflected in the affection and warmth so clearly expressed in his letter (1:3-11). Philippi had been founded by Philip II of Macedonia. Brutus and Cassius had been defeated there by Mark Antony (42 B.C.E.). It was a prominent, Latin-speaking Roman city with some Greeks and a small number of Jews.

Paul later wrote to the Philippians either from Rome or from Ephesus. Rome was traditionally considered the place of composition for the letter; however, more and more opinions favor the hypothesis of Ephesus. The fact that our present letter may be a conflation of three letters also affects the question of place of composition. If Rome is the place of origin, the date would be close to 61 C.E.; if Ephesus, it would be around 55 C.E.

Philippians 2:6-11 is generally considered to have the character of a hymn, to be of pre-Pauline or extra-Pauline origin, and to have been originally a separate, self-contained composition later incorporated by Paul into his letter.[1] Thus the hymn can be in-

---

[1] For the history of interpretation of the Philippians hymn, see Ralph P. Martin, *Carmen Christi: Philippians 2:5-11 in Recent Interpretation and in the Setting of Early Christian Worship*, rev. ed. (Grand Rapids, Mich.: William B. Eerdmans, 1967/1983), particularly for the literature before 1964 although the preface to the 1983 edition covers later developments. Later developments are also covered in the same author's commentary, *Philippians* (Grand Rapids, Mich.: William B. Eerdmans, 1980). Two important studies are those of Jerome Murphy-O'Connor, "Christological Anthropology in Phil. 2:6-11," *Revue biblique* 83 (1976) 25–50 (n. 1 includes a bibliography of recent literature); and Dunn, *Christology in the Making*, 114–25. Also see Francis T. Glasson, "Two Notes on the Philippians Hymn (2:6-11)," *New Testament Studies* 21 (1975) 133–39; Pierre Grelot, "Deux expressions difficiles de Philippiens 2:6-7," *Biblica* 53 (1972) 495–507; George Howard, "Phil. 2:6-11 and the Human Christ," *Catholic Biblical Quar-*

terpreted in terms of two settings or at two levels: the original pre-Pauline meaning or setting and the function or setting within the letter. Other Christological hymns in the New Testament include Hebrews 1:3, Colossians 1:15-20, 1 Timothy 3:16, John 1:1-14, and 1 Peter 3:18-22. The original hymn was not necessarily the same as what appears within the epistolary context. There is much agreement on the suggestion made by Ernst Lohmeyer that the *thanatou de staurou* ("even death on a cross") of verse 8 is a Pauline addition. Joachim Jeremias has suggested that three phrases are Pauline interpolations: "even death on a cross" (v. 8); "in heaven and on earth and under the earth" (v. 10); and "to the glory of God the Father" (v. 11).[2]

One of the major questions in recent interpretation of the Philippians hymn is whether or not it contains the notion of the personal pre-existence of Christ. In other words, does it contain a two-stage or a three-stage Christology? Since we are so accustomed to seeing the three stages of Christ's existence in the hymn, we almost automatically so interpret it. It is difficult not to see it there. Jerome Murphy-O'Connor challenges such a presupposition, however. At least the original hymn, Murphy-O'Connor argues, gives us only a two-stage Christology. The issue involves how one interprets the *en morphē theou* ("in the form of God") and *to einai isa theō* ("equality with God") as well as the difficult word *harpagmon,* all of verse 6. I give here my own translation of the hymn first.[3]

> (5) Keep this in mind among yourselves which was also in Christ Jesus (6) who, being in the form of God, did not consider be-

---

terly 40 (1978) 368-87; Jack T. Sanders, *The New Testament Christological Hymns* (Cambridge: Cambridge University Press, 1971).

[2]Different authors suggest varied arrangements for the original form of the hymn. For Lohmeyer's arrangement, see Martin, *Carmen Christi,* 25-30; for Jeremias's arrangement, see Martin, *Carmen Christi,* 32-35, and Murphy-O'Connor, "Christological Anthropology," 26-27; and for Martin's own arrangement, *Carmen Christi,* 36-38.

[3]For varied translations of the hymn, see Richmond Lattimore's translation in *Acts and Letters of the Apostles* (New York: Farrar, Straus, Giroux, 1982) 178; Ralph Martin's in *Carmen Christi,* 38; Murphy-O'Connor's suggestions in "Christological Anthropology," 37-39; and Sanders, *Hymns,* 9. See also the article by Roy W. Hoover, "The Harpagmos Enigma: A Philological Solution," *The Harvard Theological Review* 64 (1971) 95-119.

ing like unto God something to take advantage of, (7) but emptied himself, taking the form of a servant, being born in human likeness. And being found in his present form as a human being, (8) he humbled himself and became obedient to the extent of death, even death on a cross. (9) And therefore God raised him up to the highest and bestowed on him the name which is above every name. (10) So that at the name of Jesus every knee might bend, those in the heavens and those on earth and those under the earth. (11) And every tongue confess that Jesus Christ is Lord for the glory of God the Father.

Murphy-O'Connor abstracts from the Pauline context of the hymn and attempts to interpret the original, independent composition. The hymn falls into two fundamental parts, verses 6-8 and verses 9-11. The background for the hymn is the anthropology of the Book of Wisdom: All human beings die (Wis 2:20; 12:20; 18:12, 16, 20). Yet the fate of the just and the unjust is not the same. The just only *seem* to die (3:2-3; 4:17; 5:15). They receive the gift of immortality (2:22; 3:5-15; 5:15-16). Death was not God's intention for humankind. Incorruptibility was a privilege granted human beings from the beginning (1:13-14; 2:13). This privilege accorded Adam is the basis for being the image of God (2:23): the background here is the Genesis creation narrative (Gen 3:2-3). Death actually entered the human world only as a result of Adam's disobedience (Wis 2:24; 10:1). Thus we do not exist now in the state intended for us by God.

Murphy-O'Connor translates the difficult expression in Philippians 2:6 *(ouch harpagmon hēgēsato to einai isa theō)* in accord with the translation suggested by R. W. Hoover: "he did not regard being equal with God as something to take advantage of."[4] It is a question of something already in Christ's possession, a privilege rightly his: "Christ did not regard his *right* [emphasis mine] to be *treated* [emphasis in original] as if he were god as something to be used to his own advantage."[5]

But what gave Jesus Christ the right to be treated as if he were a god? The hymn itself does not tell us but the anthropology of the Book of Wisdom does. The human being coming forth from

[4]Hoover, "The Harpagmos Enigma," 95–119, specifically 117.

[5]Murphy-O'Connor, "Christological Anthropology," 39.

God has been granted the privilege of incorruptibility, which privilege was lost through sin. But Christ was sinless. Therefore he had a right to the privilege of incorruptibility. He had the right not to die. It is thus the sinlessness of Christ, not his pre-existence, which is the presupposition of the hymn. Christ is another Adam and has a right to the privilege which Adam lost through his disobedience. "Christ had the right to be treated as if he were god. [For Christ was in fact the image of God, *morphē theou,* that Adam had been created to be, with its attendant privilege.] Christ, however, did not turn this situation to his own advantage. . . . He did not demand the treatment that his condition merited. On the contrary . . . he permitted himself to be put to death."[6]

Though he was a perfect image of God, and thus had a right to the privilege that his perfect obedience and sinlessness justified, Christ did not use this to his advantage, but rather accepted that which accompanies the sinful condition of other human beings, namely death. He became like all other human beings and humbly accepted death. His *kenosis,* self-emptying, is this freely chosen death. In accord with an interpretation of Joachim Jeremias, the *kenosis* in the hymn refers not to the incarnation but to Christ's death and crucifixion.[7] There is nothing in the Philippians hymn then which necessitates reference to Christ's pre-existence. It is sinlessness and not pre-existence which is the basis of Christ's uniqueness. The hymn is an expression of the early two-stage Christologies, humiliation-exaltation, earthly life-risen Lord. Christ's *kenosis* was his willingness to die like others, although as the image of God he was entitled to incorruptibility. For Paul, Christ was even more humble than this. He not only submitted himself to death, but he also submitted himself to death on a cross. The hymn is aware of the utter humanity of Jesus and his freely chosen self-identification with our condition.

James D. G. Dunn also interprets the hymn as a two-stage Christology which does not assert pre-existence and whose context is a theology of Adam.[8] The Philippians hymn is an expres-

[6]Ibid., 40.

[7]Joachim Jeremias, "The Servant of God" in *Theological Dictionary of the New Testament,* ed. Kittel, 5:708.

[8]Dunn, *Christology in the Making,* 114–28. For a fuller discussion of Adam Christology, see Robin Scroggs, *The Last Adam, A Study in Pauline Anthropology* (Philadelphia: Fortress Press, 1966).

sion of the widespread Adam Christology of the Christianity of
the forties and fifties of the first century. Dunn emphasizes the
background of the hymn in Genesis 1–3 more than in the Book
of Wisdom. The contrast between being in the form of God
(morphē theou) and taking the form of a servant *(morphē doulou)*
or between an equality with God *(to einai isa theō)* and being in
the likeness of a human being *(en homoiōmati anthrōpōn)* is the
same as the contrast in Genesis 1–3 between being created in the
image of God and becoming what Adam became as a result of
the fall. Adam grasped after an equality with God (Gen 3:5).
Christ did not. Adam thus became what we now are, subject to
death, a condition Christ freely chose. Another expression of
Adam Christology in Paul is Romans 1:23, "and [they] exchanged
the glory of the immortal God for images resembling mortal man"
(also Rom 7:7-11). Adam was created in the image of God (Gen
1:26f.) and created for incorruption (Wis 2:23; Gen 3:22), but
exists in a state of slavery to sin, and thus death. Through the
sin of Adam, death has entered the world (Rom 5:12). "Snatch-
ing at the opportunity to enhance the status he already had, he
both lost the degree of equality with God which he already en-
joyed and was corrupted by that which he coveted (cf. Rom 1:21-
23; 7:9-11). Not content with being like God, what God had intended, he became like men, what men now are."[9]

The author of the hymn uses Adam language and theology and
applies it to Christ who is a contrast to the first Adam. "Christ
faced the same archetypal choice that confronted Adam, but chose
not as Adam had chosen 'to grasp equality with God.' "[10] Christ
rather chooses the likeness of sinful flesh which is subject to the
law of death (Rom 8:3; 5:12-17; Phil 2:7). *Morphē doulou* ("the
form of a servant"), *homoiōma anthrōpōn* ("in human likeness"), and *schēma hōs anthrōpos* ("to all appearances as a
human being") all describe the fallen human condition. Christ
reverses the choice of Adam and his fate is different. He chooses
to humble himself and, as a result, is exalted. Adam chose to ex-
alt himself and had been humbled. The Adam theology does not
exclude the possible influence of the servant concept in Isaiah
53:12. There the servant of the Lord empties himself out to death
as well.

[9]Dunn, *Christology in the Making*, 116.

[10]Ibid., 117.

Thus there is no necessary implication in the hymn that Christ is pre-existent. At least it is immaterial to the theology of the hymn whether he was or not. Instead, he is another Adam. Christ was no more pre-existent than Adam was. Rather he was what Adam was not: the obedient and humble one. The theology of the Philippians hymn is also reflected in 2 Corinthians 8:9 and 5:21. Because of Christ's humility and obedience God highly exalts him and gives him a name above every other name (Phil 2:9), subjecting all things to him and putting all things under his feet (1 Cor 15:27; Ps 8:16).

Murphy-O'Connor is primarily concerned about the original hymn in its pre-Pauline form. Dunn, however, clearly asserts that even in its Pauline context the hymn does not contain a three-stage or incarnational Christology. Adam Christology, widespread throughout early Hellenistic Jewish Christianity, is the most plausible context for understanding Paul's Christology as a whole.

We can thus speak of three settings for interpreting the hymn: the pre-Pauline original hymn for which we have no particular setting other than early Christian worship; the setting in the context of Paul's Letter to the Philippians in which he exhorts them to take the servanthood of Jesus as an example for their own lives; and a post-Pauline interpretation of the hymn, probably fairly early after the development of the notion of Christ's pre-existence with its incarnational three-stage Christology. Once a three-stage Christology develops, presumably after the spread of Johannine theology, the Philippians hymn can readily be interpreted as expressing that Christology, as indeed it has been interpreted through most of Christian history. As one studies the hymn, one can interpret it along the lines of both the two-stage Christology that it originally expressed and the later three-stage Christology which it also later expressed for the Church. Although personal pre-existence is probably not present in the Christology of the pre-Pauline hymn, this does not prohibit it from being so used by later Christian writers. As the Church's Christological understanding develops, some texts, such as the early hymns, just as some of the Christological titles, were of particular value because they were able to carry more and more meaning, or bear the weight of the growth in consciousness. Just as we find at times an interpretation of Scripture in Scripture (Gal 4:21-31), so the interpretation of Scripture continued after the New Testament writings themselves. The Hebrew Scriptures could be interpreted as being in accord with the Christ event and the early Christian hymns would later be interpreted in accord with the Church's growing understanding of Christ.

> Apparently, not a single one of the hymns has survived in its original form, a fact which points to the early necessity for interpreting the hymns, to their inability to bear the full content of meaning read into them at a prior time, or read out of them, or which one hoped they would bear. They express the gospel, yet they do not express the gospel quite adequately; thus certain emendations are considered necessary by the New Testament writers in using the hymns. This observation, however, is at the same time an observation about all of language. All of language is not quite adequate for bearing the meaning one hopes it will bear; thus, it is always necessary to emend, to explain, to interpret, to translate.[11]

This process of interpretation does not stop with the New Testament writers but is an ongoing function of the Church.

In the Philippians hymn, *morphē theou* ("the form of God") is contrasted with *morphē doulou* ("the form of a servant"). The contrast is not that between the two natures of Christ but between two modes of being, two distinguishable conditions. The *morphē theou* refers to Christ as an image of God, with *morphē* (form) as equivalent to *eikōn* (image) and *doxa* (glory). Christ lets go of this privileged condition in order to become what all sinful human beings are. As the author of Hebrews states it, he became like us in all things, except for sin (4:15). The *to einai isa theō* does not imply an absolute equality with God, for *isa* as an adverb implies rather "being like unto God," or "as if he were a god."[12] Christ exchanges one condition (being like unto God or being an image of God) for another one (being like unto us).

One of the most difficult words in the text to translate is *harpagmos* and its varied senses need not all be mutually exclusive. Linguistic research suggests that it be translated as "he did not regard being equal with God as something of which to take ad-

---

[11]Sanders, *Hymns,* 140.

[12]Murphy-O'Connor, "Christological Anthropology," 39.

vantage.''[13] The more commonly accepted interpretations of *har-pagmos* can be classed as: (1) *res rapta,* something already possessed, with the temptation to hold onto it, something seized or clung to; (2) *res rapienda,* something not yet possessed, but rather something to be snatched at, or to reach out and take hold of, something not yet in one's grasp but to be grasped at; (3) *res retinenda,* something already possessed, but not yet to its fullest advantage, with the temptation to exploit it to the full, something of which to take advantage.[14] These nuanced interpretations can be found in different translations: (1) "he did not cling to his equality with God" (JB); (2) "he did not think to snatch at equality with God" (NEB); and (3) "he did not use equality with God as a gain to be exploited" (R. P. Martin) or "did not regard being equal with God as something to take advantage of" (Hoover).

The Greek *ekenōsen* does not necessarily denote an incarnational act. In a two-stage Christology *kenosis* refers to the earthly life of Jesus, his servanthood, his freely chosen death, even death on a cross as Paul emphasizes. In the post-Pauline three-stage Christology, *kenosis* will more and more refer to the incarnation itself, the act by which the pre-existent Word became the incarnate Word. In the context of a Wisdom or Adam anthropology, the privilege which is not exploited to Jesus' own advantage *(res retinenda)* is his right not to die. When pre-existence is seen in the background, the privilege will be the power or status of the pre-existent Son or Word that is not clung to but let go of *(res rapta)* in the kenotic incarnation.

In the latter interpretation Christ Jesus deprived himself or emptied himself of divine power or status and was born as human beings are born and thus was found as a human being. This depri-

---

[13]Hoover, "The Harpagmos Enigma," 118.

[14]Cf. Martin, *Carmen Christi,* 134–53, xxi–xxiii. Hoover, "The Harpagmos Enigma," 118–19, does not think of the third meaning so much in terms of retaining something, although it is something already present or possessed, but more in the sense of exploiting something that is at one's disposal; the emphasis is not on what is possessed but on what is to be exploited for one's own gain on the basis of what one possesses. Murphy-O'Connor, "Christological Anthropology," 37–42, following Hoover's lead, speaks of this perspective as *res retinenda* although the emphasis is on taking advantage of what one has a right to. Martin, *Carmen Christi,* 148–53, sees this third meaning as a blend of the first two, something already possessed plus something not yet exploited to the full.

vation was freely chosen and reflected humiliation. Thus the verb *etapeinōsen* (v. 8) means to be humble, humiliate.

The pre-existent Son let go of one mode of being divine (a transcendent mode) and took on a new mode of existence or way of being divine (an incarnate mode). This "emptying" was a humiliation, certainly humility. It is this type of humility that Paul recommended to the Philippians in 2:3: "In humility count others better than yourselves." Given the divine status to which his earthly reality is contrasted, the emptying out of the divine equality or privilege was a freely chosen self-humiliation of the pre-existent Word or Son. But this choice simply shows the extent to which the Son was willing to go, to let go, to be a servant, to be one of us. He did not grasp at or hold on to the divine way of being but took or received *(labōn)* a human way of being.

Verse 8 does not rest content with pointing to Christ's emptiness or humility or identity with us. Like Hebrews it stresses this humility to make its point. Hebrews 4:15 emphasizes Christ's identity with us so far that the author had to stop and qualify the text for a moment: like us except for sin. Similarly the text here moves further than the humility involved in being born as a human being. Christ's obedience takes him even unto death *(mechri thanatou):* he was obedient, not just to death, but even unto, as far as, to the extent of death. It is almost as if this dying is over and above. Dying shows how far he was willing to go with us, as one of us. *Mechri* also connotes "until," and thus can mean that the obedience involved in his birth lasted until death, throughout his whole life, even up to death, and even the willingness to die. Jesus' being in human likeness includes an emptying of the divine power, a being born as we are, an obedience and surrender throughout his life, a willingness to die even by crucifixion. Before long, the Church's ready acceptance of Christ as the incarnation of the pre-existent One controlled the meaning of the Philippians hymn, which was put at the service of an incarnational, three-stage Christology, an interpretation to which it had not yielded within the Adamic background of both its pre-Pauline and Pauline settings.

The Question of Jesus' Pre-existence

In *The Humanity and Divinity of Christ,* John Knox articulates a modern dilemma: are the pre-existence of Christ and the humanity of Jesus incompatible? One cannot have both, according to Knox. Is he correct or did he pose a false dilemma?

Jesus did not think of himself as the pre-existent Son. Nor was the early pre-Pauline preaching conscious of Jesus as existing prior to his earthly historical life. The sonship that was attributed to him after the resurrection was associated with his post-resurrection, exalted, eschatological existence—without any sense of pre-existence. Is it possible, then, to let go of the concept of Jesus' pre-existence without doing a disservice to the Christian faith?

Before answering these questions, we must clarify what we mean by *pre-existence*. Not everyone understands this language in the same way.

Classically, *pre-existence* referred not to the pre-existence of Jesus as such, the historical Jesus, but rather to the prior existence of the Logos, which Jesus truly is. In other words, it is the pre-existence, indeed the eternal existence, of the second Person of the Trinity that is being referred to, the pre-existence of the divine Person, not the human nature. Thus, traditionally, the pre-existence of Christ simply meant that the *hypostasis* that Christ is did not begin to be with the conception of Christ or with the beginning of Christ's historical existence. This is the understanding of Thomas Aquinas: "Christ Jesus, as a human being, did not pre-exist the world" (*ST* III, 16, 9, ad 1).

This opinion, however, is not the only one to which the Christian tradition has given witness. In volume 3 I spoke of Luther's theology of the pre-existent humanity of Jesus. Karl Barth speaks of the pre-existent humanity of Christ as well: The whole God-man, Jesus Christ, divinity and humanity, pre-exists his historical birth into our time. One can speak of Jesus and not only the eternal Word prior to Jesus' entrance into our history (*Church Dogmatics,* III/2, 474–511; IV/1, 47–66).

From an exegetical perspective Pierre Benoit proposes a similar view.[15] He maintains that, for the Scriptures, Jesus Christ as a complete personage existed from the beginning of the world. The incarnation was not so much a divine Person assuming a human nature but, rather, a change from one state or condition of being to another. The New Testament understood this change in terms of the coming, descent, or manifestation of Jesus Christ.

---

[15] Pierre Benoit, "Préexistence et incarnation," *Revue biblique* 77 (1970) 5–29.

Thus Jesus was already both God and a human being before the annunciation. Jesus, not just the eternal Logos, pre-existed his conception in time. Benoit asks what type of reality is to be assigned to this pre-existence, and distinguishes it from the earthly, historical character of Christ's and our existence and also from the purely transcendent, divine existence that God is. It is another mode of existence intermediate between these two. Jesus' pre-existence as a complete being is distinct from God's mode of existence and from our historical mode of existence. Whatever the merits of views such as Barth's or Benoit's they indicate that biblically and theologically pre-existence is not always understood in the same way. Are we talking about a pre-existent Logos or a pre-existent Jesus?

An increasingly common distinction in our own day is that between an ideal pre-existence and a real or personal pre-existence: between, as Dunn described it, "the existence of an idea in the mind of God, his divine intention for the last days," and "the personal pre-existence of a divine being who was sent into the world and whose ascension was simply the continuation of an intimate relationship with the Father which neither incarnation nor crucifixion interrupted or disturbed."[16] We must be careful not to make such a distinction too clear cut, however. We ought not read too much into the Fourth Gospel, which does not yet contain the articulate, personal, hypostatic pre-existence that comes later with developing Trinitarian thought. Nor ought we read too little into the Jewish notion of pre-existence. Rudolph Schnackenburg indicates that Judaism manifested varied notions of pre-existence.[17] According to one tradition, seven things existed before the creation of the world: the Torah, penance, the Garden of Eden, Gehenna, the Throne of Glory, the Sanctuary, and the Name of the Messiah. According to another tradition, there were six things, some of which had been really created (e.g., the Torah), and some which were only in the mind of God to be created later. Thus we see various degrees of reality accorded the pre-existent entities. The Torah had more concrete actuality, but what pre-existed in the mind of God had a vivid and concrete reality to it as well.

[16]Dunn, *Christology in the Making,* 54, 59.

[17]Rudolf Schnackenburg, *The Gospel According to St. John,* trans. Kevin Smyth (New York: Herder and Herder, 1968) 1:494–500.

Another distinction, closely related to the previous one, is that between Wisdom and Word, pre-existent *sophia* and pre-existent *logos*. Pre-Christian Judaism, although it personified wisdom, did not think of it as a hypostasis or an intermediary being independent of the one God. Wisdom language was rather a way of speaking about God, of expressing God's nearness. The type of existence that Wisdom had was closer to ideal pre-existence, existing in the mind of God.

Something similar must be said about pre-Christian Jewish usage with respect to *word*. The Johannine *Logos* has its background in Jewish wisdom. Apart from the distinctive Johannine use, in Judaism itself the word of God is not an entity independent of God. The word of God *is* God, God as speaking, as related to the world, as knowable, as capable of being apprehended, as self-revealing, but the Logos of God is still always God. God's word does not have a real existence apart from God.

Wisdom provided the background for several New Testament Christologies, particularly Paul's (1 Cor 1:24, 30; 8:5-6; Col 1:15-20), and to some degree that of Hebrews (1:1-4). The contrast between Christ, the last Adam, and the first Adam was also a central Pauline theme. Dunn argues that Pauline Christology did not contain the notion of Christ's personal pre-existence.[18] Several of those passages into which we are inclined to read Christ's pre-existence (1 Cor 8:5-6; Col 1:15-20) actually express the concept of wisdom, while others present a contrast between Christ and Adam (Phil 2:6-11; 2 Cor 8:9), not Christ's pre-existence. Jesus, according to Paul, was the embodiment of wisdom but we cannot assume that we have in Paul anything like the doctrine of incarnation. Yet wisdom Christology was one of the bridges that enabled the Church to move in the direction of an incarnation Christology.

Only with the Fourth Gospel do we get an explicit statement of the incarnation and Christ's real, personal pre-existence as the Logos and Son (1:14, 30; 6:62; 8:58; 17:5, 24).[19] The prologue goes beyond Judaism and its Logos doctrine has no genuine par-

[18] Dunn, *Christology in the Making*, 176-96, 209-12, 101-28. Also see Murphy-O'Connor, "Christological Anthropology," 25-50, and "1 Cor 8:6: Cosmology or Soteriology?" *Revue biblique* 85 (1978) 253-67.

[19] Dunn, *Christology in the Making*, 239-50. Also Raymond Brown, *The Community of the Beloved Disciple* (New York: Paulist Press, 1979) 43-47.

allel. The fourth evangelist takes a new step: the transition from an ideal pre-existence to a real, personal pre-existence. The word of God is identified with a particular individual: Jesus of Nazareth. The matrix for the development of the Christian concept of pre-existence is wisdom language, the Johannine Logos doctrine, and the Fourth Gospel's particular Son of God Christology.

What we have seen, therefore, are varied ways in which the notion of pre-existence has been understood: pre-existence in the mind of God as a divine intention; a created reality existing before the creation of the world, such as Torah; the real pre-existence of Jesus of Nazareth; the pre-existence of the eternal Logos. Thus, before we jettison pre-existence language in Christology as incompatible with the human Jesus, we need to be sure what we mean by pre-existence.

Pre-existence language is meta-historiographical and metaphysical. There are reasons for not letting go of it.

1. Pre-existence forces us to face Jesus Christ as mystery. Pre-existence is meta-historiographical, and thus prevents us from reducing Jesus to the historiographical Jesus alone. There is more to reality than historiography has access to, reality which in no way diminishes the necessary role of historiographical research. The precise character of Christ's pre-existence itself remains mysterious but that is no reason to ignore it. A Christology that presumes pre-existence helps us to be drawn into the mystery that Christ is as well as the mystery that Christ reveals. With Christ we are drawn into mystery in the Pauline sense of God's plan before the creation of the world.

2. Pre-existence draws us into the mystery of Christ's *person*. In this sense it is a Christian way of expressing faith in the uniqueness of Jesus Christ. Although the uniqueness of Christ itself can never be definitively formulated once and for all, and although Christologies from below attempt to approach the uniqueness of Jesus apart from his pre-existence, nevertheless, pre-existence remains a symbol for the Christian's conviction about Jesus: that he plays a unique role in God's plan. In that plan Jesus already existed in the mind of God before the creation of the world. The pre-existence of Christ simply means the uniqueness of Christ.

3. Pre-existence draws us into the mystery that Christ reveals, namely God. The language of pre-existence is not primarily

Christological but theological language. It is a way of saying that Christ is a way of talking about God. Indeed it gives a particular focus to Christology, namely that Christology is not primarily about the man Jesus but about God. In Jesus we meet God, and the God we meet is the God revealed in Jesus. The Jesus story is a part of God's story, and no one can know God apart from this Jesus who reveals God. Jesus is God's self-revelation. Pre-existence pushes us in the right direction for understanding Jesus: he cannot be understood apart from God, from below alone. Pre-existence means that Jesus is in some sense God.

4. That which pre-exists Jesus, then, is God. Pre-existence ties the two realities together in such a way that they cannot be separated. God and Jesus cannot be understood apart from each other. Jesus is in some sense that selfsame God bending over, leaning toward, reaching out to humankind. Jesus is the embodiment of God's relationship to the world, God whose very being is to be for others, who is the One-who-is-with-us. Jesus is the nearness of God, and the pre-existence of Jesus refers to "the prior actuality of God," to borrow a phrase from Austin Farrer in a different context.[20]

The pre-existence of Jesus means the pre-existence of God and Jesus' relationship to God or identity with God. Jesus' roots are in the very being of God. What pre-exists Jesus is a (Father-Son) relationship that Jesus discloses; or better, the fact that God is relating and relational, that God *is* relationship. Jesus reveals that God is not and never was apart from us—that the very nature of God is to be with us and for us. The pre-existence of Jesus means the prior actuality of this relational God.

Thomas Aquinas and the Humanness of Jesus

In this section I develop three observations about the theology of Thomas Aquinas and then offer a suggestion.

First, Thomas's theology has a creative, developing, open, surprising spirit to it. This does not mean that Thomism has always had such a spirit. Rather, it means that Thomas himself must be seen as a developing theologian as all true theologians are, in-

---

[20]Austin Farrer, "The Prior Actuality of God," *Reflective Faith, Essays in Philosophical Theology* (Grand Rapids, Mich.: William B. Eerdmans, 1972) 178-91.

process themselves. Etienne Gilson remarks, "The general tendency among historians of medieval thought seems to have been to imagine the middle ages as peopled by philosophers rather than theologians."[21] In the same way we often see Thomas's theology as a finished product rather than a creative inquiry, an ongoing process even toward the end of his life when he resolutely decided to discontinue writing, when his mind had led him to what it could no longer grasp.

If we limit ourselves here to Thomas's Christology alone, there are several significant examples of this ongoing, developing spirit of inquiry. Question 1, article 3 of the *tertia pars* of the *Summa* concerns itself with the motive of the incarnation, the issue of whether God would have become incarnate if humankind had not sinned. The early Thomas, the Thomas of the *Sentences* (written in Paris, 1252–1256, when he was between the ages of twenty-seven and thirty-two), holds an opinion fairly close to that of his master, Albert, namely, that neither opinion on this issue is necessitating.[22] Thomas thought that either opinion could be held, that each was probable at best. He expressed direct preference for neither. Of the opinion that there would have been an incarnation even apart from the need for redemption, Thomas writes, "This can also be upheld as probable" (*Sentences,* III, 1, 1, 3). The late Thomas, of the *tertia pars* of the *Summa* (the *tertia pars* not having been begun until the spring of 1272), did express a preference. Perhaps an earlier, implicit intuition is only being made explicit. It is certainly not a case of Thomas completely changing his mind. Nor does his language in the *Summa* reject the tentative and probable character of the question. Yet, in the *Summa,* he explicitly states that the opinion that God would *not* have become incarnate is *"more* probable" (III, 1, 3). Thomas also makes this preferred opinion clear in his *Commentary on the First Epistle to Timothy (lectio 4)* and in his disputation *On Truth* (q. 29, a. 4, ad 5). If we date the latter during 1258–1259, then we see a development in Thomas's thinking between 1256 and 1258.

---

[21]Etienne Gilson, "Historical Research and the Future of Scholasticism" in *A Gilson Reader,* ed. Anton Pegis (Garden City, N.Y.: Doubleday and Co., 1957) 156.

[22]Donald J. Goergen, "Albert the Great and Thomas Aquinas on the Motive of the Incarnation," *The Thomist* 44 (1980) 523–38.

This developing character in Thomas's theology reflects itself late in his life as well. I refer here to the important question 17 of the *tertia pars,* perhaps Thomas's major contribution to Christology, on the mode of union in Christ and specifically on whether there is only one *esse* (act of existence) in Christ (i.e., the divine), or whether Christ *as* a human being had an *esse* as well. Within one year, 1272, Thomas shows himself as still progressing in his thinking, applying one of his most creative insights to Christology, and seeming to change his mind. In the disputation *De unione verbi incarnati* written earlier that year, he holds that Christ as human does have an *esse* of his own, although only in a secondary sense. "There is another *esse* belonging to the supposit, not insofar as He is eternal, but insofar as He became man in time. Although this *esse* is not accidental to the Son of God . . . it is not the principal *esse* of the supposit, but secondary" (*De unione* 4). Not long thereafter, however, in question 17 of the *tertia pars,* he states, "It is impossible that one thing should not have one act of existence," and "If, then, there were two acts of existence in Christ, and not only one, he would be two and not one," and "Consequently, with his human nature he does not acquire a new personal existence, but simply a new relation of his already existing personal existence to the human nature" (III, 17, 2). We can see Thomas struggling with the issue of the hypostatic union. In the *De unione* a solution is not yet clear to him. It only comes to him during the course of the year. A year later he decided to write no more (6 Dec. 1273). Between the writing of the *De unione* and question 17, Thomas comes to see that there is no solution to the question of the unity of Christ other than affirming one *esse* in Christ, an application of his insight into the distinction between *esse* and essence.

We could point to still a third example in Thomas's Christology, concerning Christ's acquired knowledge, where we can see development between the *Sentences* (III, 14, 3; 18, 3) and the *Summa* (III, 9, 4; 12, 2). Thomas himself acknowledges a change of mind. "Although elsewhere I have written otherwise, it must now be said that there was an acquired knowledge in Christ" (III, 9, 4; also 12, 2). In the *Sentences,* Thomas maintains that Christ had infused knowledge from the beginning of his existence and denied that the active intellect could abstract any new ideas or acquire new knowledge. In the *Summa,* however, he postulates real acquired knowledge in Christ, because Christ's perfection itself requires that his active intellect have a real function.

Because of his speculative ability Thomas is at times surprisingly open in his responses. For example, could there be more than one incarnation, a genuine incarnation of the same kind or degree that Jesus Christ is? Could the eternal Son of God assume a human nature numerically distinct from that which was Jesus of Nazareth? Could the Word be hypostatically incarnate in more than one individual? Thomas answers yes (III, 3, 7). He bases his opinion on the very power and freedom of God. The power of a divine person is not limited by anything created. Thus a divine person does not assume a human nature in such a way that it would be prevented from taking up another. "We must hold that a divine person could assume another numerically distinct human nature beside the human nature that it did assume" (III, 3, 7). However, because this human nature would lack its own distinct supposit, Thomas preferred to refer to such a situation as one human being having two human natures (not two human beings).

We must see Thomas therefore as a rigorous, open, creative, developing theologian. This is the first observation.

My second observation is that Thomas was a biblical theologian. When he first lectured in Paris (1252), he was, as was the custom, a commentator on the *Sentences* of Peter Lombard. After this, however, in 1256, at thirty-one years of age, with a dispensation from the statute that a master be not less than thirty-five, Thomas began his career of lecturing on the Scriptures as *Magister in sacra pagina*.[23] At the time, this was the title of the theologian in his formal task of lecturing on the Scriptures. Lombard was never preferred to the Scriptures, even though one began one's career with his texts. To see Thomas as a master in his own right one must look at his commentaries on Job, the Psalms, the Song of Songs, Isaiah, Jeremiah, Matthew, John, and the letters of Paul.

In asserting that Thomas was a biblical theologian I suggest that he recognized authority first in Scripture, then in patristic and conciliar teaching, and finally in philosophical reasoning.[24]

[23]See James A. Weisheipl, *Friar Thomas d'Aquino* (Garden City, N.Y.: Doubleday and Co., 1974) 101.

[24]Ibid., 110.

This is not to deny that his methods of interpretation were quite distinct from modern, critical, and historical exegesis. Of course, they were. He was a man of his times. For his times, however, he was a master of the Scriptures and a supreme exemplification of what that meant in the medieval world.

If we pay close attention to Thomas's Christology, we find that his inclination is to affirm the side of a question which Scripture seems more readily to support. The major question for Thomas as a theologian is simply which position is more in accord with Scripture.

We see this approach exemplified in the three examples above. In all three the development took place in the direction of that which Scripture seems most to suggest. Thomas affirms Christ's human knowledge seeing it as more in accord with Luke 2:52 (III, 12, 3). Likewise, Thomas's strong drive toward the unity of Christ reflects the overwhelming impression of the Scriptures: that Christ is one person.

In the question on the motive of the incarnation, Thomas formulates his eventual opinion as being more probable on the basis of Scripture. The question as to why God became one of us would be purely speculative if Scripture had nothing to say about it. On the basis of reason alone both responses would be reasonable, hence equally probable. Thomas rightly points out that we can only know the purpose of the incarnation if God has chosen to reveal it (III, 1, 3). Thus, in the end, it is a question of what the Scriptures say. Already in the *Sentences* all seven arguments in favor of the proposition that God would have become incarnate even apart from the need for redemption are speculative (III, 1, 1, 3). All four reasons for the contrary opinion (later, Thomas's preferred opinion) are biblical or patristic. They depend on Luke 19:10 and 1 Timothy 1:15 as well as a coordination of Hebrews 2:14 and Romans 5:12.

It is Thomas's opinion that, according to Scripture, the sin of the first Adam was the reason for the incarnation. Thus, "it is preferable to hold that the work of the Incarnation is ordered by God as a remedy for sin, in such a way that, if there had been no sin, there would have been no Incarnation" (III, 1, 3). For Thomas, God in fact *did* become incarnate in order to save us from the effects of sin. He could have, however, become incarnate even if there had been no sin. The question then is whether

God *would have* become incarnate apart from sin. Thomas maintains that we can only inquire into this issue on the basis of what Scripture says. The Scriptures, a comment of Augustine on Luke 19:10,[25] and the Gloss on 1 Timothy 1:15 make Thomas assert, in the *Summa,* in contrast with his teacher Albert, a particular opinion as more probable.

My third observation is that Thomas's Christology cannot be understood apart from his dedication to the humanity of Christ. In our own century, a Christology which considers the humanity of Jesus as central is usually associated with the Christologies "from below." But Thomas's Christology is not a Christology from below. It clearly presupposes the doctrine of the Trinity, accepts as a starting point the hypostatic union, and is a theology of the Word made flesh. Twentieth-century methods cannot be used as the context for understanding the text of Aquinas. We must search for his own intuition within his own texts.

One can see in Thomas's whole theology the intent to refute the Manicheans.[26] The whole history of Thomas's order of preaching friars as far back as Dominic himself had been concentrated on the Church struggle against the Albigensians (the medieval successors of the Manicheans). Thomas was writing his *Summa* for students of theology, as he had previously written the *Summa contra Gentiles* for the missionary work of his own Dominican brothers. His theology was to be faithful to the tradition, but also, one might say, a companion to the preaching mission of the order. His theology was for the sake of the proclamation of the Word, and of the Word incarnate who so respected the material order that he chose to redeem that order by entering into it himself. A theology of the incarnation would be the best refutation of Manicheism. But such a theology had to be sufficiently respectful of both Christ's union with the Godhead and his oneness with us, the twofold *homoousioi.* Thomas would not neglect that half of the problem which would be the most solid refutation of the Albigensian heresy: the humanity of Christ.

G. K. Chesterton in his own casual way sums up this fundamental point in Thomas's thought with a story about Thomas:

[25]Goergen, "The Motive of the Incarnation," 532 n. 11.

[26]Cf. Steven Runciman, *The Medieval Manichee* (Cambridge: Cambridge University Press, 1947/1982).

There is one casual anecdote about St. Thomas Aquinas which illuminates him like a lightning-flash, not only without but within. . . . On one occasion, however, he was invited to the court of King Louis IX of France, more famous as the great St. Louis; and for some reason or other, the Dominican authorities of his Order told him to accept. . . . And there could hardly be a more complete contrast, given the essentials of holiness, than between St. Thomas and St. Louis. St. Louis was born a knight and a king; but he was one of those men in whom a certain simplicity, combined with courage and activity, makes it natural, and in a sense, easy, to fulfill directly and promptly any duty or office, however official. . . .

Now a man like St. Thomas would definitely dislike being a king, or being entangled with the pomp and politics of kings; not only his humility, but a sort of subconscious fastidiousness and fine dislike of futility, often found in leisurely and learned men with large minds, would really have prevented his making contact with the complexity of court life. Also, he was anxious all his life to keep out of politics; and there was no political symbol more striking, or in a sense more challenging, at that moment, than the power of the King in Paris. . . . All that we know of Thomas tells us that he was perfectly courteous to those who spoke to him, but spoke little, and was soon forgotten in the most brilliant and noisy clatter in the world: the noise of French talking. What the Frenchmen were talking about we do not know; but they forgot all about the large fat Italian in their midst, and it seems only too possible that he forgot all about them. Sudden silences will occur even in French conversation; and in one of these the interruption came. . . .

And then suddenly the goblets leapt and rattled on the board and the great table shook, for the Friar had brought down his huge fist like a club of stone, with a crash that startled everyone like an explosion; and had cried out in a strong voice, but like a man in the grip of a dream, "And that will settle the Manichees!"[27]

Our concern is to find evidence for this in the texts of Thomas himself.

---

[27]G. K. Chesterton, *Saint Thomas Aquinas* (Garden City, N.Y.: Doubleday and Co., 1956) 97–101.

We already detect this perspective of Thomas in his prologue to the *tertia pars,* question 1, article 1, where he takes up the fittingness of the incarnation. Was it really fitting for God to become incarnate?

Thomas replies, "Of course." The nature of God is goodness. But goodness tends to communicate itself to others. Thus it is certainly fitting for the greatest good to communicate itself to creatures, which is what happened in the incarnation. Implied here is *both* the goodness of God *and* the goodness of creation. Thomas writes in the *sed contra* of that article, "It is most fitting that the unseen things of God be manifested through things that are seen, for the whole world was made for this purpose."

The major objection to the fittingness of the incarnation would stem from one's theology of creation and bodiliness. The third objection states, "Body is as far away from supreme spirit as wickedness is from supreme goodness. But it would be quite unfitting for God, who is supreme goodness, to assume wickedness. Therefore it is not fitting that the supreme invested spirit assume a body." To this objection, Thomas's anti-Manichean reply is very clear. God is uncreated, unchanging, and incorporeal. But God created changing and corporeal creatures because God is good. The created nature is established by God's wisdom and God can fittingly assume such a nature. (See also I, 44, 3 and 4; 47, 1 and 2; 65, 1 and 2.) There is nothing about an incarnation that is unbecoming to God; this is Thomas's prologue to his Christology.

A similar respect for the bodiliness of creatures is present in Thomas's discussion of Christ as head of the Church (III, 8) and particularly in the question of whether Christ is our head *as* embodied (III, 8, 2). For Thomas, the entire humanity of Christ, body and soul, exerts its influence on us. Christ is not simply head of a spiritual world. The body itself experiences the effects of grace.

Thomas's respect for the humanity of Christ is shown also in his treatment of the grace of Christ (III, 7). Was there habitual grace in Christ? Would not the grace of union supersede or make habitual grace unnecessary? No. For Thomas, Christ's human nature is not to be denigrated and he thus postulated habitual grace in Christ both because of the way his soul was united to the Word *and* because of the dignity of Christ's soul itself (III, 7, 1). For the same reason, the virtues which perfect the faculties and activities of the soul are present in Christ (III, 7, 2). The Word does not displace or replace these perfections of the human nature. (Christ did not, however, according to Thomas, have the virtues of faith and hope [III, 7, 3 and 4], since there was no need for them.)

Thomas protects the humanity of Christ from being dissolved by the hypostatic union. A basic principle of his is: "The union of natures in the person of Christ was accomplished in such a way that the distinctive properties of each nature remained" (III, 10, 1; 2, 1). On this point Thomas relies on John of Damascus. In discussing the beatific knowledge of Christ, Thomas maintains that Christ had beatific knowledge while on earth, but he also maintains that Christ as human did not fully comprehend the Word or divine essence (III, 10, 1). Both of these points rest upon Thomas's understanding of Christ's humanity. Since beatific knowledge is in accord with human nature, for it is not divine knowledge and even belongs to the perfection of human nature, it must be attributed to Christ. Yet beatific knowledge is finite and thus even in Christ remained so in spite of his union with the Word. Thomas recognizes both the limits of Christ's human nature as created and the perfection possible to it. This same principle of the integrity and distinction of the two natures places limits on Christ's power (III, 13). The person of the Word respects the integrity of the nature. The power of an agent corresponds to its nature; omnipotence follows upon divine nature; Christ as human is not omnipotent.

In questions 2–6 of the *tertia pars,* Thomas gives consideration to the mode of union in the incarnation. Then, in questions 7–15, he considers the concrete, existential, individual human nature in fact assumed by the Word. He considers both the perfections of that particular human nature (questions 7–13), its grace, knowledge, and power, and its deficiencies or defects (questions 14–15). Here we want to look at this theology of the humanity of Jesus more closely.

For Thomas, there is no *homo assumptus* (assumed human being), only the *natura assumpta* (assumed nature). Christ did not assume, however, an abstract human nature. He was rather a concrete, existing human being. The human nature assumed by Christ was qualified by its concrete existence. This is simply another way of saying that there is a distinction between the human nature assumed and the human condition assumed, namely, Christ's human nature in its concrete, existential, historical situation. Here we have the *co-assumpta* (questions 7–15), what Christ assumed along with the assumption of a human nature, the distinctive and individual condition of his humanity, what this humanity in particular was like, its contingent features, its existential shape.[28] These can be distinguished not only from the *natura assumpta* in the abstract but also from the *consequentia unionis* (consequences of the union) according to the *hypostasis*.

We must keep in mind that the *co-assumpta* (the grace, knowledge, power, and limitations of Christ's humanity) are contingencies. Their character is not necessitated one way or the other by the incarnation itself. They could have been different from what they were. They are freely chosen features of Christ's human life. Nothing speculative determines their particular character, nor does anything dogmatic. Here an argument from tradition is not definitive, for the *co-assumpta* have never been the object of dogmatic definition, as the hypostatic union and two natures of Christ have been. Thus, in this area most of all, an argument from Scripture will be particularly significant. If it is not a question of something logically conclusive, or dogmatically certain, our only basis for discussion are the facts that are available to us from Scripture.

In addition to this basic principle of the primacy of Scripture, Thomas relies upon three other theological principles to guide him in his discussion. These are what I will call the principles of perfection, *kenosis,* and credibility. First is the principle of perfection. Due to the hypostatic union itself, which cannot simply be ignored in a discussion of the *co-assumpta,* Jesus Christ in his human condition ought to have the maximum human perfection possible. As Liam Walsh writes, "The hypostatic union makes the perfection of Christ's human condition a matter of principle."[29]

Second is the principle of *kenosis,* that Christ in fact had certain limitations. The previous principle of perfection cannot be employed to deny the facts of Christ's human situation, for example that he suffered and died. There is bound to be tension

---

[28]See Liam Walsh's introduction to the *co-assumpta* in Thomas Aquinas, *Summa theologiae* (New York: McGraw-Hill, 1974) 49:xvii–xxvii. Also see R.T.A. Murphy, vol. 54 of the McGraw-Hill *Summa,* 181–88.

[29]Walsh, "Introduction," xxiii.

between these two principles, and one must steer a delicate balance between them. We can easily make Christ "too perfect," giving insufficient attention to the *kenosis,* or make him so like us that we empty the hypostatic union of any meaning. As Christ's perfection is related to his union with the Godhead, his imperfections or limitations (the *kenosis*) are related to soteriology, namely, that he came to be with us and for us. We have seen in question 1 of the *tertia pars* this soteriological context as a prologue to Thomas's Christology.

Third, Christ's humanity for Thomas must not only be real but must also be credible. He makes this point several times. Christ's true humanity cannot be left in doubt. This is the basis for some of his limitations.

Now one may or may not agree with these three theological principles, but they, along with the argument from Scripture, will provide the basis for Thomas's discussion. Because of the hypostatic union by which Christ is deserving of all human perfection possible to a human being and within the soteriological limits set by the freely chosen *kenosis,* Thomas attributes to Christ the fullness of habitual grace (III, 7, 9); three kinds of knowledge, beatific, infused, and experiential (III, 9); as well as a power which, while not omnipotent, nevertheless surpasses that of all other creatures (III, 13). To these perfections we shall return, but we shall first turn our attention to Christ's defects or limitations which Thomas discusses in two questions, the bodily defects (III, 14) and defects of soul (III, 15).

Should the Son of God have assumed bodily defects within his human nature (III, 14, 1)? The principle of perfection would imply not. But that principle is here qualified by the other two principles. Thus Thomas gives three reasons why it was fitting for Christ to share in the weaknesses and bodily deficiencies of human existence, such as death, hunger, thirst, and the like. First, because he came to make reparation for sin and these human realities are the effects of sin. They impute no sin to him but only imply his willingness to take on the effects of sin. Second, these limitations are a support to our faith in the incarnation. Here the principle of credibility is important. Human nature is not known to us or experienced by us apart from these bodily limitations. Thomas writes, "If the Son of God had assumed a human nature without these defects, it would seem that he was not a true human being, and that he did not have true but imaginary flesh, as the Manicheans said" (III, 14, 1). Here we see the opposition to the Manicheans explicitly expressed as well as the principle of credibility. Third, Christ's freely chosen bodily limitations allowed him to be an example to us of patience in bearing human suffering. Although he had a right to human perfection, even bodily perfection, and although such perfection would have been most appropriate considering the *hypostasis* that Christ is, nevertheless, other qualifying reasons made it appropriate that he not be completely without human limitations. These limitations, however, were freely chosen; it was not necessary that he choose them.

In this whole discussion we see Thomas's principles of *kenosis* and credibility at work. We also see, however, the fundamental basis for them. They are simply called upon in order to explain the Scriptures. In studying question 14, we find that the biblical references are central, not ornaments to an argument. Thomas admits hunger, thirst, suffering, and death in Christ because of Scripture. He quotes Hebrews 2:18 ("For because he himself has suffered and been tempted, he is able to help those who are tempted") and Romans 8:3 ("God has done what the law, weakened by the flesh, could not do: sending his own Son in the likeness of sinful flesh . . . ").

Thomas grants that Christ's divinity was hidden by these defects and limitations, but affirms that they revealed his humanity, and the humanity is a way of arriving at his divinity (III, 14, 1 and 4).

Next (III, 15) Thomas considers the defects or limitations of Christ's soul in contrast to those of his body. He attributes to Christ neither sin nor ignorance (III, 15, 1–3), but he does attribute the human emotions (III, 15, 4). He quotes Augustine to this effect: "For the one who had a real human body and a real human soul did not have counterfeit human feelings" (*City of God,* 14, 9). Christ experienced genuine pain (III, 15, 5), sadness (III, 15, 6), fear (III, 15, 7), wonder (III, 15, 8), and anger (III, 15, 9). Thomas so qualifies these emotions that they do not reflect nor are they conducive to sin in Christ. Yet, he argues, Christ felt these passions of the soul. Again, Thomas cites Scripture: Psalm 87:4; Isaiah 53:4; Matthew 26:38; Mark 14:33; Matthew 8:10; John 2:17.

Thomas attributes genuine emotional responses to Jesus as well as physical limitations. These two human characteristics reflect the *kenosis*. But in accord with the principle of perfection, Thomas does not attribute any lack of grace or any lack of knowledge to Jesus. For the sake of our salvation, Christ freely accepted human limitations that were not necessarily intrinsic to human nature. Yet, in order to effect our salvation, it was also required that Christ have perfect human knowledge and grace. Therefore, "Christ ought to assume those defects which follow upon the sin common to the whole of human nature but are yet not irreconcilable with perfect knowledge and grace" (III, 14, 4). There are three kinds of limitations. The first are those incompatible with the principle of perfection as it manifests itself in Christ's complete knowledge and life of grace (e.g., ignorance, proneness to evil, and difficulty in doing good). Christ did not assume imperfections such as these. Second, there are those disabilities which are not common to all but are manifest in particular people and have their own specific causes (e.g., leprosy and epilepsy). Thomas does not attribute defects such as these to Christ. But third are those limitations common to us all which are a result of sin, for example, death, hunger, thirst. According to the principles of *kenosis* and credibility, Christ accepted all these defects. They are common to all and do not imply lack of knowledge and grace.

Although Thomas speaks most explicitly about the *kenosis* when he discusses Christ's humanity (III, 7–15), his theology of the *kenosis* is discernible in his consideration of Christ's passion (III, 46–52) which was in fact the supreme exemplification of that principle. In response to the objection that Christ ought not have died by crucifixion, Thomas responds according to the fashion we have outlined: Christ did not assume degrading limitations, such as a lack of knowledge or grace. He did not resist, however, suffering which was inflicted on him from the outside, such as all the pains of the passion (III, 44, 4). In fact, he endured all classes of suffering, even though the least amount of suffering was sufficient for redemption (III, 46, 6).

We can now summarize Thomas's theology of the *kenosis* of Christ in six points:

1. Both Christ's human nature, the *natura assumpta,* and the contingent limitations of that nature in the concrete, the *co-assumpta* or Christ's human condition, were freely chosen realities on Christ's part (III, 14, 2–3; 15, 7, ad 2).

2. The motive for this freely chosen self-limitation and assump-

tion of human deficiencies was primarily our redemption (III, 1, 3; 14, 1; 36, 4; 34, 2). The Christology of the *kenosis* is placed within the context of soteriology.

3. Since even the assumption of a perfect human nature, or the assumption of the least of sufferings, could have sufficed for redemption, the *kenosis* manifests the extent to which Christ was willing to go for our sake and also his desire to make his human nature credible, that is, like unto ours. He chose to be one of us, or like us in all things but sin. It is on this basis that Thomas interprets the text of Luke 2:52: as Christ grew he behaved accordingly, in accord with his age, in order to show that he was really human (III, 7, 12, ad 3). This is also the reason why it was appropriate that his birth be humble and hidden. Otherwise the reality of his humanness would have come to be doubted (III, 14, 1). To this effect Thomas also quotes Augustine: "If he had not passed through the different stages from babyhood to youth, had neither eaten nor slept, would he not have strengthened an erroneous opinion and made it impossible for us to believe that he had become truly human?" (*Epistle* 87). This is also why he worked no miracles as a child, lest his incarnation be taken as only seeming to be real, only apparent and imaginary (III, 36, 4, ad 3).

4. The only truly valid criterion in terms of which we can determine the character and extent of the *kenosis* is the canon of Scripture. We see Thomas quoting Scripture over and over, not by way of proof texts for dogmatic conclusions, but as the context within which the question is discussed. It is for biblical reasons that Thomas concludes that Christ was subject to the Father (III, 20, 1), not because he was unequal to the Father but because Scripture so indicates in John 14:28, Matthew 19:17, Philippians 2:7-8, and John 8:28.

5. Thomas has genuine theological respect for the humanness of Jesus and in fact emphasizes his identity with us and our human condition as much as he reasonably could. In this, he articulates another principle of his theology: in his dealings with us God treats us in accord with our natures. Likewise, in the incarnation God respected the human nature of Christ. God may perfect it but never destroys it. The underlying philosophical principle is that whatever is received is received according to the mode of the receiver. In this case the receiver was Christ's human nature. This

is why Thomas argues that the human soul of Christ, or the human and earthly Christ, was not omnipotent. The hypostatic union took place in such a way that the distinction of natures remained. Each nature retained its characteristics. Omnipotence follows from divine nature but not from human nature (III, 13, 1). What Christ received was received according to a finite and human modality.

> What is received from a higher nature into a lower one is held according to the mode of the lower nature *(per inferiorem modum)*. . . . Because, therefore, the soul of Christ is of a lower nature than the divine nature, the likenesses of things are not received into it with the same perfection and power that they have in the divine nature. Thus it is that the knowledge of Christ's soul is, with respect to its way of knowing, lower than divine knowledge. . . . And therefore the soul of Christ, since it is a creature of finite power . . . cannot do all things (III, 13, 1).

These same principles underlie Thomas's understanding of the will of Christ. The Son of God assumed a complete human nature. Thus he had a human will. It was a will of its own even if it acted in harmony with the divine will (III, 18, 1). The Son of God allowed Christ's human nature to function according to its nature. For example, even though Christ willed to suffer, he naturally shrank back from the pain involved, again as the Scriptures say (III, 18, 5). Thomas respected the integrity of Christ's humanity. He indicates on several occasions that Christ's divinity was contained. It did not overflow into his body. Nor did it remove his vulnerability and mortality (III, 15, 5, and 3; 45, 2; 54, 2). In fact, the incarnation and its accompanying *kenosis* expressed Christ's wish to manifest his divinity *through* his humanity (III, 40, 1, ad 1).

6. Christ's simple manner of life was suitable for a God enfleshed. The kenotic incarnation manifested not so much humiliation but a humility (III, 40, 3). In fact, it was through the humility manifested in his passion and death that Christ merited the glory accompanying his resurrection (III, 54, 2).

In discussing Christ's ascension Thomas elaborates briefly on the notion of Christ's descent as well (III, 57, 2). There are two ways of applying descent to Christ: his descent from heaven in the incarnation and his descent into hell or the nether world after his death. The first Thomas calls an emptying, *exinanitio,* a *kenosis.* Here he refers to the Philippians hymn. Christ's incarnation evidently was a "having been emptied" *(exinanitus)* and an assumption of our "littleness" *(parvitas).* "He assumed our earthly nature into the unity of his person" (III, 57, 2, ad 2).

I stated above that I was going to make three observations about Thomas's Christology and one suggestion. We have now come to the suggestion. Following the theological leads of Thomas, I suggest that Jesus did not have continuing beatific knowledge while on earth and that he did have the theological virtues of faith and hope. But how can we suggest these conclusions which differ from those of Aquinas while using the insights of his own Christology? Thomas attributes beatific as well as infused and experiential knowledge to Jesus and denied that Jesus lived by faith and hope.

Let us check the three observations with which we began. First, Thomas's Christology is a surprisingly open and developing Christology. It is based on the *mysterium Christi* which is always incapable of being articulated definitively. We saw this development in his explicitation of the motive of the incarnation, in his coming eventually to the insight of one *esse* in Christ, and in his later attribution of an experiential knowledge to Christ. There is no reason to think that Thomas would not change his mind if something justified or necessitated it. What might this be?

Our second observation about Aquinas was that he was a biblical theologian. A decisive criterion for him in any discussion was Scripture. It carried more weight than speculative arguments. Where he does manifest development in his Christological thinking, the later position seems to be more in accord with the Scriptures and thus a more satisfying conclusion. We may, therefore, assume that Thomas today would be more than open to the developments in the biblical sciences and what they suggest or even demand in terms of Christology. This does not mean that Thomas would be blindly accepting of the critical approaches to Scripture. His interests would most likely be far more than historiographical alone. Yet the distinctions basic to Catholic biblical studies today between the Jesus material, the oral tradition, and the written tradition, and the awareness that not all of the biblical statements attributed to Jesus in the Johannine material are *ipsissima verba,* would only help and not hinder Thomas in his search for the truth about Christ. In the end, to follow the example of Thomas forces one to make choices in accord with Scripture as the criterion of theology (of course Scripture as interpreted from within the Church).

Third, we observed that one of the fundamentals of Thomas's Christology was his respect for the humanity of Jesus and his theology of the *kenosis*. It is this that would urge Thomas in the direction of attributing ordinary human ignorance to Christ as a condition co-assumed along with the human nature. This does greater justice to the humanity of Jesus, is more in accord with the Scriptures, and is not ruled out by the intense and hypostatic union to the Word which overflows into the fullness of grace.

Let us note what Thomas had to say about the *kenosis* itself. Christ freely chose to assume together with a concrete human nature the contingent limitations of human existence. His motive was to identify with us for the sake of our salvation. The criterion for our determining the extent of the *kenosis* is Scripture. Thomas stresses the human vulnerability of Jesus as much as possible. But human ignorance is not unbecoming a God enfleshed. It only reveals further the humility of the one who loves us. Thomas sees in the incarnation a refutation of Manicheism and he sees the *kenosis* as a reality central to a credible and redemptive incarnation. Invincible human ignorance and nescience, a universal quality of our humanness although not intrinsic to our nature, would not be unfitting to a God who wants to be one with us.

Although Thomas's discussion of the knowledge of Christ might leave many contemporary Christologists unmoved, he argues in question 9 of the *tertia pars* in accord with a contemporary objective: the desire to preserve the full and real humanity of Jesus. Thomas *wants* all that is human to belong to Christ. Article 1 of question 9 is the context for his discussion. The question there is whether Christ had any knowledge other than divine, *any human knowledge at all.*[30] For the objection could be raised

---

[30]Hugh of St. Victor had held the position of absolute omniscience in Christ. Christ's knowledge was the same as the uncreated knowledge of the Lord. Peter Lombard modified this position and postulated two kinds of wisdom in Christ, pertaining to two natures, with a distinction between the intensiveness of Christ's human knowledge which was not as intensive as divine knowledge and the extensiveness of his knowledge which was co-extensive with divine knowledge. Lombard's opinion prevailed and was the opinion of Alexander of Hales and Albert

that human knowledge would be superfluous. But Thomas not only attributes human knowledge to Christ, he attributes to him all three kinds of human knowledge (i.e., beatific, infused, acquired). Thomas is no anthropological minimalist in his Christology. Our problem is whether Jesus had any knowledge at all beyond the ordinary. Thomas's problem was whether he had any beyond the divine. In his discussion Thomas defends the threefold knowledge of Christ as *an affirmation of Jesus' humanity*.

The second objection (III, 9, 1) argues: A lesser light is obscured by a greater one. Compared to God's uncreated knowledge all created knowledge is like a lesser light. Therefore no knowledge other than the divine shone forth in Christ. But that depends upon how one sees the relationship between the greater and the lesser. Thomas replies to the objection: Certainly the light of the sun obscures the light of a candle, for both are sources of light and the one a greater source. But if of two lights one is the source and the other a reflector, then the lesser is not obscured by the greater but is made brighter by it, as air reflects the sunlight. Christ's human knowledge reflects the divine life within him and is not superfluous because of it.

Operative in Thomas's discussion of Christ's knowledge is the principle that his human nature ought not be imperfect (III, 9, 3). Here the principle of perfection dominates rather than the *kenosis* which manifests itself in Christ's bodily and emotional life. In his discussion of Christ's acquired knowledge Thomas argues that nothing implanted by God in human nature is lacking to Christ. As a result, Christ's human nature had an active as well as passive intellect; and since God does not create anything futile, Christ's active intellect was operative and he acquired knowledge in this ordinary way. Thomas also acknowledges here that he had held a different opinion when as a younger man he had commented on the *Sentences* (III, 8, 4; 12, 2).

Does the attribution of ignorance to Christ deny a real effect within the human nature of its hypostatic union in the Word? No. Thomas himself writes, "The soul of Christ, which is united to the Word in person, is more closely *[propinquius]* joined to this Word of God than any other creature" (III, 10, 4). Human

---

the Great. Thomas goes much further in attributing acquired knowledge to Christ, not the common opinion of the Middle Ages. The background for Thomas's discussion is thus quite different from our own.

ignorance would neither negate this nor the fullness of Christ's habitual grace.

There is no need to comment further on Thomas's discussion of Christ's knowledge. He wrestles in a somewhat contrived way with biblical texts that are hard to explain in the light of relative omniscience, such as Mark 13:32 (III, 10, 2) and Luke 2:52 (III, 12, 2). One can argue that Christ did experience transitory beatitude, had some infused as well as acquired knowledge, and that these need not exclude ignorance. Yet Thomas is unwilling to attribute ignorance to Christ (III, 15, 3).[31]

Once one is willing to apply Thomas's understanding of the *kenosis* not only to Christ's physical and emotional life but also to his intellectual life, then the basis for denying faith and hope in Christ no longer exists (III, 7, 3 and 4). Christ was a man of faith (particularly trust in God) as well as a prophet of hope.

We can retain both Thomas's interpretation of hypostatic unity (III, 2–6 and 17) and his theology of the *kenosis* in his discussion of the concrete human condition assumed by Christ (III, 14–15). What we cannot retain, and I would argue that the always thinking, developing, biblically conscious Thomas so sensitive to the humanness of Jesus would himself no longer retain, is the opinion Thomas often asserts in his Christology that Christ is both a wayfarer and a beholder, *simul viator et comprehensor,* both a pilgrim to God on earth and one who already possessed the heavenly beatitude (III, 15, 10; also 7, 8; 11, 1 and 2). This suggestion in no way denies Jesus' unique relationship with the Father, his own intimate knowledge and experience of God, his own personal union with the Word, his own oneness in being with the Word, his own life of grace. It only makes him even more one of us, a fellow pilgrim.

In Christ, God and the human have been brought so closely together that it can truly be said that our original destiny has been restored, that another *adam* has been given to us; all this has happened through grace, and yet in such a way that the human race itself has participated in it and, through Christ, has merited salvation. Christ remains the mediator for Thomas, the supreme ex-

---

[31]The distinction between ignorance and nescience as such is not important here (I/II, 76, 1). Thomas applied neither to Christ. Also, ignorance could connote sin in the medieval world, another reason for not attributing it to Christ. Thomas, however, distinguished vincible and invincible ignorance.

emplification of the relationship between grace and freedom, because he is both God and one of us.

In Conclusion

In the previous chapter we explored the concept of Jesus' divinity. We came to realize that his divine nature did not make him a different kind of being than you and I are. We too are divine.

But was Jesus' humanity a different kind of humanity than ours? No. He not only had (assumed) an abstract human nature but a concrete human existence. He assumed not only our human nature but also our human condition.

In this chapter we saw the Philippians hymn as one expression of Pauline Christology. In its Pauline setting the hymn portrays Jesus as the truly human one. It is not Jesus' humanity but ours that may be open to question. As a perfect image of God, Jesus is able to give content to what being truly human is all about.

Even though pre-existence as we ordinarily think of it in theology was probably not part of the original content of the Philippians hymn, its interpretation in terms of a three-stage Christology later came to predominate. It is something like seeing the Pauline Jesus through Johannine glasses. But even here, in contrast to so many modern Christologists, I argue that a doctrine of pre-existence as such need not disparage or negate the true humanity of Jesus. The doctrine of pre-existence has become something of a scapegoat for the weakness of traditional Christologies. Yet pre-existence only means "the prior actuality of God."

Next we turned to Thomas Aquinas as an example of classical Christology. We saw how Thomas valued the humanity of Jesus, how his theology of the hypostatic union need not prevent Jesus from being human as we are human, how his theology of the incarnation took the "consubstantial with the Father" and the "consubstantial with us" with equal seriousness. Allowing Thomas's instincts full scope we see Jesus as a fellow pilgrim with us on our journeys to God.

There are still points that need to be explored further: Jesus' power, knowledge, and sinlessness. But what is becoming apparent is the intent of both biblical and classical Christology to see Jesus' humanity as being the same kind of humanity as ours— even if he may have been distinctively more humane than we are.

4

Two Contemporary Approaches
to the Humanity of Jesus

Although the mode of union between the human and the divine in Jesus was distinctively hypostatic, according to classical Chalcedonian Christology, Jesus' being divine was not as such a unique event in human history. We too can be divine, through grace, as we saw in chapter 2. Nor is Jesus' humanity a radically different kind of humanity from ours. He partook fully of our human condition, a reality the classical tradition also attempted to explicate even if not always adequately so, as we have seen in chapter 3. For contemporary Christology, however, there is no turning back from this central intuition of the full and real humanness of Jesus Christ. Christology requires not only an account of Jesus as the incarnate Word, but an adequate theology of the humanity of Jesus as well. It is to this task that we turn in this chapter and the next. In this chapter we consider two contemporary efforts to do justice to Jesus as consubstantial with us: kenotic Christologies and the theology of Piet Schoonenberg.

A Kenotic Incarnation

Kenosis is not a precise expression with only one meaning. Its varied uses are not necessarily incompatible, although some may use the word in one sense while being critical of its use in another.

Speaking strictly, *kenoticism* refers to the thought of a particular group of nineteenth-century theologians, such as Gottfried

Thomasius and H. R. Mackintosh, for whom *kenosis* was a key Christological concept. Speaking less strictly, it is applied to Christologies of any century that make use of *kenosis*. For example, there is a kenotic dimension to the Christologies of Hilary of Poitiers and Martin Luther, and in the twentieth century *kenosis* is still being used as an aid to Christology.

We can distinguish between those theologians for whom *kenosis* is a tool for interpreting the death of Christ and those for whom it is a tool for interpreting the incarnation. The nineteenth-century theologians interpreted the incarnation as a kenotic act on God's part. In the twentieth century, however, John Macquarrie applies *kenosis* particularly to the cross of Christ, and Luther's theology of the cross leads some to describe his theology as kenotic.

In the present Christological climate, we must also distinguish the use of *kenosis* in those Christologies which are from above and those which are from below. For the nineteenth-century kenoticists, and for those for whom *kenosis* primarily refers to the incarnation, a kenotic Christology remains a Christology from above. In the twentieth century, however, *kenosis* is being used deliberately in some Christologies from below, where it refers primarily to the life as well as the death of Jesus. What is common to all theologians who use the concept of *kenosis* is the desire to respect or emphasize the humanness of Jesus. In that sense they all produce theologies of the humanity of Christ.

Twentieth-century kenoticism, to a greater or lesser degree, can be associated with names like Russell Aldwinckle, Dietrich Bonhoeffer, John Macquarrie, and Lucien Richard, to name only a few. Lucien Richard[1] describes the purpose of his Christology as a search for both personal and social transformation in the light of the teaching and person of Jesus (8). He labels his Christology as explicitly kenotic (12) and as a Christology from below (36), and especially as this is exemplified in the cross (36). *Kenosis* does not refer to a divine self-emptying in the incarnation, but rather applies primarily to acts of *human* self-emptying and suffering. The kenotic character of the Christ event is rooted in the kenotic nature of human reality itself (190). Kenotic Christology is grounded on kenotic anthropology (190).

[1]Lucien Richard, *A Kenotic Christology, in the Humanity of Jesus the Christ, the Compassion of our God* (New York: University Press of America, 1982): numbers in parentheses refer to pages in this text.

Russell Aldwinckle's[2] kenotic Christology (also explicit) is distinctive from that of Richard. His guiding concerns are both the genuine humanness of Jesus and the traditional affirmation of the divinity of Jesus (6). A Christology from below is the necessary starting point for Christology, but it is only the starting point (103); faith demands that one arrive at a Christology from above as well (106). A Christian can never remain with the human Jesus alone but must come in the end to affirm that *God* became one of us—a theology of incarnation (106, 268). And this theology of incarnation which can hold together both Christology from below and Christology from above is the doctrine of *kenosis* (88, 182).

John Macquarrie's theology[3] respects the importance of the *kenosis* concept although his Christology cannot simply be labeled kenotic as such. He accepts the current emphasis on the humanity of Jesus as absolutely indispensable.[4] At one time he used the death of Jesus as the starting point of Christology.[5] The death of Jesus under Pontius Pilate is the best-attested fact of critical biblical scholarship and also a fact which presumes the humanity of Jesus. In addition, however, the death of Jesus helps us to see how one who is fully human can also disclose God. Does the incarnation not take place with the cross rather than at the moment of conception?[6] Incarnation for Macquarrie is a process in which the finite human life of Jesus and the divine life of absolute love draw closer and closer until, in the midst of death, the human life is raised to the level of the divine. Such is not a theology of the incarnation in its traditional sense, nor a kenotic Christology in its nineteenth-century sense, but a recognition of *kenosis* as the way of bringing together the human and the divine in Christ.

---

[2]Russell F. Aldwinckle, *More Than Man, A Study in Christology* (Grand Rapids, Mich.: William B. Eerdmans Publishing Co., 1976): numbers in parentheses refer to pages in this text.

[3]Cf. John Macquarrie, *Jesus Christ in Modern Thought* (London: SCM Press, 1990). Also see nn. 5–7 of this chapter.

[4]See in particular ibid., 3–26, 245–50, 339–47, 359–74.

[5]See in particular John Macquarrie, "A Dilemma in Christology," *The Expository Times* 76 (1965) 207–10.

[6]See esp. John Macquarrie, "True Life in Death," *Journal of Bible and Religion* 31 (1963) 207.

God is absolute letting-be, and letting-be is the ontological foundation of love. Letting-be is also self-giving or self-spending, so that God's creative work is a work of love and self-giving, into which he has put himself. In so far as created beings themselves manifest creativity, love, self-giving, they tend to be like God. This self-giving is supremely manifest in the particular being, Jesus Christ. Just as there is a self-emptying, or *kenosis,* of God as he pours out Being, so Christ empties himself in the life that is portrayed in the gospels. But how could this relative self-emptying in a finite particular being manifest the absolute letting-be of God? To this, it must be replied that death is the one absolute in human life. . . . Christ's self-giving, his love or letting-be, becomes complete and absolute in the accepting of the cross.[7]

Dietrich Bonhoeffer would not have described his theology as kenotic, yet the motif of *kenosis* is present in his theology. John A. T. Robinson has suggested that "the 'kenotic' theory of Christology, based on this conception of self-emptying, is, I am persuaded, the only one that offers much hope of relating at all satisfactorily the divine and the human in Christ. . . . It was some such Christology, I believe, toward which Bonhoeffer was working and of which he left such tantalizing intimations behind him."[8] Yet, in his 1933 lectures on Christology, Bonhoeffer had discussed and critiqued kenotic theory.[9] His starting point was the *exinanitio* (humiliation) of Lutheran orthodoxy. "The subject of the *exinanitio* is, according to Lutheran orthodoxy, not the one who is *becoming man* but the one who *has become* man. In other words, the incarnation is not an act of the Logos hum-

---

[7]John Macquarrie, *Principles of Christian Theology* (New York: Charles Scribner's Sons, 1966) 278.

[8]John A. T. Robinson, *Honest to God* (Philadelphia: Westminster Press, 1963) 74. Also see Ronald A. Carson, "The Motifs of *Kenosis* and *Imitatio* in the Work of Dietrich Bonhoeffer, with an Excursus on the *Communicatio Idiomatum,*" *Journal of the American Academy of Religion* 43 (1975) 542-53.

[9]Dietrich Bonhoeffer, *Christ the Center,* trans. John Bowden (New York: Harper and Row, 1966) 97-102. For a discussion of the Lutheran doctrine on *kenosis* as well as later developments, also see Pannenberg, *Jesus, God and Man,* 307-23.

bling himself. . . . The humiliation is an attribute of the Incarnate, not an attribute of the Logos as such."[10]

The humiliation consists in Christ's restraint from exercising divine power for the duration of his earthly life. This restraint is interpreted in different ways by two schools of Lutheran thought: (1) the kenoticists who held to a real renunciation or evacuation of the divine properties, and (2) the cryptics who held to a concealment of the divine powers but not an actual renunciation of them.

Bonhoeffer described how the doctrine of *kenosis* was taken up afresh in the nineteenth century; but, in contrast to the Lutheran tradition, in nineteenth-century kenoticism the Logos itself rather than the incarnate Jesus was the subject of the humiliation. "The sequence of events is no longer Logos-man-humiliation (as in Lutheran orthodoxy), but Logos-humiliation-man. . . . The subject of the renunciation is the Logos, not the Logos incarnate."[11] Bonhoeffer judged the modern kenoticism a failure. Yet is it, as J.A.T. Robinson suggests, still some form of kenotic theory toward which Bonhoeffer was working?

Ronald Carson suggests that Bonhoeffer's Christology is kenotic in all but name.[12] Surely Carson is on the right track. If we think of Bonhoeffer's Lutheran background, his analysis of humiliation Christology in the 1933 lectures, his theology of the cross and the cost of discipleship, the nature of discipleship as the imitation of Christ's earthly *kenosis,* as well as the central image in Bonhoeffer's Christology of Jesus as a man for others, we have a kenotic Christology—a kenoticism in accord with Luther's theology transferred to a modern and secular world. "To be a Christian does not mean to be religious in a particular way, to cultivate some particular form of asceticism (as a sinner, a penitent or a saint), but to be a man. It is not some religious act which makes a Christian what he is, but participation in the suffering of God in the life of the world."[13]

[10]Bonhoeffer, *Christ the Center,* 97.

[11]Ibid., 99.

[12]Carson, "The Motifs of *Kenosis* and *Imitatio* in the Work of Dietrich Bonhoeffer," 548.

[13]Dietrich Bonhoeffer, *Letters and Papers from Prison,* trans. Reginald Fuller (New York: The Macmillan Co., 1966) 222–23.

The kenoticists of the nineteenth and early twentieth centuries have been the subject of frequent criticism, and yet they deserve further consideration. In their own time, many held that they had gone too far; in our time, the criticism is that they have not gone far enough. In their time they were criticized for having questioned the immutability and impassibility of God; in our time they are dismissed too easily as still being proponents of Christology from above. To their credit, it must be said that they developed a Christology from above (a Logos Christology) that did greater justice to the humanity of Jesus and the biblical record than had many previous Christologies. Nor is it clear in our own age that Christology from above is to be simply discarded: it too has its basis in the New Testament.

These kenoticists were located primarily in Germany and England, with counterparts in Russia. They cannot, of course, be equated with each other. In general, however, it can be said of their theologies that they are Christologies from above, that they presuppose the pre-existent Logos, and that it is the Logos who is the primary subject of the *kenosis*. The incarnation itself, not just the earthly life and death of Jesus, was a kenotic event. In the incarnation, the Eternal Word voluntarily limited itself to a historical human consciousness and human faculties. Gottfried Thomasius distinguished between two sets of divine attributes: on the one hand omnipotence, omniscience, and omnipresence; and on the other, holiness, righteousness, and love. The former set the eternal Logos chose freely to set aside, whereas the latter were those attributes capable of being expressed through the human nature of Christ.

The German and British kenoticists include to varying degrees Gottfried Thomasius (*Christi Person und Werk,* 1857),[14] Charles Gore (*Dissertation on Subjects Connected with the Incarnation,* 1895), H. R. Mackintosh (*The Doctrine of the Person of Jesus Christ,* 1912); also, in a more modified fashion, P. T. Forsyth (*The Person and Place of Jesus Christ,* 1909), and more recently Vincent Taylor (*The Person of Christ in the New Testament Teaching,* 1958).

[14]For a translation of Thomasius, see *God and Incarnation in Mid-Nineteenth Century German Theology,* ed. and trans. Claude Welch (New York: Oxford University Press, 1965), which includes writings of Thomasius, Isaak Dorner, and Alois Biedermann.

Although the Russian and Orthodox kenotic Christologies of the time cannot be simply subsumed under the same category as the Protestant and Anglican Christologies, they suggest the emergence of the same kenotic spirit, as in the writings of S. H. Bulgakov, M. M. Tareev, and Vladimir Soloviev.[15] In Russian thought, the concept of *kenosis* is not only an aid toward interpreting the life of Jesus and the incarnation, but plays a part in the theology of the Trinity as well.

Although criticism of kenotic Christologies abound,[16] it is difficult to avoid some theology of *kenosis*. Either one must deny any notion of pre-existence, the doctrine of the incarnation as central to Christian faith, and all Christology from above or do violence to the biblical testimony and critical New Testament scholarship. Otherwise, one must find a place for a freely chosen self-limitation on God's part in God's actions and presence *ad extra*. Although there are many who are willing to go in the direction of one of the former two options, the reality appears to be more with the latter—a kenotic incarnation, which does not dismiss the kenotic character of the entire life and death of Jesus as well. *Kenosis* is a category which can help us both in our theology of the incarnation and in our theology of the cross.

> Whether we use the word kenosis or not—and in view of the many theories which the term covers, it may be wise not to do so—the fact remains that Jesus of Nazareth does not exercise all the functions of deity, nor was He in His historical actuality in the full possession and exercise of what we have called the metaphysical attributes. This view does not spring from any modernizing attempt to play down the significance of Jesus or to deny the Christian claim. It is a fair deduction from the testimony of Scripture itself.

[15]For a discussion of Russian Orthodox kenotic thought, see Nadejda Gorodetsky, *The Humiliated Christ in Modern Russian Thought* (London: SPCK and New York: Macmillan, 1938).

[16]We cannot take the time to respond to the variety of criticisms here, many of which do merit consideration. For varied criticisms, see D. M. Baillie, *God Was in Christ* (New York: Charles Scribner's Sons, 1948) 94–98; Eugene R. Fairweather, "The 'Kenotic' Christology," in F. W. Beare, *Commentary on the Epistle to the Philippians* (London: Adam and Charles Black, 1969) 159–74; Knox, *The Humanity and Divinity of Christ,* 101–16; William Temple, *Christus Veritas* (London: Macmillan, 1949) esp. 141ff.

Again, if Jesus is truly man, since by God's intention He too is a finite creature, then if God is to become man, God must adapt himself to the limitations of the finite creature, limitations which are of God's ordaining as far as the finite creature is concerned. Any doctrine of the Incarnation must take full account of these facts. This means that Christian theology must work with the concept of divine self-limitation.

This implies that when we speak of the divine fullness in a human being, this cannot mean that the finite becomes infinite. This would be a contradiction in terms. It can only mean that the finite, while remaining finite, becomes the vehicle of the divine presence and activity as far as finite reality can embody this.[17]

Although only in modern times has Christology been explicitly developed along kenotic lines, the kenotic element cannot be interpreted as only a modern phenomenon. We see its antecedents in the theology of the Reformation and in the Christology of Thomas Aquinas. Lutheran kenotic thought has associated the humiliation and *kenosis* with the life and particularly the death of Jesus. Luther in no way denied the traditional doctrine of the incarnation, which his understanding of paradox helped him to illuminate, but in his thought *kenosis* primarily referred to the cross. In Thomas Aquinas, on the other hand, for whom the passion of Christ was the supreme exemplification of his human identity with us, *kenosis* can actually be seen as one aspect, one of the principles, in his theology of the incarnation, as we saw in the previous chapter. For the sake of credibility and for the sake of our salvation, Christ co-assumed along with his particular human nature the physical and emotional defects and limitations which are a consequence of sin. Thomas's Christology is not a kenotic Christology but *kenosis* is an aspect of his theology of the humanity of Christ. Both Thomas's and Luther's Christologies are Christologies from above, but Thomas's is a metaphysical theology of the hypostatic union, Luther's an existential theology of the cross. For Luther, Jesus on earth possessed the divine qualities but set aside their use, although they remained available to him. There was no self-emptying on the part of the Logos, but rather on the part of Jesus of Nazareth.

[17]Aldwinckle, *More Than Man,* 192–93.

The concept of *kenosis* was anticipated in various ways even in the patristic period. Thomasius claimed Hilary of Poitiers as an early kenoticist. Thomasius was right in that *kenosis* (or more properly *krypsis,* concealment) functioned in Hilary's Christology, yet Hilary was no direct forerunner of the nineteenth-century kenoticists. No one in the patristic period actually associated the self-emptying with a self-limitation on the part of the Logos or a relinquishment of the attributes of the divine nature.

Yet Hilary's Christology[18] is kenotic in a real sense. Traditional in his Christology and anti-Arian in his Trinitarian doctrine, Hilary distinguished three stages in the history of Christ: pre-existence, *kenosis,* exaltation. The *kenosis* of Christ was strongly affirmed (*De Trinitate* 8, 45). Yet this was never a renunciation of the divine nature. Christ is one, and the subject remains the pre-existent Son. In the *kenosis,* rather, Christ refrains from showing himself in his complete identity with the Father, although his divine nature at times shines through, as in the miracles or in the transfiguration. In other words, the fullness of the unlimited divine nature is present in Christ, even if inhibited or concealed. There is no permanent renunciation of the divine properties nor any self-limitation on the part of the eternal Son.

The union of the eternal Son with the human nature is so strong that the actual condition of Christ's humanity is a freedom from ordinary human needs, even eating and drinking. Yet Christ did eat, drink, and suffer. These activities, however, were more like "miracles" than what we often call the miracles, which came so natural to Christ. The state of transfiguration was the natural state of Christ's humanity; it revealed (or unconcealed) who he truly was. His identity with our condition required that he refrain from showing this natural state of glory. With Hilary, we find in Christ a truly human nature, but a divinized human nature, as well as a *kenosis* which prevented that human nature from manifesting itself in all its glory. Hilary's Christology is kenotic, but not in the modern sense.

---

[18]Cf. Aloys Grillmeier, *Christ in Christian Tradition,* vol. 1, *From the Apostolic Age to Chalcedon (AD 451),* rev. ed., trans. John Bowden (London: Mowbrays, 1975) 392–400; Paul Galtier, *Saint Hilaire de Poitiers, le premier docteur de l'Eglise Latine* (Paris: Beauchesne et ses fils, 1960) 108–58; Piet Smulders, *La doctrine trinitaire de S. Hilaire de Poitiers* (Rome: Analecta Gregoriana, 1944) 179–206, esp. 195–206.

Although there is nothing of the modern doctrine of *kenosis* in the patristic period, Hilary's Christology did indicate an awareness of the difficulties of elaborating, in a two-nature Christology, how the union of the natures functions in Jesus Christ on earth. Besides *kenosis,* some form of the doctrine of divinization was also central to Hilary's Christology, a doctrine particularly significant among the Greek Fathers. Among the Cappadocians, Gregory of Nyssa helped to bring home the value of the doctrine of divinization to Christology.[19] As I will suggest later, Christ's humanity was divinized but his divinity kenoticized. Both divinization and *kenosis* contribute to a Christology—a kenotic incarnation, a divine indwelling, and an ongoing divinization.

Gregory emphasized the distinction of natures in Christ. He articulated the unity of Christ in terms of a "mingling" which effected a divinization. His bold simile was that the human Christ was absorbed into the Godhead "like a drop of vinegar in the sea." Because of the co-mingling, the human Jesus was not confined within the limitations and properties of humanity. The transformation or divinization of Christ began with his conception. Gregory's provocative language makes us aware that in Christology we must concern ourselves not only with our fallen human condition but also with nature divinized by grace.

With a sensitivity to contemporary biblical research on the earthly, historical Jesus, with an awareness of a biblical basis for a theology of incarnation and its importance in the history of Christian thought, and with an appreciation of the many constructive contributions to Christology in our own day as well as prior to our times, the time has come for us to bring together some conclusions about the incarnation. To be sure, the dominant part of Christology is the message that Jesus of Nazareth as incarnate Word symbolically communicates. This message is proclaimed by his life and death, is vindicated by his resurrection, is grounded in his incarnation, and continues through the power of the Spirit. Yet our concern here is only with one part of Christology: the incarnation.

Kenosis is a word that can be applied analogously to several aspects of the Christ-event. It can be applied to the incarnation as God's act, to the life and ministry of Jesus, and to his death

---

[19]See Grillmeier, *Christ in Christian Tradition,* 370–77.

and cross. It need not be limited to only one of these events but can be descriptive of the Jesus phenomenon as a whole.

Although the Philippians hymn provided the language, the theological use of that language need not be confined to its usage in that hymn in either its pre-Pauline or Pauline setting. Post-Pauline uses can also be valid, not as interpretations of the pre-Pauline or Pauline hymn but as an aid to the developing theological understanding of Christ within the Church. In other words, the theological usefulness of *kenosis* need not be restricted to a particular exegesis of the Philippians hymn. The hymn has given the Church language which it has used beyond its meaning in the hymn itself.

The hymn probably manifested a two-stage, Adam Christology, with no reference to a prior or pre-historical existence on Christ's part. Once, however, a three-stage Christology developed in the Church, with its accompanying notions of the pre-existence of the Word and the incarnation, and once the three-stage Christology became not only *a* Christology but *the* Christology, it was natural for the Church to read into the Philippians hymn a means for articulating its three-stage Christology. Or, one might argue that the hymn is an expression of a three-stage Christology, but that the *kenosis* or humiliation does not refer to the incarnation but to the life and death of Jesus. But neither interpretation prevents the Church from legitimately applying *kenosis* later to the conception of Jesus. The word and the image it evokes is useful beyond the confines of its original historical application. The Philippians hymn itself is not the basis for a kenotic Christology, even if some kenoticists have previously interpreted it as such. It does, however, provide the language.

The situation would be different if there were no biblical basis at all for a three-stage Christology, if a three-stage Christology only developed from a misreading of the Philippians hymn. But Johannine Christology is the biblical basis for incarnation. Once a Johannine Christology became dominant, it was misread into the Philippians hymn. Today we recognize that the basis for a theology of the incarnation is the Fourth Gospel, but this does not mean that one cannot use language from elsewhere in the New Testament to help us articulate such a theology. Even in the Fourth Gospel, *sarx* implies *kenosis*.

The self-giving and fully conscious humbling that *kenosis* implies can help us to understand the life, death, and coming-to-be of Jesus of Nazareth. *Kenosis* suggests a conscious and freely chosen self-emptying, self-giving, self-limiting, self-sacrificing act.[20] "Jesus saw God-likeness essentially as giving and spending oneself out. Precisely because Christ was in the form of God he recognized equality with God as a matter not of getting but of giving."[21] One can easily see that Jesus' entire life and ministry had a kenotic character: servanthood. One can also readily see why the cross, only one event in the mystery of Jesus Christ, came to stand symbolically for the whole Christ-event. The cross is a clear summation of the mystery—God as being-for-others. But not only do the life and death of Jesus put flesh and blood on the image of *kenosis,* so does the divine act by which God chose to be united hypostatically to a human nature in the incarnation. That event reveals the nature of God as being-for-others. In one sense it is a condescension. In another sense, it is a revelation: God is love. Thus *kenosis* can be applied both to the earthly Jesus and to the pre-existent Word. Indeed, the former reveals the latter, and the latter reveals our God. Jesus is an earthly, historical embodiment of that which God always is. Jesus is a freely chosen, self-giving act of God.

When we attribute self-limitation not only to the earthly Jesus but also to the act of God which constitutes Jesus' coming-to-be as one of us, several questions emerge: Can God be so limited? Can God become so circumscribed and localized? Would not the localization of God, if it be truly God, dissolve or destroy the humanity of Jesus?

There is nothing in the Christian theology of God that prevents God from being self-limiting. Such self-limitation does not imply God's not being God, or God's becoming less than God is. Rather it is a question of God's being God, being that being-for-others that God is, not withdrawing from being divine but revealing what being divine means. How does God reveal in the concrete, finite, tangible course of history what it means to be God and what it means to be love? There is nothing unfitting or impossible about God's choosing to be limited *in the other*. To deny such a possibility to God would be to deny God's infinitude.

---

[20]I have written of this previously in *The Power of Love* (Chicago: The Thomas More Press, 1979) 192–233.

[21]Richard, *A Kenotic Christology,* 104.

God's choosing to be in the other, and to be self-limiting in order to be present in the other, does not imply the particular limitation of being circumscribed. God's local presence is never God's only presence, or exclusive presence, or a denial of God's omnipresence. God never becomes present somewhere in such a way as to be unable to be present elsewhere. God's real and local presence does not exhaust God's power. God's presence in Christ is one instance of God's universal presence, although God is uniquely present in Christ.

God is fully present in Jesus Christ, but not exclusively so. To be really and fully present does not mean to be spatially or historically confined. Thus God's choosing to be self-limiting in and for the other is not the choice of becoming finite in God's very own being but becoming finite in the other.

But what does this mean? The analogy of grace helps us to understand God as present to creatures and also how God's presence is not destructive of the nature of creatures. Taking the history of God's presence to God's people and the theology of grace which we sketched out briefly in chapter 2, we see God as present but God's infinite capacity for presence never being exhausted. That God is hypostatically united to a human nature in Jesus Christ does not limit God in God's own being. God does not choose to become limited by nature but only in the other, and this limitation is not a limitation *of God* as such. Grace, by which God is present to creatures *as* creatures, does not limit God. It rather implies God's capacity to be present to another.

But why describe God's presence through grace as a self-limitation on God's part at all? Because that is what is involved if God is going to be present to the other *as* another. In other words, God freely chooses to respect the nature of creatures at the same time that God longs to be present to them. God chooses limits in order to be with creatures without destroying them, to be with them as they are.

We can return here to Thomas's Christology. A principle Thomas borrowed from John Damascene was that the distinctive properties of each nature remained in the hypostatic union (*ST* III, 10, 1; 2,1). Yet it is not a question simply of *whether* Jesus was God, but in what way or sense he was. He was obviously not God confined to earth. Nor was he God in all God's transcendence. Jesus was God as incarnate—another mode of divine presence. It is a new mode of presence because it is God's freely choosing to be present (hypostatically) in the other. But to be present in the other is to respect the otherness of the other. That grace does not destroy nature is a basis of Thomas's Christology. Not even the grace of union destroys the human nature of Christ. What is received is received according to the mode of the receiver, and in this instance the receiver is the human nature of Christ—which enables a new mode of divine presence.

Grace, and here the grace of union is no exception, tells us that God can be present in, to, and with creatures, as creatures. Union with God, even hypostatic union, does not destroy the creatures; it completes them. God chooses, in sharing the divine nature, to be limited not as God *is* but as God is *in others*. Grace is an example and analogy of God's freely choosing self-limitation in order to be in the other. "To say that fullness of God is in Jesus Christ can only mean the complete indwelling of God as far as this is possible within the limits of a finite human existence."[22]

Grace is a proper analogy for the hypostatic union, even if the latter is a unique instance of the former and a different kind of union. In the life of divinizing and sanctifying grace, God is God. God is present in the other, the other's nature as other is preserved, humanness is not destroyed, and God has chosen to be limited for our sake.

In our effort to probe the *mysterium* of the incarnation further, we must take seriously a caution voiced by Bonhoeffer (without allowing it to foreclose further inquiry), to distinguish between the *who* question and the *how* question. For Bonhoeffer, only the *who* question, "Who are you?" is appropriate; not the question, "How is this possible?"[23] A theology of the incarnation must be seen primarily as a response to the *who* ("You are the Son of the living God") and only secondarily as an effort to explain how that is possible. Faith affirms that in Jesus we meet God without having to explain exactly how such a meeting is possible. Theology simply attempts to show that it is not impossible.

An adequate Christology today must be both a Christology from below and a Christology from above. These two approaches are often set up as mutually exclusive or over against each other. Yet we should be suspicious of a too facile dichotimizing. Are

[22]Aldwinckle, *More Than Man,* 88.

[23]Bonhoeffer, *Christ the Center,* 27–40.

they rather not complementary? Is not the Christ-event so profound and mysterious that several, potentially conflicting methods might be necessary to appreciate it? Can the truth be grasped by one type of Christology alone? Did not Alexandria and Antioch both have an insight into the Christological question such that tradition was not able to surrender either? A Christology from below, at our period in history, clearly keeps us in touch with the historical reality of Jesus, with Jesus' humanness. It is the best defense against Docetism and helps us to come to faith in an age of unbelief by retracing the steps by which the disciples themselves who knew Jesus in the flesh came to proclaim: Jesus is Lord. On the other hand, retracing those steps also helps us to come to see inadequacy in a Christology from below by itself alone, to see that the Church itself already within the New Testament period came out of its experience to a Christology from above. Christology from above is that to which Christology from below leads. Only a Christology from above can answer the *who* question unambiguously: this person is God. The danger in a Christology from above is that we will bring a preconceived notion of divinity to it, rather than allowing Jesus to disclose to us who his God is. The danger of a Christology from below is to assume a preconceived notion of what humanity is, based on our experience of fallenness, and to reduce Christology to a consideration of only the historiographical Jesus. But all of these approaches can remain only anthropology or historiography or philosophy and miss the *novum* (the newness or uniqueness of Jesus).

Christian tradition forces us to deal with two aspects of the mystery of Christ: the unity of Christ, that Christ is one, one person; and the humanity of Christ, that Christ is one of us. A theology of the incarnation cannot separate Christ from God, nor from us. It simply asserts that Christ is the most intimate union possible between God and us—not that there could not be another incarnation but that no other incarnation could surpass the unity between God and us that is manifested in Jesus Christ.

A theology of this (hypostatic) unity must be such that it reinforces the full and real humanness of Jesus, his oneness with us. And the theology of the humanity of Jesus must be such that it does not deny or make negligible the real effect or effectiveness of Jesus' union with God. In other words, Christology must be both a theology of the union (its Alexandrian pole) and a theology of the humanity (its Antiochene pole). The union has an effect and at the same time respects Jesus as being human. Jesus cannot be two distinguishable persons (heretical Nestorianism) nor less than fully human (Apollinarianism).

What is obvious is that God does not manifest divinity as enfleshed in the same way in which God might do so apart from being enfleshed. Enfleshment is only one way in which God reveals God's self and is present. God as immanent is not the same mode of being divine as God as transcendent. The incarnation is another mode of existence for God, another way of being divine.

This is in no way Trinitarian modalism. We are not talking here about different modes of the Trinity or the Son as pre-existent. Rather we are talking about another mode of existence assumed by the Son, the incarnate mode. At a point in time the Son becomes enfleshed, takes to himself a human nature, and is God as incarnate rather than God as pre-incarnate or pre-historical. God has freely chosen to become really related to his creation.

In defining one person and two natures as the limits within which Christian theology could attempt to articulate its understanding of the incarnation, Christian tradition sought to preserve both the oneness and the humanity of Christ. We cannot speak as if Christ were one person prior to the incarnation (the pre-existent Son), another person while on earth, and perhaps still a different person after the resurrection. Christ is ultimately one and the same person throughout the two or three stages of his existence, although each stage is a different mode of existence. Likewise then we cannot speak as if Jesus were both "God" and "a man," as if he were two distinguishable substantial beings joined together through some unanimity of heart or will.

If we say that Jesus is not "God and *a* man" (not a *homo assumptus* but a *natura assumpta*), it is only to affirm that Jesus is ultimately one. He is obviously a man, a human being. In fact, he is fully a man, a truly human being. The bottom line of an approach to Jesus from above or through the hypostatic union is to say that in Jesus there was no existing human being whom one could call Jesus prior to the union of the two natures. There never was, even momentarily, a human being that was not already in some sense God. Jesus is more accurately described as the incarnate Son of God than as an adopted son of God. In other words, what we have in Jesus is a new creation.

Jesus is a creature.[24] He was created as a singular human nature for God. He only came to be as a human being at the same moment that God came to be enfleshed as that particular human being. God created the human existence or nature of Jesus Christ so that God might be incarnate and thus be present to the world in another way. The hypostatic union asserts that Jesus was not a creature prior to the incarnation, but rather was created for the incarnation and as an incarnation.

In creating Jesus of Nazareth, God freely chose to create a creature in whom and through whom God might be more present to the world. God chose a new mode of existence in order to be incarnate. In doing so, God revealed God's essential self as love, as being for others. In the incarnation, God freely chose to be for others—whatever restrictions or limitations this kind of presence might imply. All of Jesus' human and earthly choices to be for others reflected the congruence between Jesus and God. Jesus' freely chosen self-definition is the self-definition of God: I Am (is) the One-who-is-with-you. Jesus' human nature and existence reflect and manifest his divine nature, although as a human being, in a human way: in him God is incarnate, enfleshed, revealed. In him, God is with us. God created Jesus in order that through him God might be with us, even if within the confines and restrictions of a human nature.

The *communicatio idiomatum* is a manifestation of this real congruence between God and the human in Jesus. The qualities of Jesus' human life—compassion, fidelity, generosity, humility,

---

[24]Thomas deals with Christ as a creature in two articles in his *Summa,* within the question on proper Christological language (III, 16, 8 and 10). For Thomas it is better to say "Christ, as man, is a creature" (16, 10) than to say simply "Christ is a creature" (16, 8). Thomas takes a cue from Jerome that careless expressions lead to heresy. "For this reason not even the expressions we use should conform to those of heretics lest we should give the impression that we favour their error" (16, 8). The Arians are known to have taught that Christ, even as divine, was a creature. Thus the simple statement "Christ is a creature," with no qualification as to whether one is talking about Christ as God or as a human being, can be misleading. "In consequence it should not be stated without qualification that Christ is a creature or is subordinate to the Father; such statements should be qualified by the phrase, 'according to his human nature' " (16, 8). In the expression "Christ, as man, is a creature," the qualification is more likely to be understood as referring to the human nature and not the hypostasis, and is then true (16, 10).

and joy—reveal and perfectly reflect the attributes of God. They define for us the kind of love that God is. They reveal God to us. Through Christ and in Christ we come to know the Father. Jesus enables us to encounter God. No pre-conceived definition of love or divinity here, but rather God as self-disclosing and thus choosing to become vulnerable for our sake. To say that Jesus is divine is to say that he is absolute love (compassion, fidelity, generosity, humility, joy—being for others) in the flesh. If one asks who God is, or what God is like, or what God would look like in the flesh, we point to Jesus. That is what God looks like if enfleshed, and that is what we are to look like in the flesh. What God looks like if enfleshed is what we are to look like if we are to be mirrors of God or the likeness of God. Jesus is God as God emptying God's self into human history in an unsurpassable way. Jesus is love made incarnate. In this incarnation Jesus is both God and human. The question is not: How could Jesus be both human and divine? but rather: How can anyone not be? Sin obstructs the possibility, but there is nothing about humanity as such which is incompatible with its becoming also divine.

There is a strong tendency among Christians and in Christology to reject the incarnation as necessary for Christian faith. Does the proclamation of the Lordship of Christ necessitate the proclamation of the incarnate Word? Obviously not. The earliest Christians proclaimed Jesus as Lord, but Johannine Christology came later. Yet this does not completely answer our question, for we are no longer "the earliest Christians." Thus we face other questions. Is being earlier better? Cannot a more profound insight or understanding come later? Is it possible or even desirable to reduce the historical Christian faith to its earliest formulation? Is not the question still: Who do you say that I am? Is Jesus God or isn't he, and if so, in what sense? Did Christian history make a mistake, or is it simply that its formulations are less able to speak effectively in our times? None of these questions are easily answered, and all are important. What then do we say of a "Christianity without incarnation"?[25]

Incarnation is one interpretation of the Jesus event, not the only interpretation possible. Christological pluralism fills the pages of

---

[25]I refer here to the collected essays edited by John Hick, *The Myth of God Incarnate* (Philadelphia: The Westminster Press, 1977). See in particular the first essay, by Maurice Wiles, "Christianity without Incarnation?" 1–10.

history as well as of the New Testament itself. It is not only a question of whether we can remain open to other Christologies (as indeed we must), but also a question of why we reject what we reject. We can ask what a pre-Nicene, non-Chalcedonian, two-stage Christology looks like. Is it adoptionist? Does it reject the Fourth Gospel as also normative for Christian faith? Can it avoid reducing the theology of Jesus to historiography alone? The suggestions that the doctrine of the incarnation is too time-bound and no longer relevant or that it is simply unintelligible are questionable.[26] If our concern is to be less exclusively insistent on Jesus as *the* way for all peoples, this is valid in any age cognizant of cultural and religious pluralism. But does this concern require a Christology without incarnation?

It can be fashionable to be critical of the Chalcedonian effort. Yet Chalcedon manifests centuries of intellectual struggle with the meaning of Christ. Are we sure that it has no more value? "The so-called definition defines only in a negative sense, by excluding the extremes of both christological approaches, without being able to offer any positive christological understanding."[27] But is this assertion not a misunderstanding of the purpose of such conciliar definitions? They are not intended to propose once and for all (positive) theologies of Jesus Christ but to set the limits within which further theological inquiry takes place. Chalcedon offers no theology of Christ, nor any theology of the hypostatic union, and to expect its dogma to do so will force us to conclude that it is inadequate. Each council is a starting point for theology as well as a closure to a particular theological debate. The Church considered Arianism and Apollinarianism closed issues, but never intended to advocate for all times one theology of God or Christ. Further theology would simply not be free to deny the equality of the pre-existent Son with the Father or the full humanity of Jesus or the unity of Jesus as one person. The function of Chalcedon's formulation was negative, to rule something out, or to set some limits, so as to resolve a controversy—and this was its positive contribution.

Certainly it is possible to experience the Lordship of Christ or believe in the divinity of Christ without being tied to particular

---

[26]Ibid., 3–5.

[27]Ibid., 28, from the essay by Frances Young.

language, even that of the two natures. But we must recognize that there is a difference between a Christian for whom certain theological language lacks meaning, a pastor for whom the theological language may be meaningful but not catechetically or homiletically primary, and the theologian who rejects its validity. The theologian must be critiqued on theological grounds. The doctrine of the incarnation is not necessarily at the top of the hierarchy of truths to be preached, but that is not to say it is untrue, unintelligible, or out of date.

Nor should the language of incarnation be taken too literally, as scientific or historiographical description. It is rather theological or religious language, God-talk, never adequate. Christian tradition has never made the ontological equation Jesus = God, even though it is frequently thought to have done so. In its care with respect to Trinitarian as well as Eucharistic theology, God is never reduced to Christ, nor the presence of Christ to the Eucharist. There is always "more" to God or Christ. But this is not to deny that Jesus is ontologically, hypostatically, tied into God, that Jesus *is* in some sense God, that Jesus' *isness* may be an uncreated act. Theological language, even philosophically theological language, is never what moderns might describe as scientific language. It always reflects personal knowledge and faith. The incarnation, if it be true at all, is a historical but clearly meta-historiographical event.

The incarnation refers to God's presence in history. But one must distinguish between (1) the event or process, what happened; (2) theological interpretations, language, hermeneutics; (3) the significance of the event, for a particular interpretation is not the last word about its significance or relevance; and (4) verifiability, which scientific historiography can neither prove nor disprove. The incarnation is a meta-historiographical, theological interpretation of the Christ-event which in itself is open to pluralism. Various theologies may assign varying significance to it. Belief in incarnation does not predetermine soteriology in all its details, does not necessarily make Jesus an exclusive savior. Thus a theology of the incarnation is still a viable and valuable part of Christology. The incarnation is not so much a specific event as it is a process, realized throughout the entire life of Jesus Christ, and summed up in the paschal mystery of his death and resurrection. The word *incarnation,* in other words, does not refer only to the event at the origin of Jesus' life in which the Word united to itself hypostatically a human nature and became the man Jesus, but also refers to the continuing realization and manifestation of that union throughout the entirety of Jesus' life. It is the life of Jesus that is the gradual embodiment or enfleshment of the hypostatic union. Christmas cannot be separated from Good Friday, Easter, and Pentecost. "The Incarnation is the whole life of Christ, from his conception in the womb, through all his further life of action, completed finally in his death, resurrection and being established as Lord and Sender of the Paraclete; it is prolonged everlastingly in his uninterrupted sending of the Holy Spirit.[28] The act by which God becomes one of us is a process by which God's becoming one of us is accomplished.

This helps us to appreciate the variety of valid but analogous ways in which the word *kenosis* is applied to Christ. Although it has different implications, *kenosis* refers to the conception, life, and death of Jesus—all manifest a freely chosen self-limitation. There is no need to choose one or the other; Christ is all of them. Likewise with incarnation: God becomes enfleshed in the conception (whether virginal or not) of Jesus and throughout his life and ministry. If anything, the incarnation is most fully accomplished on the cross, as John Macquarrie has suggested: "At what moment did the Incarnation, the union of God and man, take place? . . . Must we not rather say, at the Cross?"[29] Yet incarnation cannot refer to one event exclusively, but rather to the life lived, as a totality. God's uniting a human nature to God takes time, because temporality is a constitutive dimension of what it means to be human. The enfleshment not only takes up space (the body of Christ) but takes up time as well (the history of Christ). God does not become fully incarnate in a human nature instantaneously. The incarnation is not finished at the moment of conception; it has only begun. And although the moment of conception is significant, it is not the only nor even the most significant event in the life of the incarnate Word. The (hypostatic) union of God and a human nature in Christ is a biography, a story, a process. This is true simply because what is received is received according

[28]Edward Schillebeeckx, *Christ the Sacrament of the Encounter with God* (New York: Sheed and Ward, 1963) 28–29, also 20.

[29]Macquarrie, "True Life in Death," 207.

to the mode of the receiver, and God respects the nature of creatures. God is united to us as human beings in accord with our human nature, which is not atemporal or ahistorical. God became united to a history. Throughout his life Jesus had continually to actualize who he already was—the Son of God. It was never something done. The incarnation was inaugurated at the conception, but consummated on the cross. In another sense it is still going on.

As a process, the incarnate life of Jesus as a whole has a "before" and an "after." The story of God's action and presence in Christ cannot be understood apart from the whole pre-history of Jesus, the action and presence of God within the Hebrew people. The story of Jesus is a part of this history of God coming to be with God's people, being revealed as the One-who-is-with-us. In a secondary but real way, the incarnation can be extended backwards: it sums up the prior historical activity of God.

It can also be extended forward beyond the death-resurrection event, the continuing presence of Christ, the ongoing activity of the Spirit, the human body of Christ that is Church, the Eucharistic action—all of these are "extensions of the Incarnation." The story of Jesus is not over even with his resurrection. Nor is God's involvement with the world. In Christ, the world has become constitutive of our understanding of God. He is now the God of Jesus of Nazareth. God is not who God is apart from us. There is never the possibility of separating God from us—God's freely chosen self-definition as the One-who-is-with-us.

The incarnation, speaking analogously, is a social and even cosmic process, in some sense co-extensive with space-time. This is one of Teilhard de Chardin's fundamental intuitions: "Is the Kingdom of God a big family? Yes, in a sense it is. But in another sense it is a prodigious biological operation—that of the Redeeming Incarnation."[30] Whether we choose to "extend" the meaning and language of incarnation that far or not, we must nevertheless still admit that what God was doing in Christ is a supreme exemplification of the more universal reality of God's presence. The incarnation, even for God, takes time.

If we come back to the incarnation in its more precise use, God's being united to a human nature hypostatically in Jesus, there are

---

[30]Pierre Teilhard de Chardin, *The Phenomenon of Man,* trans. Bernard Wall (New York: Harper Torchbook, 1959) 293.

three further suggestions to be made. First, union according to hypostasis means that the ultimate ground of Jesus is God: Jesus' deepest self is the divine self, and this divine self pre-exists Jesus, and creates Jesus in order to be both hypostatically and kenotically one with him from the beginning. Second, the union, which is both hypostatic and kenotic, not only grounds Jesus but frees him to be human. God permits Jesus to have a completely human consciousness and will. Third, the union is so strong that the divine life not only overflows into and affects the human life *(communicatio)* but the human life and experience is taken up as God's very own. In Christ, God freely chose to suffer and to reveal God's own *passibilitas*.

Union according to hypostasis does not mean the predominance of the divine nature of Christ over the human nature during his earthly life. Union according to hypostasis means rather that Christ's hypostasis, *ousia*, ground, or act of existence is the Logos. The human nature belongs to the Logos. The Logos, however, does not, in uniting itself to a human nature, displace any element of that nature. There is a fully human soul in Christ. This soul is not the ultimate foundation of who Christ is; yet that ultimate foundation in no way jeopardizes the full functioning of the human soul. To say this is to agree that Apollinarianism is a distortion of who Christ is. What is affirmed in a union according to hypostasis is meta-psychological, or metaphysical. In other words, there is both a metaphysical starting point and a psychological starting point for Christ, and the one need not preclude the other.

We see here the contribution of both the Alexandrians and the Antiochenes to Christology. Following the Antiochenes, and their anti-Apollinarian concern, we must think of Jesus' humanness as complete and genuine. Christ had human knowledge and consciousness. The hypostatic union does not necessitate absolute or divine or perfect knowledge in Christ. It manifests rather a respect for the complete human nature. But Jesus' human psychology does not predetermine his ultimate ontological foundation. Ultimately, Jesus is God, but God as God has freely chosen to be present in specifically human terms.

Our age is an age of psychology, both by insight and preoccupation. Our concern is Jesus' psychological self. A doctrine of hypostatic union in no way destroys Jesus' human self. Yet psychology oversteps itself if it tries to answer metaphysical questions—questions which may be of less concern to us but were the preoccupation of another age. We each have a psychological structure and a metaphysical structure. Is my ultimate ground the fact that I am a created or uncreated act of existence? This may not be a pressing question in our age. For medieval theology it was. Our concern does not make their answer invalid, nor does their concern make our insights invalid. We ordinarily think of the incarnation as a subordination of the human Jesus to the divine Logos. We realize today rather that it began with the subordination *(kenosis)* of the Word to the humanity, and only ends with the subordination of the human Jesus to the Father, and the assimilation (divinization) of the human into the divine life.

There is both a metaphysical and a psychological basis to Jesus' human life. One does not negate the other. "Hypostatic union" refers to the *ousia* that Christ is, not his human psychology. The Logos chose to let the human be human. Here the Christology of Theodore of Mopsuestia is helpful. Through both a kenosis and a hypostatic union, a union that let the human be human, the Logos became a human being as if by indwelling. The Logos came not to destroy a human nature, but as if dwelling within a human nature, intimately united yet completely respectful, like grace. Indwelling and grace are analogies. The presence of God to someone through sanctifying grace does not destroy their human psychology, nor is human psychology an adequate test of the metaphysical presence of grace. In Christ we have a psychological self (the human soul) and a metaphysical self (the Logos) intimately united. In Jesus, there is one ultimate foundation, one hypostasis, and that is the Logos. Yet that Logos chooses to unite a human nature to itself and limits itself so as to be united to the human as if dwelling within it—letting it be human, respecting its human growth and development, and letting its human selfhood come to be. We can speak about the human person of Jesus, realizing here that person is not to be understood in the ontological sense of hypostasis, but in a modern psychological sense of a relational, individual, and conscious self. Yet, out of respect for tradition and to avoid confusion (as if Jesus were two rather than one), it may be better to say that Jesus is ultimately a divine Person, who has let go of his transcendent mode of being in order to become one of us. Jesus is a new creation.

There is no need to ascribe omniscience or omnipotence to God in the incarnate mode of being. Although we are not accustomed to attributing human ignorance to Christ, there is nothing to prevent us from doing so. The author of the *De Sectis,* toward the close of the sixth century, wrote: "Most Fathers admitted that Christ was ignorant of certain things; since he is in all things consubstantial to us, and since we ourselves are ignorant of certain things, it is clear that Christ also suffered ignorance."[31] Most theologians in the past, however, refused to attribute ignorance to Christ. For some, ignorance was associated with sin. Others saw a relationship between gnosis and salvation. For others, a hypostatic union required a perfect human nature. But these views only continue to manifest the theological pluralism of the Church. There is no such thing as one theology of the hypostatic union.

We have been puzzling over the humanity of Jesus and how it may have been affected by union with the Godhead, but we also need to ask how the divinity of the Godhead is affected by its substantial union with a concrete human nature. If it is indeed a substantial union, in the hypostasis of the Word, then the Word itself is also affected by the union. The Logos is now the ultimate subject of the human experiences. Jesus' pain is God's pain.

There is no reason to hesitate ascribing feeling to God. We do so, of course, by analogy. We are not saying that God feels in the same way that we do. Neither do we say that God thinks as we do. Yet we can apply thought to God really, and not simply figuratively. Thought points to something real in God, even if we do not know what divine thinking is like. God's ways are not our ways, yet we have never been offended by suggesting that God thinks or wills. So feelings too are not unbecoming a God who loves us and freely chooses to become one of us. The pain of Christ only reveals the suffering of God. The cross is God's very own anguish made visible. But to these thoughts we shall return in the next chapter. We now look at another contemporary approach to the humanity of Jesus.

The Christology of Schoonenberg

Piet Schoonenberg's Christology must be placed in the context of his early writings and the theological issues that concerned him

[31]Cf. John Meyendorff, *Christ in Eastern Christian Thought* (New York: St. Vladimir's Seminary Press, 1975) 86.

throughout his theological career. One of these issues was that of the relationship between God and the world. His early work also reflected the influence of Teilhard de Chardin. For Schoonenberg, it was never a question of God *or* the world, or of a God *apart from* the world, but rather of God *in* the world, without reducing God's transcendence to immanence alone.[32]

How one approaches the relationship between God and the world in general sets the context for how one approaches the relationship between God and the human person in particular, which in turn provides the key for a theological understanding of the relationship between the divine and the human in Jesus Christ. The theology of God, Christian anthropology, and Christology are interrelated. Thus, for Schoonenberg, Jesus Christ, although unique, can still be seen as the "chief exemplification" of God's relationship to the human. Any *"either* God *or* human" approach to Jesus Christ is immediately suspect as a false theological dilemma.[33] Even in anthropological terms, one does not speak about God *or* the human, or even of God *and* the human, but of God *in* the human. God is present to the world and humankind from within their very own structure: this is one of Schoonenberg's fundamental theological perspectives.

Another such fundamental perspective is that we only come to God, to our knowledge of God, from the world, from below so to speak, and this is true of our revealed knowledge as well. Revelation proceeds from God's self-disclosure from within history and creation. Thus, theologically, we never speak about God-as-unrelated but only about God-in-relationship: this is always the starting point for Scripture as well, in which one does not find some concept of "God-in-himself."

This theological perspective leads Schoonenberg to insist strongly in Christology that our point of departure can only be Jesus Christ, the one in whom we find God from within the world, the Word incarnate, and not the pre-existent Logos.[34] This is not

---

[32]See such early works as *Covenant and Creation* (Notre Dame, Ind.: University of Notre Dame Press, 1966); and *God's World in the Making* (Techny, Ill.: Divine Word Publications, 1967).

[33]See *The Christ,* 13–49.

[34]Cf. ibid., 80–91, 106–08; and Piet Schoonenberg, "Trinity—the Consummated Covenant: Theses on the Doctrine of the Trinitarian God," *Studies in Religion* 5 (1975–1976) 111.

a repudiation of any doctrine of pre-existence, but a refusal to allow the pre-existent Logos to be the starting point for Christology. We come to our knowledge of the pre-existent Word through Jesus Christ, and not the other way around. Christology then must begin from below.

Schoonenberg's theological life-project has been Christology. This has its roots of course in other theological and anthropological principles and also has an effect on the theology of the Trinity. But Christology is in the center. In the international theological community, Schoonenberg's name became associated with Christology in 1966, with the publication in Dutch of three articles in *Tijdschrift voor Theologie,* a theological journal which had been started only five years earlier.[35] The core article was by the Augustinian Ansfried Hulsbosch with responses from the Dominican Schillebeeckx and the Jesuit Schoonenberg. Following this dialogue, Schoonenberg continued to refine his position, and his *Christ* appeared a couple of years later, in 1969 in Dutch and in 1971 in English. It is to the fruit of these past twenty-five years of Christological reflection that we now turn.

In order to appreciate Schoonenberg's Christology, one must understand that it rests upon two (or three) convictions that form the parameters for its development. Christology must remain faithful to its heritage, and it must also interpret that heritage for our period of history. That heritage includes both Scripture and tradition. The two parameters of fidelity to the past and creativity in the face of the future both underlie the question asked in *The Christ:* "What does a real, creative loyalty to our faith in Jesus as the Christ demand?"[36] For Schoonenberg it demands

[35]The original articles never appeared in English. For further discussion of the Christology of Schoonenberg and of the 1966 dialogue see: Robert North, "Recent Christology and Theological Method," *Continuum* 7 (1969–1970) 63–77; idem, "Soul-Body Unity and God-Man Unity," *Theological Studies* 30 (1969) 27–60. Both of these articles are summaries of the 1966 Dutch symposium and are in substance reprinted in *In Search of the Human Jesus* (New York: Corpus Books, 1970). See also Steven Pujdak, "Schoonenberg's Christology in Context," *Louvain Studies* (1977) 338–53, one of the better expositions of Schoonenberg's Christology by someone thoroughly versed in it; Mark Schoof, "Dutch Catholic Theology: A New Approach to Christology," *Cross Currents* 22 (1973) 415–27; R. C. Ware, "Christology in Historical Perspective," *The Heythrop Journal* 15 (1974) 59–66.

[36]Schoonenberg, *The Christ,* 50.

a serious integration of both biblical and Chalcedonian Christology. One does not sacrifice either leg of one's reconstruction. Schoonenberg's Christology attempts to be faithful to both the biblical and the classical historical images of Christ. The third basis of the Christological project is theological hermeneutics. An explicit elaboration of the latter has become even more central to the theological project of Schillebeeckx. But hermeneutics is also one of the overarching aims of Schoonenberg: "The theologian's task as I see it is not only to describe the history of Christian tradition until now but also to engage himself in it, to continue the history of faithful interpretations by his own faithful interpretation."[37]

The point of departure for Schoonenberg's hermeneutical reconstruction of Christology is the unity or oneness of Christ's person: Jesus Christ is one person.[38] This is perhaps the most undisputed point in Schoonenberg's Christology. Yet it ought not to be passed over lightly. Christological discussion, particularly modern discussions, can contain a crypto-Nestorianism, just as traditional discussion often appears to us as a crypto-Docetism. Although we moderns affirm the unity of Christ's person, we often talk as if Christ were two people rather than one, the human Jesus and the divine Jesus. Often our linguistic distinction between Jesus and the Christ or Jesus and the Risen Lord inclines us in the same direction, as if we were talking about two people rather than one person. Schoonenberg recognizes that the obvious evidence of Scripture is that Jesus Christ is one person. This was likewise affirmed by the Council of Chalcedon and even earlier by the Church's rejection of Nestorianism as an adequate basis for Christology. The oneness of Christ's person was the major contribution of the Alexandrians to Christology.

"Jesus Christ is a human person"[39] is Schoonenberg's next and perhaps most disputed affirmation. His starting point and overriding concern is not only the oneness but also the humanity of Christ. He wants Christ to have what all other human beings have.

Here Schoonenberg shows his desire to be faithful to both Scripture and the Council of Chalcedon. For he argues: (1) that Jesus

[37]Piet Schoonenberg, "Evolution and Theology," in *L'Origine dell'uomo* (Roma: Academia Nazionale dei Lincei, 1973) 332.

[38]Schoonenberg, *The Christ,* 66–68.

[39]Ibid., 71–74.

is a human person is as much a presupposition of the New Testament as the fact that he is one person, and (2) whether Jesus' personhood can be called human is a question not decided in the negative by Chalcedon. The first point would be difficult to dispute, although one might argue that the technical theological language of personhood and *hypostasis* is post-biblical and hence is not to be further specified on a biblical basis alone. Yet it would still seem important to recognize that for the Scriptures Jesus was a human being as we are except for sin, and that Jesus Christ was a human person would be a presupposition of the New Testament. The argument here would hinge on what one means by human person, what content or definition one is giving to it.

Schoonenberg's second point hinges on one's interpretation of the Chalcedonian formulation. How do we get to the truth of what Chalcedon was teaching? Just as with Scripture, so there must be a hermeneutics of conciliar statements. Schoonenberg asserts: "An initial hermeneutical principle may be formulated this way: we need to rethink constantly all assertions made in the past. . . . This principle is based on the conviction that the expression of an insight is never and cannot be ever *only* the expression of that insight, in a chemically pure state, so to speak. . . . So all our expressions are historically conditioned."[40]

In order to determine whether Schoonenberg's interpretation of Chalcedon is correct we must return to the Chalcedonian statement itself. We might argue that the text in the context of its period of history was affirming that the one person Jesus Christ was a divine person. But Schoonenberg argues that we must take the text as it stands in order to see what it explicitly affirms. Let us see for ourselves.

> Following therefore the holy Fathers we unanimously teach that the Son, our Lord Jesus Christ, is one and the same, the same perfect in divinity, the same perfect in humanity, true God and true man, consisting of a rational soul and a body, consubstantial with the Father in divinity and consubstantial with

---

[40]Schoonenberg, "Evolution and Theology," 337. For the hermeneutics of the Chalcedonian definition, also see Karl Rahner's essay, "Chalcedon—End or Beginning," under the title "Current Problems in Christology," in *Theological Investigations,* vol. 1, trans. by Cornelius Ernst (Baltimore: Helicon Press, 1961) 149–200.

us in humanity, "in all things like as we are, without sin" (Heb. 4:15), born of the Father before all time as to his divinity, born in recent times for us and for our salvation from the Virgin Mary, Mother of God, as to his humanity. We confess one and the same Christ, the Son, the Lord, the Only-Begotten, in two natures unconfused, unchangeable, undivided and inseparable. The difference of natures will never be abolished by their being united, but rather the properties of each remain unimpaired, both coming together in one person and substance, not parted or divided among two persons, but in one and the same only-begotten Son, the divine Word, the Lord Jesus Christ, as previously the prophets and Jesus Christ himself taught us and the Creed of the Fathers handed down to us.[41]

If we look closely at the text itself, Schoonenberg is correct. Of course, it must be interpreted; but, while it affirms frequently that Jesus Christ is one, and one in two natures, true God and truly human, it nowhere explicitly affirms that the one person of whom it speaks is the personally pre-existent divine person. We have come to assume this meaning, but is that an assumption we can continue to make? In the text itself, *physis* and *hypostasis* are used but not themselves defined. Our tendency is to read the text through the eyes of Leontius of Byzantium and a still later interpretation of the anhypostatic humanity of Jesus. But the text itself affirms one *hypostasis* without calling that *hypostasis* exclusively divine or human. That Jesus Christ is one person in two natures is the doctrine of Chalcedon. The anhypostatic character of Jesus' humanity is Chalcedonianism but not Chalcedon. According to Schoonenberg, "Jesus Christ is one person. He is a human person. Can he then still be called a divine person? He is so called in the Chalcedonian pattern, but not precisely in the individual formula of Chalcedon itself—only by those who prepared and elaborated Chalcedon."[42]

We may not yet be in full agreement with Schoonenberg, but we should feel free to at least move further to see what his

[41]See Denzinger, 301–02. This translation comes from Josef Neuner and Heinrich Roos, *The Teaching of the Catholic Church* (New York: Alba House, 1967) 153–54.

[42]Schoonenberg, *The Christ,* 74–75. On Leontius of Byzantium and Leontius of Jerusalem, see Goergen, *The Jesus of Christian History,* 151–54.

Christology proposes. He suggests that Jesus Christ is a human person. Such is the implicit understanding of Scripture, and as such is not explicitly ruled out by the teaching of Chalcedon. How does Schoonenberg then understand this human personhood of Jesus and does it exclude a divine personhood as well? Only a further elaboration of Schoonenberg's Christology can answer the question whether it is truly faithful to Chalcedon or not.

Given that the Chalcedonian formulation may not exclude a human personhood in Jesus Christ even though the traditional post-Chalcedonian pattern so interprets it, we can still rightly ask why Schoonenberg insists on Jesus' being a human person and not simply having a human nature. One reason is his firm commitment to the humanity of Jesus, so central to contemporary Christology, and another is the modern concept of person.

Does a firm commitment to Jesus' humanity necessitate more than ascribing to him a full human nature? Does it imply something about Jesus' person as well? A prominent path taken in contemporary Christologies which recognize the human consciousness of Jesus is that of distinguishing between his psychological consciousness or ego or self and his ontological ground or self. Such a distinction preserves the classical ontological understanding of personhood (and Jesus' personhood as divine) and allows for the modern attribution of a fully operative human psychology to Jesus (a part of his human nature). Yet Schoonenberg rejects this fairly common ontological/psychological split: "If in Jesus Christ the human ego or act-center stands psychologically outside his ontological person, it is then clearly not the ego or act-center of Jesus. And if therein the ontological person of Christ is not itself conscious and does not speak to us, then Jesus as man is in this regard not different from us and the Christ or the Son has disappeared behind the man Jesus without being of significance for our salvation."[43] Perhaps Schoonenberg speaks too strongly. It is possible for there to be an ontological ground (person) which is not psychologically the conscious center or self. Yet his proposal clearly has the advantage of presenting a personhood more integrated into the life of Jesus. So he combines the ontological and psychological aspects of personhood rather than dividing them, thus making Jesus a human person. "Presupposed is a

[43]Schoonenberg, *The Christ*, 70.

Christology which starts from the true and unabridged humanity of Jesus. Consequently the man Jesus not only *has* a human 'centre of activity' or a human 'psychological ego,' but he also *is,* psychologically *and* ontologically, a human person, a human ego, a human subject of conscious and free acts, a subject of human decision and history.''[44]

Schoonenberg's proposal clearly carries with it the advantage of overcoming a duality in Christ. Yet the proposal he rejects (based upon distinguishing the ontology and psychology in Christ) is theologically defensible. His proposal is an orthodox interpretation of Chalcedon, even if not the classically normative nor only orthodox interpretation of Chalcedon. Whether one follows Schoonenberg's theological proposal partially rests upon whether one sees the more traditional interpretation as in danger of "ontological docetism," Schoonenberg's expression for some extreme forms of the tradition.[45]

Why does Schoonenberg go to the extent that he does in affirming human personhood in Jesus and reading one strand of the tradition as an ontological form of Docetism? Because of his conviction of both the oneness and the complete humanness of Jesus. But also because of his definition of what personhood implies. How can he affirm human personhood in Jesus? Because his starting point for understanding *person* is its modern and not its classical philosophical definition.[46] This point is crucial as to whether one will follow Schoonenberg or not.

One might argue against such a shift of meaning for a technical theological term. Again, however, to Schoonenberg's advantage is his emphasis on hermeneutics: Christology is intended to unfold the Christ mystery for *our* world. The modern understand-

[44]Schoonenberg, "Trinity—the Consummated Covenant," 115.

[45]Schoonenberg, *The Christ,* 60, 73. For Schoonenberg, the expression "ontological docetism" only refers to the extreme views of those who deny a human act of existence or *esse* in Christ, namely, Capreolus and Louis Billot.

[46]This distinction between classical and modern understandings of *person* applies at this point only to the theology of Jesus Christ and not the theology of God or Trinity which is another theological issue. With respect to this distinction, I also highly recommend John C. Dwyer, *Son of Man and Son of God* (New York: Paulist Press, 1983) esp. 77–98, 119–54. Also see Karl Rahner, *Foundations of Christian Faith,* trans. William V. Dych (New York: Seabury Press, 1978) 289–92.

ing of *person* is different from the medieval understanding, but it is nevertheless the understanding with which modern ears hear the proclamation of Christ. To modern ears, the refusal to affirm human personhood of Jesus is heard as Docetism. The people end up with a docetic Christ. This is not to say that the classical tradition was in fact docetic. It is simply to say that a significant linguistic shift has taken place which must be taken seriously in the proclamation of the gospel. Schoonenberg here is not repudiating the tradition, but using a traditional term in a new way. *Personhood* not only implies ontological subsistence but psychological consciousness, freedom, and intersubjectivity as well. This was not true for the Thomistic metaphysical understanding of *person*. In Trinitarian theology, "three persons" never meant three consciousnesses, wills, or subjects. As we saw in the previous volume of this series, *person* was an ontological concept and reality.[47] Yet according to Robert Ware, "It is impossible in the present day to speak of person and continue to divest the concept of individual consciousness and freedom. It is to Schoonenberg's credit that he has faced this issue squarely."[48]

Schoonenberg's Christology moves along clearly chosen steps. The steps we have so far delineated are: (1) Scripture testifies to both the oneness and the human personhood of Jesus Christ, (2) the Council of Chalcedon's formulation does not exclude human personhood being attributed to Christ, (3) to separate Jesus into an ontological self and a psychological self in order to preserve both divine personhood and human consciousness and freedom does a disservice to both the unity and the humanity of Jesus, and (4) Christology ought incorporate within it the modern concept of person and not limit itself to the traditional ontological definition only. If one accepts those steps (and I would argue that there are sufficient reasons for doing so), then one comes in an orthodox but modern way to Schoonenberg's further conclusions.

Given the human personhood of Jesus, Schoonenberg rejects the post-Chalcedonian, Leontian non-personhood *(anhypostasia)* of the humanity of Jesus.[49] He rather develops a theory of reciprocal *enhypostasia*. This begins by reversing what Leontius had

[47]Ware, "Christology in Historical Perspective," 67.

[48]Cf. Goergen, *The Jesus of Christian History,* 109, 132–43, 207–23.

[49]See n. 42 above.

maintained, that the human nature (anhypostatic, not a *hypostasis* in itself) was enhypostatic in the Logos (its personhood was the personhood of the Word). Schoonenberg, rather than seeing the *hypostasis* as being exclusively that of the Word, and having given his argument for the human *hypostasis* of Jesus, suggests a reversal and speaks about the *hypostasis* of the Word as being the human *hypostasis* of Jesus Christ—the *enhypostasis* of the Word in the human Jesus rather than the other way around.[50] Not the human Jesus but the pre-existent Word is anhypostatic.

Schoonenberg's more developed and recent theology emphasizes a reciprocity between the human Jesus and the divine Word, something of a mutual interpenetration.[51] As he maintained earlier, the Word is enhypostatic in the human person Jesus Christ, but the human person Jesus Christ is also enhypostatic in the Word. Schoonenberg still maintains that Jesus is a human person and still rejects the *personal* pre-existence of the Word, but also speaks of a reciprocal *enhypostasia.*

The *enhypostasia* of the Word in the human personhood of Jesus, Schoonenberg's most creative contribution to Christology, implies that the pre-existent Word *becomes* person only in and through the human personhood of Jesus Christ. This is a point to which we shall come shortly. But, in addition to this novel perspective, Schoonenberg also maintains in a more traditional vein that the human personhood of Jesus is enhypostatic in the Word as well. For Schoonenberg this means that the human person Jesus Christ is sustained by God as God's very own self-revelation, that the Word of God is, so to speak, the ground of Jesus' being.

God's being is not only immanent in the man Jesus (the *enhypostasia* of the Logos in Jesus Christ), but due to God's transcendence, Jesus Christ is also present and immanent in God (the *enhypostasia* of the human person Jesus Christ in the Godhead). God contains or grounds Jesus, and thus God's Logos is also the *hypostasis* of Jesus' humanity in a real sense. It is almost as if Schoonenberg is now able to preserve the positive contribution of the ontological/psychological distinction mentioned earlier

[50]For the early articulation of Schoonenberg's theory, prior to his development of the notion of reciprocal *enhypostasia,* see *The Christ,* 58–61, 80–98.

[51]For Schoonenberg's later development of the theory of reciprocal *enhypostasia,* see "Trinity—the Consummated Covenant," 115; and "Spirit Christology and Logos Christology," *Bijdragen* 38 (1977) 364–65.

without its negative duality affecting the oneness of Christ. For, can we not say: If we take personhood in the more modern sense, Jesus is a human person, and this implies the *enhypostasia* of the Word in Jesus and a rejection of the personal pre-existence of the Word. But if we take personhood in its more traditional sense, even if Jesus is a human person in the modern sense, we can still speak of the *enhypostasia* of Jesus in the Word, in the sense of God and the Word as the foundational reality and subsistent ground of Jesus' very own being. This latter still does not necessitate the personal pre-existence of the Word: there is no attribution at all of two persons to Jesus Christ. There is a real and reciprocal *enhypostasia,* even if *hypostasis* is being used in two different senses (in the more modern sense when speaking of the *enhypostasia* of the Word in Jesus Christ and in the more traditional sense when speaking of the *enhypostasia* of Jesus Christ in the Word).

The language of *enhypostasia* remains theologically technical. But a question lying underneath it is whether Schoonenberg's theology still contains anything like a *real* incarnation. Jesus Christ is a human person for Schoonenberg. Is he also divine? And if so, in what sense? For Schoonenberg, in Jesus Christ, God's Word has become incarnate, through "the self-identification of God's being with a human person."[52] Jesus Christ is a human person created in and through the incarnation itself.

Jesus Christ is a human person. In what sense is he also a divine person? There was an unfortunate and ambiguous statement in Schoonenberg's Christology, reflective of the 1966 discussion,[53] which some have taken as characteristic of his Christology: "Jesus' divine sonship is his humanness to the utmost."[54] If the statement as it stands is taken in a reductionistic sense, then there

---

[52]Schoonenberg, *The Christ,* 88; also "Reflections on the Prologue of John's Gospel," a lecture delivered at Aquinas Institute, Dubuque, Iowa, 25 October 1979. Also see "A Sapiential Reading of John's Prologue: Some Reflections on Views of Reginald Fuller and James Dunn," *Theology Digest* 33 (Winter 1986) 403–21.

[53]In the 1966 discussion, Hulsbosch had made a proposal along the lines that the divinity of Christ consists in the perfection of his humanity. Cf. North, "Soul-Body Unity and God-Man Unity," 27; Schoof, "Dutch Catholic Theology," 418–19.

[54]Schoonenberg, *The Christ,* 7.

is nothing left of the traditional understanding of Jesus' divinity. The only ontological content to Jesus' divinity is his perfected humanity, but Jesus is not really divine in any traditional sense. On the other hand, the statement can be understood as similar to the thinking of Teilhard de Chardin, who spoke of the non-antagonistic relationship between divinization (or Christification) and humanization.[55] Divinization is not to be reduced to humanization, but neither is it antagonistic to it or destructive of it. Indeed, divinization humanizes and personalizes. Grace perfects nature. I interpret Schoonenberg in this latter, non-reductionistic sense, both because such is this statement's immediate context in *The Christ*[56] and because of Schoonenberg's early concern for the thought of Teilhard de Chardin.[57] This implies, however, that while divinization (grace) humanizes, divinization (and Christ's divinity) and humanization (and Christ's humanity) are still ontologically distinguishable realities. The statement as its stands ("Jesus' divine sonship is his humanness to the utmost") is in need of clarification. Is Jesus in some real sense divine, and if so, in what sense? This becomes the challenge Schoonenberg's Christology must face lest he be led into Adoptionism.

Schoonenberg maintains that Jesus Christ is not only a human person, but that he is also a divine person, although not in the way that such an assertion has been traditionally understood, in the sense of the pre-existent Word being a divine person. What Schoonenberg wants to avoid (and does avoid) is bringing into the picture, into Jesus Christ, a divine personhood that will compete with Jesus' human personhood, and thus either make of Jesus two persons or eradicate his human personhood.

> I myself want to see Jesus as having all a human person has and therefore being a human person. But, on the other hand, I want not to deny that he is a divine person nor to make him to be two persons. Now it seems to me that as long as we maintain the Logos to be a divine person prior to the incarnation,

[55]See Teilhard de Chardin, *The Divine Milieu.*

[56]The immediately preceding sentence in *The Christ,* 7, concludes: "Our divinization is our humanization." This statement too can be ambiguous and interpreted reductionistically but has the much wider context of Schoonenberg's early writings and the thought of Teilhard.

[57]E.g., Schoonenberg, *God's World in the Making.*

we have either to deny that he is a human person—as classical
christology does—or to consider a duality of persons in him—
the position ascribed to Nestorius and certainly rejected by Chalcedon.[58]

The Logos is divine before the incarnation for Schoonenberg, but
not yet a person in the modern sense. Setting aside for the moment the character of the pre-existent Word, the personhood of
the earthly and glorified Jesus is both human and divine, or thean-
dric. The one person is to be called divine-human.[59] Schoonenberg has made the point clear from the beginning. This way of
speaking in no way implies a duality of persons, nor is it improper
attribution. For Schoonenberg the one person Jesus Christ, the
earthly and glorified Christ, Jesus' personhood is both human
and divine, at the level of personhood, and this is possible because there is no prior personhood of the Word with which he
must deal. Jesus Christ is an incarnation of the divine Word, but
not of a divine person. The *one* person (Schoonenberg's first
Christological thesis—the oneness of Christ) is both *human* (his
second thesis, that Jesus is a human person) and *divine* (his third
thesis which we are still exploring).

Have we done justice yet to the divinity of Christ? Is Jesus
Christ in any real sense divine? If not an incarnation of a pre-
existent divine *person,* in what sense is Jesus' personhood divine?
We must go further.

For Schoonenberg, Jesus is the Word incarnate, and the Word
is both pre-existent and divine (as in the Johannine prologue) but
not a person, *hypostasis,* in the modern sense, or as Schoonenberg employs the word. This does not necessarily deny that the
pre-existent Word is in some sense hypostatic in the traditional
sense, as a subsisting relation. But one must be consistent in the
use of language, and therefore Schoonenberg prefers to speak of
the pre-existent Word as a mode of being rather than as a person. The Word prior to the incarnation does not yet have *personal* existence in Schoonenberg's sense.

> I do not deny the pre-existence of the Word, but I try to qualify
> the way in which it pre-exists. Doing so, I do not want to deny

[58]Schoonenberg, "Reflections on the Prologue of John's Gospel," 17.

[59]Ibid. Also, *The Christ,* 81–82, 87.

or to diminish in any way the full divinity of the Word. I only contend that the divine Word's distinction from God—which I see as an intra-divine distinction—is not yet a distinction of divine person to divine person before the Incarnation.[60]

We must go back here to the foundation of Schoonenberg's theology. Schoonenberg does not reject God's Word as being a divine person before the incarnation out of some desire to reject Christian tradition. Rather his hermeneutical concern is to remain faithful to the tradition while attempting to re-express it in another period of history. And one of his presuppositions has been that we come to our knowledge of God from the world, from below, and thus to our knowledge of the pre-existent, eternal Word from the incarnate Word. The incarnate Word, Jesus Christ, must be our starting point. We move from an understanding of the incarnation to the Trinity, and not the other way around.

We have already made two biblically based and theologically argued points about Jesus Christ, the incarnate Word: (1) Jesus Christ is one person; (2) Jesus Christ is a human person. We move from this awareness to our understanding of the Word's prior existence and activity. The divine Word is not added to the human Jesus in such a way that Christ would no longer be one, or no longer be fully and ontologically human. The way we speak about the Word's pre-existent divinity is already determined by the way in which we have spoken about Jesus Christ. The pre-existence must be understood in its relation to Christ, and not the other way around.[61]

But personal pre-existence, the Word eternally existing as a divine person, makes it impossible for Jesus Christ either to be one person or to be a human person. Therefore the mode of being of the eternal Word is not that of a divine person although it is divine. The pre-existence of the Word is qualified only in so far as necessary to protect the human personhood and oneness of Jesus Christ.

The divine Logos is God, but God as speaking and acting and present *ad extra*. The Logos is the presence of God. The Logos is not a person or *hypostasis* in Schoonenberg's sense but rather

[60]Schoonenberg, "Reflections on the Prologue of John's Gospel," 14.

[61]Schoonenberg, *The Christ,* 80–91. Also see idem, "God's Presence in Jesus: An Exchange of Viewpoints," *Theology Digest* 19 (1971) 29–38.

a *mode of subsistence* (which is similar to the meaning of *hypostasis* in the classical sense).[62] The Logos in the Johannine prologue is not a divine person but rather a personification of a divine mode of subsistence, God as self-disclosing. For Schoonenberg, the Logos and the Spirit are divine, subsistent modes of being.

The Word is not a person, has no personhood, in its divine mode of being. It only becomes a person in the truest, fullest sense in and through its incarnation in Jesus Christ. Jesus Christ *is* the incarnation (hypostasization, *enhypostasia*) of the Word. The Word as person, as personal existence, is Jesus Christ. Jesus Christ is the person of the Word but the Word has become person in Jesus Christ. The personhood of the Word and the personhood of Jesus are one and the same; there is but one person, and that person is human and divine. The Word became flesh and became a person in Jesus Christ. "Jesus Christ is sustained by God in this mode of being, without in any way being impaired in his human personality. Conversely in Jesus this mode of God's being becomes person."[63]

Schoonenberg's rejection of earlier kenotic Christologies is founded on the fact that they, like classical Christologies, start from a theology of the pre-existent divine Word as a person (from above), and thus there is a divine person even after the self-emptying. They do exclude a psychological dual personality in Christ but not an ontological dual personality. They are not able to affirm both the oneness and the human personhood of Christ

---

[62]Schoonenberg's preferred expression for the "persons" of the Trinity is "mode of subsistence" or "mode of being." This is not completely novel. Karl Barth prefers the phrase "modes of being or existence," *Church Dogmatics* I/1 (Edinburgh: T and T Clark, 1936) 400-40. Karl Rahner prefers "manners or modes of subsistence," *The Trinity* (New York: Herder and Herder, 1970) 103-15. And John Macquarrie interprets the Trinity as three "modes of Being": Primordial Being, Expressive Being, and Unitive Being, *Principles of Christian Theology* (New York: Charles Scribner's Sons, 1966) 174-93. Schoonenberg's usage is not to be equated with these others' but these reinterpretations show the rethinking going on in Trinitarian theology as well. Hermeneutical reconstruction in Christology eventually leads to reconstruction in the theology of the Trinity. For some critique of Rahner's and Schoonenberg's theology of the Trinity, see Yves Congar, *I Believe in the Holy Spirit,* trans. David Smith (New York: Seabury Press, 1983) 3:11-18.

[63]Schoonenberg, "Trinity—the Consummated Covenant," 115.

to the same degree. To their credit, however, they have opened up for reconstruction the concept of divine immutability.[64]

Schoonenberg does not deny that God is immutable, but chooses to attribute mutability to God as well. "God is immutable *and* mutable, and both at the same time. He is immutable in his divine being and mutable in his self-communication, which coincides with his being. These statements are not contradictory if we notice that 'becoming' and 'change' in God are quite different from becoming and change in creatures."[65] The language of becoming and process can be applied to God (but only in a particular sense). Schoonenberg does not shirk from taking the biblical language seriously: the Word *became* flesh. The Word *became* the Son.

Schoonenberg does not attribute mutability to God in the same sense in which that is done in Anglo-American process thought.[66] God's becoming or changing for Schoonenberg does not imply that God is receptive or receiving; there is no enrichment of God as such by which God is self-surpassing. God's mutability involves only a movement of giving and self-communication. Schoonenberg states it thus: *"I am not saying* that God becomes God, realizes himself, or 'becomes more God,' only that God, by relation to our history, becomes more 'our' God; the change which takes place in him and which affects him in the depth of his being consists neither in his acquiring nor in his losing anything whatever, but in giving, or rather in his self-giving."[67]

Schoonenberg's theology of God starts with God as mystery, as love, and as perfect.[68] God is mystery, and thus we are not, properly speaking, thinking about God but toward God. God is both mystery and love, but "the God whose love is greater than

[64]Schoonenberg, *The Christ,* 76–80, 106–08.

[65]Schoonenberg, "Spirit-Christology and Logos Christology," 370. Schoonenberg discusses God's mutability most thoroughly in "Process or History in God?" *Louvain Studies* 4 (1973) 303–09; summarized in *Theology Digest* 23 (1975) 38–44; and also in "God as Relating and (Be)Coming: A Meta-Thomistic Consideration," *Listening* 14 (1979) 265–78. Also see *The Christ,* 83–86 n. 16.

[66]For Schoonenberg's sympathetic but critical evaluation of process theology, see his "Process or History in God?"

[67]For this quotation, see Steven Pujdak, "Schoonenberg's Christology in Context," 342 n. 21.

[68]Schoonenberg, "Process or History in God?," esp. 315–19.

we are able to conceive."[69] God is both mystery and perfect, but God changes because God is perfect.[70] God's mutability consists entirely in God's self-giving. One might say, God changes or becomes because God is pure act.

Scholastic theology denied that becoming was attributable to God because becoming implied potency rather than act. Schoonenberg is not attributing potency in the passive sense to God. God's becoming is purely active and creative. "Becoming" in God and in creatures is different, perhaps analogous, but more properly "in a polar way."[71] God's becoming is pure giving and communicating, God as self-relating. "So God's self-relating is not only analogical to ours, being the highest degree of relatedness which is possible; it is also polarly opposed to every form of relatedness between finite beings, God's relations being purely active and giving and those of creatures involving passivity and receptivity as well."[72] God is really related to the world, and God changes because of that relationship, but that mutability is simply a manifestation of God's perfection, implying neither gain nor loss in God, implying only God as creating, giving, revealing, becoming more our God, becoming our savior, and this is a real becoming even if only attributed to God in a way that is the contrasting pole of the way in which we become. "God . . . relates and changes as the creator whereas we do so as creatures."[73]

If we can use the word *become* of God, then one of the ways in which God becomes is in and through the incarnation, by which God becomes more our God and in which the Word becomes Son and a divine person.

"Change, emergence, and becoming must also be recognized in God, albeit in a completely divine way," Schoonenberg asserts.[74] God's self-giving and self-communication involves God's

[69]Ibid., 319.

[70]Ibid., 317.

[71]Schoonenberg, "God as Relating and (Be)Coming," 267–70.

[72]Ibid., 271.

[73]Ibid., 274. See Langdon Gilkey, *Reaping the Whirlwind* (New York: Seabury, 1976) 307f.; and Donald Goergen, *The Power of Love* (Chicago: The Thomas More Press, 1979) 192–213, for reflection on God's freely chosen self-limitation, although in Schoonenberg there is not "self-limitation" in God. This is not his way of speaking. Yet he speaks of "becoming."

[74]Schoonenberg, *The Christ*, 84, the note.

self-identification with the human person Jesus Christ, which brings about in God a new person.[75] The Word or Logos, as we have seen, has no personhood or *hypostasis* in its divine nature; it rather becomes a person in the man Jesus. The pre-incarnate Logos, as a mode of divine subsistence, assumes another mode of subsistence and becomes the human person Jesus. The Word is not a person prior to the incarnation. The human person Jesus Christ is, however, the embodiment, the personification, the self-identification of the divine Word. In the incarnation the human person Jesus is divine and the divine Word becomes a person—a divine-human person.

Before the incarnation, the Word is not yet the Son.[76] The Word becomes the Son. In the Johannine prologue, Father/Son terminology is introduced only after the reference to incarnation in verse 14. Only after the incarnation are the Father and Son distinct as two *persons* (and Son for Schoonenberg always means the incarnate Word, the earthly and glorified Christ). The Word in its identification with the history of the man Jesus became a subject personally distinct from God as Father. The one God became Father and Son in and through the conception and history of Jesus. The divine-human person that Jesus Christ is can be called the Second Person, for God in his second mode of being as Logos has become identified with, substantially present in, and ontologically one with this Jesus. In and through human history God *becomes* a Trinity, a plurality of persons.

Schoonenberg has not yet developed his theology of the Spirit to the degree that he has his theology of Jesus and the Word. Yet several intimations suggest the direction that he will take.[77] Like

[75]Ibid., 88.

[76]In a similar vein, see Marcellus of Ancyra and Simeon the New Theologian. Cf. Joseph T. Leinhard, "Marcellus of Ancyra in Modern Research," *Theological Studies* 43 (1982) 486–503; and Symeon the New Theologian, *The Practical and Theological Chapters and The Three Theological Discourses* (Kalamazoo, Mich.: Cistercian Pub., 1982) 110–11.

[77]Cf. "God's Presence in Jesus: an Exchange of Viewpoints"; "Trinity—the Consummated Covenant"; and "Spirit Christology and Logos Christology." For Schoonenberg, the Father is a person, one person, with two extensions, or modes of subsistence, and these two are persons only analogously, by analogy to the person of the Father. After the incarnation, the Word becomes a person in a new way. The personhood of the Spirit is still more distantly analogous, more removed from what we mean by person, not person in the same way as Father and Son are.

the Word, the Spirit is a mode of subsistence or mode of presence. The Spirit is not person prior to the incarnation, but is rather another mode of God's being. As the Word becomes person at the incarnation, the Spirit becomes person (becomes more than an extension of God's person) at the glorification of Christ. At the glorification the Spirit becomes the Paraclete in and through its presence in the community and the Church. The Spirit does not become person and is not person in the same way that the Word is in Jesus Christ. The Word subsists in the divine-human person of Jesus, and the Spirit subsists and becomes personal in the Church. With the giving of the gift of the Spirit, God becomes tri-personal.

As in the early Church, the theology of the man Jesus moves theological reflection in the direction of Trinitarian thinking. Christology eventually necessitated a new theology of God and the doctrine of the Trinity.[78] This is the proper trajectory of theology. But, once the Church had developed a theology of the Trinity, the tendency was to do Christology from the starting point of the Trinity (from above) rather than the other way around (from below).

Given the theological and methodological point made earlier about Schoonenberg, namely, that we only come to our knowledge of God from below, it is no surprise that Schoonenberg rejects God-talk about the Trinity-in-itself as unrelated to us and the history of our salvation. Schoonenberg's theology of the Trinity is always "salvational." We cannot know God-in-himself as distinct from who God is in relationship to us. To conclude to such a "transcendent Trinity" reflects a false understanding of God's immutability: God is tri-personal in history; God is immutable; therefore God is tri-personal in his pre-historical, transcendent nature. Our concluding to a plurality of persons in God on the basis of God's historical self-communication, however, cannot be absolutized by saying what God "originally" was or was not. For Schoonenberg, "on a Trinity in God from eternity and by necessity we as creatures cannot make any statements, either in the affirmative or in the negative."[79] Schoonenberg nei-

---

[78]For Schoonenberg's reflections on the Trinity, see especially "Trinity—the Consummated Covenant." For another provocative treatment on the Trinity, see Eberhard Jüngel, *The Doctrine of the Trinity, God's Being Is in Becoming*, trans. Horton Harris (Edinburgh: Scottish Academic Press, 1976).

[79]Schoonenberg, *The Christ*, 86, n. 16.

ther affirms nor denies an "immanent Trinity," as abstracted from the economy of salvation. The only Trinity of which we can speak is the salvational Trinity. The starting point for a theology of the Trinity is the human personhood of the man Jesus.

Thus, for Schoonenberg, all we can say is that God becomes a Trinity. There is a real "becoming" in God. The Logos was in God before creation, became the Word through creation, and became the Son through the incarnation. One must always keep in mind Schoonenberg's use and definition of *person,* which involves consciousness and freedom. The three modes of subsistence (three "persons," *hypostaseis,* relations in the classical sense) are not personal vis-à-vis each other. Only when the Word becomes flesh and the Spirit is given to the Church do they become truly personal vis-à-vis God (the Father).

We have up until now spoken of God in God's transcendent life (God, Word, Spirit) and of God in history and salvation (God, Son, Paraclete), but we have not spoken of God as "Father." Although God is personal in God's transcendent life,[80] God is not yet "Father" in the sense of the Father (Abba) of Jesus Christ,[81] until the incarnation. God, Word, and Spirit became Father, Son, and Paraclete. There is no I-Thou relationship in God, in the divine nature, prior to the incarnation. The pre-existent Logos and God do not relate as two divine persons. They only relate as Father and Son in and through the history of Jesus of Nazareth.

Schoonenberg's explorations into the theology of the Trinity bring his Christology to a close: Jesus Christ is *one* person. Jesus Christ is a *human* person. Jesus Christ is *Son of God,* the preincarnate divine Word enfleshed and person-ified. Jesus Christ is truly divine by God's freely chosen ontological self-identification of God's Word with the man Jesus. Jesus Christ is divine by nature, God's very own Son, in whom God's Word became a person (Son) and God's Son became the incarnate mode of God's being. In the next chapter we continue to explore the humanity of Jesus which Schoonenberg and the kenotic Christologists make a prerequisite for any contemporary theology of Jesus Christ.

---

[80]Schoonenberg, "God as Person(al)" in *A Personal God?,* Concilium 103 (New York: The Seabury Press, 1977) 80–93.

[81]Cf. Bernard Cooke, "Non-Patriarchal Salvation," *Horizons* 10 (1983) 22–31, for his suggestions about referring to God as "Father."

5

Contemporary Prerequisites
in Dialogue with Classical Christology

In volumes 1 and 2 of this series, we attempted to explore and understand the biblical, earthly, historical but meta-historiographical Jesus of Nazareth.[1] In volume 3 we explored the unfolding of the Christian tradition and the Jesus of this Christian history following upon the emergence of Johannine Christology.[2] In this volume we are attempting to bring together the insights of these previous volumes in order to understand even more deeply this one Jesus.

In volume 1, chapter 1, we uttered a strong no to Docetism and the pull toward Docetic Christologies. In chapter 1 of this volume we uttered an equally strong no to Adoptionism and the push toward Adoptionist Christologies.[3] We have opened the door to explore both Jesus' divinity and his humanity in relationship to our humanity. Jesus is both human and divine. So are we—through grace. Yet Jesus remains distinctive within the human race. His human experience of God was his own distinctive, unique experience. His solidarity with God reached an unsurpassable intensity, according to Christian faith. His union with God has classically been called hypostatic. Jesus is really human, as we are,

[1] See Goergen, *The Death and Resurrection of Jesus,* 155–59, 183–203, for the distinction between historical and meta-historiographical.

[2] Goergen, *The Jesus of Christian History.*

[3] See pp. 17–20 above. Also Goergen, *The Mission and Ministry of Jesus,* 32–45.

not only abstractly but existentially, a full participant in humanity's history. Yet classically he has been called sinless even though it was fallen humanness that he inherited.

In this chapter I would like to seek further clarification on four difficult issues: Jesus' knowledge, Jesus' power, Jesus' uniqueness, and Jesus' sinlessness.

Jesus' Knowledge

In our discussion of Jesus' knowledge, consciousness, and self-understanding we must take seriously both the *kenosis* and the *hypostasis,* the self-emptying, self-identifying solidarity with humanity, and the ultimate, ontological, foundational union with God. Jesus had to learn as we learn. He acquired knowledge through experience. Although perceptive, perspicacious, and knowledgeable with respect to the Hebrew Scriptures and traditions of his people, although having prophetic insight and sensitivity, although a teacher of wisdom, Jesus, in both his religious knowledge and his self-knowledge, grew and developed throughout his life. This growth was an effect of *kenosis* and accompanied his humanity. Whether or not we can pin Jesus' self-understanding down precisely, we can still say that his life and mission were not clear to him from the start. He came to understand what it was that God was calling him to do and be. This does not imply that "he became God." He was (ontologically) who he was before he came to know, realize, or understand it. The future was not always known to him. He approached life in faith and with hope.

But just as we take seriously the humanity of Jesus and the *kenosis,* so we must take seriously the divinity of Jesus and the *hypostasis.* If Jesus was in some sense (ontologically, hypostatically) God, this cannot have had no effect. It cannot simply be dismissed as of no relevance. Although the classical, metaphysical language is only a human way of speaking, and indeed only one way of speaking about Jesus' union with God, it refers nevertheless to something real. At the deepest levels of his life and thought, personality and selfhood, Jesus was in direct contact or communication with divine energy and the divine reality. This cannot be insignificant and inconsequential. Jesus' knowledge, and particularly self-knowledge, would be affected by such an intense or unique union.

Although Jesus is truly one of us, this does not mean that he is like us in all ways. We often live our human lives in a sinful mode; Jesus did not. And although Jesus is consubstantial with God, this does not mean he is like God in God's transcendent mode of being. Both Jesus' mode of being divine and his mode of being human were distinctive. His humanity was hypostatically one with God and his divinity was kenotically able to let him be one with us. Incarnation implies both: truly divine, even if not in a transcendent but rather in an incarnate mode; and truly human, even if not in a sinful, but rather in a sinless mode, in accord with his hypostatic unity. Both the *kenosis* and the *hypostasis* that Jesus truly was affect our interpretation of his way of knowing. Jesus neither knew nor taught that he was equal to God, nor was he simply oblivious to the role he would play in human history.

In any effort to draw conclusions about Jesus' own self-understanding, we must realize that we can be only suggestive and tentative. As we said in volume 1: (1) consciousness itself is a very flexible, fluid, living reality, and (2) Jesus was a very un-self-preoccupied person.[4] Jesus was alive, and thus his self-understanding cannot be pinned down with precision. We can say that he was very God-conscious (he loved God with his whole heart and with all his strength) as well as people-conscious (he came to serve and not to be served). As a prophet, he was socially conscious (God belongs to the poor) and eschatologically conscious ([the reign of] God is at hand).[5] Our access to Jesus does not primarily come from the later titles of Christian faith nor from the categories of Jewish thought, but through his own experiences of prayer *(abba),* ministry (preaching, healing), and friendship (John, Lazarus, Mary, Martha). In fact, the predominant element in Jesus' consciousness and self-understanding was not himself but (the reign of) God. Jesus' preaching and prayer give us clues to understanding him and how he saw his mission. "Let us go on to the next towns, that I may preach there also; for that is why I have come" (Mark 1:38). "The time is fulfilled, and the reign of God is at hand; repent, and believe in the gospel" (Mark 1:15).

[4]Goergen, *The Mission and Ministry of Jesus,* 157–59, 218–29.

[5]Ibid., 151–70, 218–48. For my interpretation of Jesus' use of the expression "reign of God," see ibid., 225–27.

What we have then in our effort to understand Jesus are not clear and decisive statements on Jesus' part, but rather "intimations" and "signs" which draw us to faith, insight, and understanding. We find Jesus expressing human tenderness, prophetic anger, affection for God, marvelous power, great courage, bold authority, forgiveness of sin, anticipation of suffering, passionate faith, pure hope, compassionate love, deep gladness, solidarity with the people, a sense of mission, personal relationships, genuine wisdom, a feeling for God. It is not a question of whether Jesus saw himself precisely as a prophet, or the Messiah, or *the* son of God. Jesus saw himself as belonging to God, doing God's work, and proclaiming God's word. He was God's servant, alive with God.

Jesus did not come all at once to an understanding of his mission and his Father's will for him. It is not so much a question of an evolving consciousness or psychological development, nor a question of our being able to pinpoint his development on the basis of the biblical records available to us. Nevertheless we can speak of "critical points," or "turning points," or significant events when Jesus seemed to manifest more understanding, such as (1) his baptism, what accompanied and followed it, and his return to Galilee preaching with a sense of mission he had not previously had; (2) the lack of reception as well as misunderstanding that his proclamation received, and as the Caesaraea Philippi incident symbolizes, Jesus beginning to warn the disciples of impending danger and suffering; (3) his decision to face Jerusalem, and all that it symbolized, as he resolutely set forth to face a prophet's fate there. We can see in these critical events a deepening understanding on Jesus' part of what God was asking of him.

Jesus was an un-self-preoccupied person. Our questions about his personal identity did not concern him. When he did speak of himself, his language could be metaphorical or cryptic, as when he described himself as a bridegroom (Mark 2:19). He spoke quite clearly as one having authority. He was a man of great freedom, able to be himself, independent of social pressures and conventions.

Jesus was not omniscient. Yet he spoke authoritatively on behalf of God. It may be helpful to bring together some of our previous suggestions, organizing them around titles commonly applied to Jesus: (1) prophet, (2) servant, (3) Messiah, (4) son of humanity, (5) Lord, (6) Word, and (7) Son. As we indicated in volume 2, in our discussion of the title "Lord," we can call to mind the distinction between a pre-resurrection and a post-resurrection meaning for some of the New Testament expressions; the distinction between Jewish Christianity and Gentile Christianity as the frame of reference for the expressions; as well as the fluid, flexible character of some of the expressions and the more restricted capability of others.[6]

1. *Prophet.* Jesus was seen by the Jewish people of his day as falling within the prophetic tradition: as a prophet like John; or like the prophets of old, such as Jeremiah; or as another Elijah (Mark 8:27-28; Luke 9:19; Matt 16:14). Jesus probably saw himself primarily in those terms (Mark 6:4; Luke 4:16-27; 13:33). He saw himself as a prophetic preacher (Mark 1:38), and he interpreted his exorcisms as a manifestation of the power of God at work within him (Luke 11:20).

Jesus' consciousness was not only prophetic, but social and eschatological as well. He befriended outcasts and sinners (Mark 2:15-17). The preoccupation of his preaching was (the reign of) God (Mark 1:15; Matt 6:10; 11:12; Luke 11:20; 17:20-21; many parables).

It can be credibly suggested as well that Jesus saw himself as a prophet like Moses, and that the Moses/Exodus/wilderness tradition in the spirituality of the north was more formative of his self-understanding than the David/Zion/Temple spirituality of the south. He certainly interpreted his mission as more akin to that of a prophet like Moses than that of a king like David.

After the resurrection, an event and experience which could not be completely contained within the category of prophet, the remembrance of Jesus' prophetic style and the people's perception of him was retained (Acts 3:22; 7:37; Mark 1:10; 12; the references above). The post-resurrection meaning of prophet was no different from the pre-resurrection understanding: Jesus was a man of the Spirit, inspired and empowered by God. The category of prophet was meaningful for Jewish Christians, but it carried less significance for Gentiles. Because of its inability to convey the full significance of the resurrection of Jesus, as well as its thoroughly Jewish character, its use became more limited and res-

---

[6]Goergen, *The Death and Resurrection of Jesus,* 174–79.

tricted. It never became the primary proclamation of the Church. Yet there is probably no expression closer to Jesus' own self-understanding, unless perhaps that of a teacher of wisdom.[7]

2. *Servant.* Jesus undoubtedly saw himself as a servant of God (Mark 10:45a), even if we leave open the precise ways in which he may have understood his servanthood (e.g., Mark 10:45b).[8] Jesus saw himself as a prophet, but probably also as more than a prophet. He saw himself as called to suffer and die, and probably saw this suffering as part of his mission and prophetic vocation (Luke 13:33; and the core behind the Marcan passion predictions), even if he anticipated vindication. He belonged to God, and loved his God with his whole heart, his whole soul, and all his strength (Deut 6:4; Mark 12:29-30), and his neighbor as much as himself (Lev 19:18; Mark 12:31).

That Jesus saw himself as a servant of God need not imply that he saw himself as *the* servant, in the sense of the Deutero-Isaian servant, to a great degree because there probably was no concept of *the* servant in Judaism.[9] We see the richness of the servant tradition in Israel, its significance for Jesus, as well as the probable significance of the Book of Isaiah for Jesus, the prophetic book most frequently quoted in the New Testament (cf. Luke 4:16-22). Yet this does not mean that Jesus saw himself precisely as the servant in Isaiah 52-53, since the Deutero-Isaian servant is a modern concept. But neither does this exclude the influence of Isaiah 52-53 on Jesus. All the richness of the servant image was available to Jesus, someone who saw himself as called to do Abba's will (cf. Matt 6:10; Mark 14:36).

The concept of servanthood in Israel carried a flexibility and wide applicability with it. The prophet, the priest, the king, as well as Israel as a whole were all called to be servants of God. Thus it is a concept with significance for Jesus as well as for the early Church's understanding and interpretation of Jesus (Mark 1:11; Matt 8:17; 12:18-21; Luke 22:37; Acts 3:13, 26; 4:27, 30; 8:32-35; Phil 2:7; Heb 9:28; 1 Pet 2:21-25). This concept assisted the early Church in its understanding of the earthly mission and ministry of Jesus as well as his suffering, rejection, and death by

[7]Cf. Goergen, *The Mission and Ministry of Jesus,* 151-57, 193-202, 267-77.

[8]Goergen, *The Death and Resurrection of Jesus,* 62-67.

[9]Ibid., 42-67.

crucifixion. It is to the life and death of Jesus that the interpretative value of the concept of servant primarily applies. It also assisted Jesus in his own understanding of his mission, ministry, life, suffering, and death. He was called to be a faithful servant of God, a true Israelite, a prophet and servant.

3. *Messiah.* One of the most difficult expressions of all is that of Messiah. It is significant to Christianity; it is the subject of much controversy; yet there is little evidence on which to base a conclusion about Jesus' messianic self-understanding. The question of Jesus' messianic consciousness is probably unanswerable.[10]

Although most of the people in Jesus' day seem to have seen him as a prophet, some undoubtedly saw him as fulfilling messianic expectations. Certainly those among his followers who were Zealots so saw him. Perhaps Peter did, and maybe James and John, disciples who continued to misunderstand Jesus' teaching about his suffering to come and who did not fully grasp some of what he taught (Mark 8:27-33; 10:35-45). Perhaps other members of the crowds who followed Jesus did think of him as Messiah, whatever it may have been that historically lay behind the memory of the triumphant march on Jerusalem (Mark 11:1-10), not to mention some members of the opposition, Roman and Jewish, by whom Jesus was at least perceived as a false Messiah or a messianic threat.

The more difficult question is again Jesus' own self-understanding. About this one can draw no firm conclusions. With those who deny Jesus a messianic consciousness, we can say that Jesus did not see himself as Messiah in either the priestly (Levitical) or royal (Davidic) ways in which messiahship was more commonly understood in Judaism. His consciousness was more prophetic than messianic. Yet his prophetic sense and identity need not have excluded the sense of a messianic mission as well, even though such awareness would have been secondary. Indeed, the prophets of old provided those texts which had come to be interpreted in a messianic sense in the time of Jesus. If Jesus thought of himself in messianic terms, it was more along the lines of a prophetic (Mosaic) role. The question then is whether Jesus would have interpreted that role to be messianic, whether he would have

[10]Cf. Goergen, *The Mission and Ministry of Jesus,* 157-70.

reinterpreted the expected role of Messiah along prophetic/Mosaic rather than royal/Davidic lines.

If Jesus thought of his role in messianic terms at all, he naturally expressed reserve lest it be misunderstood. It may be that he simply did not identify with messianism, however, and that messiahship was completely a post-resurrection, Christian reinterpretation of Jesus. In either case, Jesus' preferred way of speaking about himself was as "the son of humanity."

Even if we think of Jesus' self-understanding along less exalted ("lower") lines, we must admit that the authority with which he spoke (Mark 1:22), his close identification with God (Luke 11:20), and the way people responded to him all have a definitive character (Mark 8:38). And although one ought not too quickly to bring dogmatic tradition into one's exegesis, one must still admit that if Jesus is hypostatically in union with God, such a union would be of some effect on Jesus' conscious life. This would not imply that Jesus saw himself as the Messiah or as equal to the Father, but it is plausible that he could have seen in himself messianic fulfillment. Even so, it may have been only by way of intimation or intuition that Jesus felt himself to be who he was. "It is not necessary—and is hardly probable—that this fundamental experience should from the beginning have taken the form of an intellectual certitude, of a clear concept."[11]

Whether Jesus would have understood his mission in explicit messianic terms or not we may never know, nor is it important to know. After the resurrection, however, Jesus was clearly proclaimed as the Messiah—a messiahship interpreted along the lines of the concrete history of Jesus, his suffering and death. The proclamation of Jesus as "the Christ" (Messiah) would have more meaning for Jews and Jewish Christians than for Gentiles. Its significance can be seen in the fact that eventually the expression became part of Jesus' proper name: Jesus Christ. Its post-resurrection application to Jesus may have had its roots in Pilate's inscription on the cross, "the king of the Jews" (Mark 15:26; Matt 27:37; Luke 23:38; John 19:19). This title was at the basis of the early Christology recorded in Acts 2:36: "God has made him both Lord and Christ, this Jesus whom you crucified." In the earliest

---

[11]Jacques Guillet, *The Consciousness of Jesus,* trans. E. Bonin, (New York: Newman Press, 1972) 44.

Christologies, Jesus' messiahship was associated more with the expectation of the parousia, his return, and the resurrection than with an interpretation of his earthly ministry.

4. *Son of Humanity.* The New Testament evidence suggests that "son of humanity" was not an expression by means of which others referred to or addressed Jesus, as was the case with prophet, Messiah, teacher, and Lord. Rather the expression, found frequently and exclusively on the lips of Jesus himself, suggests Jesus' own way of speaking.

As I have discussed previously, the "son of humanity" problem is complex.[12] The two major directions of interpretation have been to see the expression as a title for an apocalyptic, quasi-messianic, celestial figure still to come, or as having its roots in Galilean Aramaic and being a characteristic of Jesus' way of speaking. The latter is the more probable. The basis underneath the "son of humanity" sayings in the Synoptic Gospels is Jesus' own particular way of using the expression. Also, in pre-Christian Judaism there is insufficient evidence that the "son of humanity" functioned as a title for a messianic or quasi-messianic figure. In the Gospels as they now stand, "son of humanity" does function as a title and refers to Jesus. Jesus' own usage, however, was Aramaic, as a general expression referring to humankind, as an indefinite reference, and probably also as a polite form of self-reference. It manifested Jesus' identity and solidarity with others. The apocalypticization of the expression took place after the resurrection, perhaps late, during the period of Gospel formation, and perhaps under the influence of Daniel 7. All of this I have already discussed in volume 1.[13] I am inclined here to make a further suggestion.[14]

---

[12]Cf. Goergen, *The Mission and Ministry of Jesus,* 180–202.

[13]Ibid., 180–202.

[14]Cf. Barnabas Lindars, "Re-enter the Apocalyptic Son of Man," *New Testament Studies* (1975) 52–72; A.J.B. Higgins, *The Son of Man in the Teaching of Jesus* (Cambridge: Cambridge University Press, 1980). Although I do not agree with either Lindars or Higgins fully, their unique interpretations are highly suggestive and merit consideration. Lindars contributes the notion that the quasi-titular New Testament use can be traced back to Jesus himself; it is neither pre-Christian nor completely post-resurrection. Higgins contributes the emphasis that the expression does not refer to a messianic individual but to a future *function.*

If "son of humanity" manifests a characteristic way in which Jesus spoke, and if it is also a way in which Jesus spoke about himself, manifesting both his solidarity with humankind and his own sense of mission, then the expression contains within it all that lies within Jesus' own self-understanding. It is a way in which Jesus spoke about himself and therefore contains what Jesus thought about himself, both as one of us and as one called by God. The enigmatic character of the expression is rooted in the enigmatic character of Jesus' self-understanding.

This would suggest that, in the life of the earthly Jesus, the meaning of the expression changes with Jesus' understanding of himself. It will have no one fixed meaning. It means all that Jesus understood himself to be, at any one point in his life. The expression is not so much a clue to Jesus' self-understanding as Jesus' self-understanding is the clue to its meaning. The expression has no particular content, apocalyptic or otherwise, other than what Jesus put into it; it is simply Jesus' way of speaking.

Thus, at the critical points or turning points in Jesus' life, the expression itself will bear more meaning. Jesus, growing up in Nazareth, may have used it. With the inauguration of the preaching in Galilee, the expression would carry not only Jesus' sense of humanity, but also his sense of personal authority and his distinctive relationship to *abba*. Later in his mission, as Jesus came to sense more fully his impending fate, the expression would suggest Jesus' conviction about his suffering and death. It could also bear the weight of his conviction about a future vindication. In other words, Jesus' self-understanding and "the son of humanity" expression can undergird the varied present, suffering, and future uses of the expression as reflected in the Gospels. It could also reflect Jesus' sense of a possible role in the future judgment. There is thus a bridge between the ordinary, unmessianic meaning in Jesus' use of the Aramaic expression—the "low" self-understanding it implies—and the quasi-messianic, titular meaning found in the Gospels—the "high" understanding it conveys—and that bridge is Jesus of Nazareth himself.

Thus the expression is messianic to the degree that Jesus' consciousness was messianic.

Jesus' use of the expression was flexible. In the preaching of the Church it became fixed and titular. Once fixed, it became less useful and was never a prominent title in the post-biblical period.

Yet the New Testament retained the expression because, like *abba,* it was so characteristic of the earthly Jesus. Underlying its use by the Church was the early Christian conviction of the role that Jesus would play in the judgment to come. Especially under the influence of Daniel 7 and growing apocalyptic speculation, it expressed the conviction that Jesus would return.

Nothing excludes then the possibility that Jesus thought of himself in a quasi-messianic role on earth (a prophet like Moses), yet as one who would suffer and die (a servant of the Lord), and then be vindicated and play a role in the future, in the judgment—another quasi-messianic, future, functional, celestial role (Mark 8:38). The typical way of conveying all of this for Jesus at different points in his life was through his use of the "son of humanity" expression.

5. *Lord.* We have already discussed the title "Lord" in volume 2.[15] The Aramaic *mari* was used of Jesus by others in his lifetime (Mark 7:28). When so used, it reflected ordinary Palestinian usage. It manifested respect for Jesus as a teacher and healer and as one having authority. The expression was not used by Jesus to refer to himself, and thus it does not help us to pursue Jesus' self-understanding. Jesus rather referred to himself as a prophet, was ambiguous and hesitant about accepting references to himself as Messiah, and most often spoke of himself simply as "a son of humanity." He did not, however, reject the references to himself as Lord (Mark 7:28; Matt 8:2, 6-8, 25).

After the resurrection, the content of the term "Lord" changes. Here we have one of the clearest examples of a wide flexibility with respect to meaning: the meaning when applied to Jesus in his own lifetime; the post-resurrection meaning among Jewish Christians to refer to the resurrection, exaltation, and future coming of the risen Jesus, Lordship in an exalted and eschatological sense; and the meaning among Gentile Christians with particular application to Jesus' present activity, having cosmic significance as well.

Lordship, along with Christ, was able to express a Christological interpretation of Jesus (Acts 2:36). In other words, Lordship was able to express that there is more to Jesus than Jesus of Nazareth alone; that Jesus cannot be finally and fully grasped

---

[15]Goergen, *The Death and Resurrection of Jesus,* 174–79.

apart from the reality of the resurrection; that "Jesus' life" comprises two stages, both of which he is, the selfsame Jesus. Both Christ and Lord helped the early Christians to proclaim the resurrection of Jesus and his future coming, to articulate a Christology of Jesus. "Lord," even more than "Christ," had a broader appeal, beyond Jewish Christianity. "Lord" thus became a highly significant title for the Church and was the basis for a two-stage understanding of Jesus. "Christ" became a part of Jesus' name and "son of humanity" more or less disappeared, but the title of "Lord" continued to capture the developing understanding of faith in Jesus.

6. *Word.* The expression *logos,* so significant to the history of Christology, as we saw in volume 3, is infrequent as a biblical expression.[16] As a reference to the pre-existent Word, it is confined to the prologue of the Fourth Gospel. Jesus never spoke of himself nor thought of himself in such terms—as an incarnation of some pre-existent *logos* or *sophia. Logos,* as a means for articulating the Church's understanding of Jesus, was a latecomer to Christology (late first century) and reflected the Christology of the Johannine community.

The Logos expression, with its probable roots in Jewish and Hellenistic wisdom, is of no use in a search for Jesus' self-understanding. Yet it eventually played a major role in the Church's understanding of Jesus. It enabled the Church to move from a two-stage Christology to a three-stage Christology with its doctrine of incarnation.

Just as the expression "Lord" was the vehicle by which the Church could express an early post-resurrection understanding of Jesus as a man whose life involves two phases, so "Word" was the vehicle by which the Church later expressed a further, fuller understanding. At the resurrection, Jesus became Lord and was revealed as the Christ. Later, however, not only was Jesus understood in terms of his resurrection from the dead, but also in terms of incarnation—the Word becoming flesh.

Both expressions, "Word" and "Lord," were limited. They were flexible enough to be applicable to two stages of Jesus' life, but by themselves could not carry the burden of all three stages— only "Son" had that wide a flexibility. "Word" helped the

[16]Goergen, *The Jesus of Christian History,* 9–35.

Church to bring together the first two stages—the pre-existent Word and the Word incarnate—but the Church never spoke about "the risen Word" or "the exalted Word." One could and did speak of the risen or exalted Lord, but not of the pre-existent Lord. The Word became flesh; Jesus became Lord. Word was the vehicle for a Christology of incarnation.

7. *Son of God.* James D. G. Dunn has written, "None of the other titles or ways of assessing Christ . . . has had both the historical depth and lasting power of 'Son of God.' "[17] Of all the titles, it assists us in our search for Jesus' self-understanding and is also applied by the Church after the resurrection to all three stages of the Jesus story: it has the capacity to express Jesus' self-understanding and the Church's understanding of Jesus, to express both a two-stage Christology and a three-stage Christology. Its meaning in each of these situations is not exactly the same; the expression is used differently, analogously, yet it is truly applicable. "Son of God" has a richness and flexibility that goes beyond other Christological expressions.

Jesus knew himself to be "a child of God," perhaps *the* child of God. Even if Jesus' *abba* consciousness is judged as not absolutely unique, *abba* is still distinctive of Jesus' way of praying. It was characteristic of Jesus and manifested a filial awareness on his part of his intimacy with God. When Jesus thought of himself as God's son, it was not with the implication of deity or divinity in any later Trinitarian sense. Jesus did not think of himself as equal to the Father, nor as pre-existent Son. Yet sonship was a way in which he understood his relationship to God, and *abba* captured that distinctive, intimate, special filial consciousness.

The basis for the early Christian interpretation and proclamation of Jesus as God's Son, however, does not seem to have been Jesus' own use of *abba* or his sense of sonship, but rather the resurrection. For Christians, the decisive Christological moment was the resurrection: the moment at which Jesus became God's Son in power (Rom 1:3-4; Acts 13:30-33). The Sonship of Jesus followed upon his having been raised from the dead. This was an eschatological Sonship. It may not have been the earliest way in which the Christians proclaimed the resurrection (the earliest seems to have been that Jesus was both Lord and Christ), but

[17]Dunn, *Christology in the Making,* 12.

when Sonship came to be used in the Church, it referred to the resurrection of Jesus, and it said more than Jesus himself had implied in his use of *abba.*

The decisive Christological moment (the moment when Jesus' Sonship was perceived by the Church to have had its beginning) was pushed further and further back.[18] The early application of the title "Son of God" to Jesus implied a two-stage Christology—Jesus raised from the dead. In the Gospel of Mark, Jesus becomes Son of God at the beginning of his ministry, at his baptism: Jesus was Son of God already on earth, prior to his death and resurrection. In the infancy narratives of both Matthew and Luke, Jesus becomes Son of God at the moment of conception: there never was a time on earth when Jesus was not God's Son. None of these different Christologies thus far implied any pre-existent sense of Sonship. This was most clearly introduced with the Fourth Gospel, in which Jesus' status as Son no longer depended on or flowed from the resurrection.[19] Sonship then became the basis for a three-stage Christology or an incarnational Christology. In the Synoptic Gospels there is no incarnation.

Thus we can see that Sonship was widely, variously, and richly applied, although not always in the same sense. Jesus himself saw himself as God's Son. The Church also understood Jesus to be God's Son, and applied the expression analogously to Jesus as of the resurrection (the earliest use), because of his death (Paul), from the beginning of his ministry (Mark), from the moment of his conception (Matthew, Luke), as the incarnation of the pre-existent *Logos* (John). The Church's further probing the Sonship of Jesus led to even further developments in the second and third centuries.

"Lord" and "Christ" had been the earliest ways in which the Church expressed its faith in Jesus. They proclaimed the resurrection and were the basis of early two-stage Christologies. Eventually "Christ" became a part of Jesus' proper name. "Jesus Christ is Lord" remained the central proclamation. Such expressions, however, did not facilitate the Church's further understanding of Jesus as having a pre-historical as well as post-historical existence. "Logos" or "Word" was the vehicle for such an un-

[18]Goergen, *The Death and Resurrection of Jesus,* 255–56.

[19]Goergen, *The Jesus of Christian History,* 9–35.

derstanding. "Son of God," however, was the most comprehensive expression.

Today we continue to search for expressions, old and new, by means of which we might best express our faith in Jesus. Jesus is both "Son of God" and "son of Mary." This latter expression, very ancient, already significant to Leo I, has new capacity today to affirm the humanness of Jesus and Jesus' solidarity with us. As "Son of God" and "son of Mary" Jesus is revealed in his twofold solidarity and deepest levels of identity.[20] Likewise, Jesus' biblical name, Immanuel (Isa 7:14; Matt 1:23) has particular power today, telling us who Jesus is by placing him within the context of the history of God's coming closer and closer to be with his people.

If we return to Jesus' own self-understanding, however, our primary concern here, Jesus' consciousness was prophetic, perhaps also messianic, although not in the senses in which that was commonly understood within Judaism. Jesus' self-awareness was more than simply prophetic, however. He manifested a sense of authority, finality, and distinctive relationship with God. He was both God's servant and Son. He "belonged" to God. He tended both to reveal and to conceal all of this by his use of that ordinary but enigmatic expression, "son of humanity"—an expression as enigmatic as the person to whom it referred, an expression which also suggested Jesus' sense that he "belonged" to the people, as does Jesus' God.[21]

In the end, the question of Jesus' consciousness or self-understanding is misplaced. It is to have already misunderstood Jesus. The question is not what Jesus may have been thinking about himself, but what God was thinking about Jesus, what God was doing in relationship to us through this particular human being—Jesus as God's nearness to us. There is no question that Jesus was a physical being, but the details of his physicality (his height, weight, shape, etc.) are not of theological importance to us. Likewise, there can be no dismissal or diminution of Jesus' psychic life, but the details of his psyche are not of great theological import either. What is of importance is the God being revealed through the human reality of Jesus.

---

[20]Goergen, *The Mission and Ministry of Jesus,* 109–45, 218–29, 278–81.

[21]Ibid., 227.

The Power of Jesus

One of the qualities of Jesus' ministry which stands out in the biblical records is his power and authority. How is one to understand such power in the context of a theology of Jesus that is both incarnational and kenotic? If we accept the freely chosen, self-limiting character of the Logos's historical incarnation, it is not necessary to attribute omnipotence to the human, earthly Jesus. The Logos is incarnate *as* a human being. At the same time, if the hypostatic union meant anything, such an intimate union between Jesus and the Word, whereby Jesus ontologically was the Word, must have some effect on Jesus' life and will. We must steer a middle course between attributing all power to Jesus and denying him any power beyond the ordinary. The power of God in Jesus Christ is both restrained and operative. Although miracles are a prominent part of the biblical record, so is Jesus' self-restraint. The narratives of Jesus in the wilderness (Matt 4:1-11; Luke 4:1-13) already indicate the kind of son of God he was going to be.[22] Yet, in Luke's account, the verse immediately after the close of the episode in the wilderness states "And Jesus returned in the power of the Spirit into Galilee, and a report concerning him went out through all the surrounding country" (Luke 4:14). In what did this power of the Spirit consist, and how did it manifest itself in the life of Jesus?

Thomas Aquinas himself held a middle position with respect to the power of Jesus (*ST* III, 13). According to Thomas, God is omnipotent, but not Christ. Thomas followed his principle that the union of the natures in Christ did not destroy the distinction of the natures. The power of Jesus to act corresponds to nature, the principle of activity. Thus Christ, as a human being, is not omnipotent. This agrees also with one of Thomas's fundamental philosophical principles: what is received is received according to the mode of the receiver (*ST* III, 13, 1, ad 2). Christ's power on earth was limited.

Thus we ought not to be surprised to find in Jesus both the ordinary human limitations which constrict and constrain all of

---

[22]See Piet Schoonenberg, "He Emptied Himself, Philippians 2:7," in *Who Is Jesus of Nazareth?*, Concilium 11 (New York: Paulist Press, 1965) 55, 57-62, where he emphasizes that the *kenosis* is a renunciation by Christ of what we think the life of God's Son ought to be.

us, and what appear to be at times extraordinary manifestations of spiritual power. Nor are we able to determine more precisely on scientific or historiographical grounds the particular character of these manifestations of power, for the biblical records here are filled with difficulties. The miracle stories in the Gospels are not primarily reports of Jesus' activities but are rather recognition opportunities.

When we come to a miracle story in one of the Synoptic Gospels, we can ask three questions or consider three levels at which the miracle can be understood: (1) the Jesus level or level of factuality—what actually happened; (2) the level of the written tradition and redaction—what function the miracle story plays in the Gospel as a whole; (3) the level of personal, moral, or spiritual meaning—what the text is saying to me. Each miracle narrative can be approached at all three levels.

We can ask critical and historiographical questions of the text to determine what may have actually happened on these occasions. Not all such questions will be answered. We must be satisfied with what we can learn. The tradition testifies to deeds or works of Jesus that are as authoritative and as provocative as his words. The search for objective knowledge[23] about Jesus cannot dismiss out of hand the historical basis of these events. As we discussed in volume 1, the healings and exorcisms are well attested as being based on the life of Jesus.[24] This does not mean that every detail of these narratives is rooted in the life of Jesus. Jesus cured people of various illnesses. The miracle stories manifesting his power over nature which go beyond the healings and exorcisms contain more legendary features. Even these may be based on some historical event. However, it is historiographically more difficult to determine what actually happened on these occasions. What happened was embellished and developed during the stage of the oral tradition.

It is necessary at a certain point to bracket the historiographical data, the historical character, or even the factuality of these events—to put aside some of our questions as unanswerable or perhaps irrelevant—and to go to another level in order to understand the narratives. Not "what happened?" but "what function

---

[23]Goergen, *The Death and Resurrection of Jesus,* 183–203.

[24]Goergen, *The Mission and Ministry of Jesus,* 170–76.

does the narrative play in the written Gospel?'' Here we are involved in questions of literary and redaction criticism. We will not pursue these critical questions with respect to any one Gospel or any one miracle in particular. Rather we will note a significant function that the miracle stories perform in all the Synoptic Gospels—recognition opportunities. I will use the Gospel of Mark as an example. We can see the Gospel of Mark as divided into prologue (1:1-13); public life, associated with Galilee (1:14–10:31); and the passion narrative and ministry in Jerusalem (10:32–16:8).

Who Is Jesus? (The Gospel of Mark)

This itinerant and charismatic preacher and teacher, healer, and exorcist, manifests something new (2:18-22), and his new teaching reflects authority (2:27; 3:4). One cannot help at this point but wonder—who is this? Perhaps some of us have already truly recognized him. At least we can probably admit that this person is "from God," as the Gospel of Mark presents him.

The demon in 1:24 had already proclaimed, "I know who you are, the Holy One of God." Similarly, the demons in 5:7 proclaim him to be "the Son of the Most High God." The miracles, from the viewpoint of the narrative, are recognition opportunities for the hearer or reader. Note how they build and stir our wonder.

1:23-28	Jesus cures a demoniac.
1:29-31	Jesus cures Simon's mother-in-law.
1:32-34	There were many cures and exorcisms.
1:40-45	Jesus cures a leper.

Do we not recognize who this Jesus is?

2:1-12	Jesus cures a paralytic and forgives his sins.
2:23-28	Jesus shows his authority over the Sabbath.
3:1-6	Jesus cures a man with a withered hand.
4:1-34	Jesus teaches in parables.
4:35-41	Jesus calms a storm.

Do we recognize how this last miracle goes beyond any of the previous ones, which were healings and exorcisms? Certainly if we as readers and hearers did not recognize Jesus in the previous miracles, we must have recognized him in this latter even more amazing manifestation. Whenever unclean spirits saw him, they shouted, "You are the Son of God" (3:11). Mark says, in effect, "Do you yourself not yet see this?"

Lest there be any doubt, chapter 5 continues with three more such opportunities for recognition. The cure of the Gerasene demoniac whose demon's name was Legion (5:1-20) is no simple exorcism, but a singularly difficult one. (Do we see with whom we have to do here?) A hemorrhaging woman is healed simply by touching Jesus' cloak (5:25-34). This is far beyond the previous healings as the exorcism of the Gerasene was a step beyond previous exorcisms. (We must surely by now recognize who this man is.) Jesus raises the dead daughter of Jairus to life (5:35-43). This miracle is now of a completely new order. Chapter 4 concluded with Jesus' power over nature, chapter 5 with his power over death. Can there be any further question?

This progression makes it impossible for us not to recognize Jesus. The response to the question of who Jesus is becomes more and more obvious in chapter 6.

> He prays (6:46).
> He teaches (6:2, 6, 34).
> He heals (6:56).

Our curiosity is raised by that of the people who are still trying to figure him out (6:14-16). Only the demons so far have really recognized him. The people continue to be amazed (6:2, 33, 51, 56). He sends out his disciples (6:7-13). But chapter 6 also describes the progression of recognition opportunities, two opportunities beyond anything so far (for the really blind and slow learner).

> 6:30-44   Jesus multiplies five loaves and two fish for at least five thousand people.
> 6:45-52   Jesus walks on water. This is not just calming the storm. Surely this man is son of God in some unique way.

In chapter 7 Jesus cures the daughter of a Syrophoenician woman from a distance (7:24-30). He does not even go to her home.

In case there remains doubt, however, before Mark puts Jesus on the road toward Jerusalem, chapters 8 and 9 provide the climax of this (Galilean) section of the Gospel. Notice how well-ordered this last chance for one's own profession of faith is.

8:1-10   There is a second multiplication of the food, this time of seven loaves and a few fish for about four thousand people. (Whom do you think this man is for Mark?) Notice Jesus' question to his disciples in 8:21, "He said to them, 'Do you not yet understand.'"

8:23-26   Jesus cures a blind man. The question of Jesus to the man (8:23) is, "Are you still blind? What do you see?" It takes some doing; but at last the blind do see clearly.

8:27-33   Jesus questions the disciples in the region of Caesaraea Philippi. We have discussed this incident at length in volume 1. Do we now see, however, that this is an opportunity presented to us as well, to see like Peter (finally someone besides the demons recognize him), but not like Peter who rejects the suffering that lies ahead which is also being disclosed. This incident is almost the climax of the recognition opportunities in the Gospel. We can now recognize Jesus, the Messiah, and be his disciple. But not only will Jesus suffer; so will his disciples (8:34-38).

Chapter 9 is the true climax. Jesus is revealed in all his glory. Does this revelation come as any surprise?

9:2-8   Jesus is transfigured before his disciples and they (we) see who he truly is—one who lives in the presence of God. He comes from God. We have here one who is greater than Moses and greater than Elijah. Jesus continues to emphasize, however, that he must suffer (9:12-13). When he is recognized (8:27-30; 9:2-8), he teaches that he must suffer (8:31; 9:12-13).

9:14-29   The climax in Galilee has taken place. There will be nothing like this in Galilee again, until Jesus returns there on the clouds of heaven. Yet Mark gives us another demonstration of Jesus' authority and power in the healing of this epileptic demoniac, another recognition oppor-

> tunity (9:14-29), followed by Jesus teaching that
> he will be put to death (9:30-32).

The pattern underneath the structure of the Gospel is as follows: recognition (by the disciples, primarily after the resurrection) → proclamation of the gospel (the life, death and resurrection of Jesus) → recognition (by us who now profess our faith as well) → discipleship (we who throughout history number ourselves among his disciples for we have truly recognized Jesus as Risen Lord).

In chapter 10 the story shifts toward Jerusalem. But, by now, we should all recognize *who* is going there. With the demons and with his disciples we can say: the Christ, the Son of God. And we must also admit that we have been forewarned that he/we must suffer.

Recognizing Jesus

We must continue to be aware of the significant difference between objective knowledge and personal knowledge, between knowledge *about* someone and the encounter *with* someone, between historiography and faith.[25] The Scriptures are rooted upon personal knowledge, encounters with the Risen Lord. They invite us to that same encounter, to personal knowledge, and to faith. The Gospels are constructed to enable us to recognize Jesus. They do not pretend merely to inform us about Jesus. Rather they presuppose or look toward a personal encounter with Jesus.

The nature and role of recognition in literature and in Scripture has been discussed in a significant work by Diana Culbertson. She writes:

> There is an experience in life we call recognition. It is a kind
> of knowledge by which we apprehend meaning in a pattern of
> events or realize that the meaning we had once assigned to those
> events has been shattered. It is distinguished from simple cog-
> nition in which we become aware intellectually of a fact or an
> idea, but not necessarily of its implications. Recognition also
> differs from perception in that a fact or event is seen in a way
> that involves the whole of the perceiver's personal awareness,

[25]Goergen, *The Death and Resurrection of Jesus,* 183-203.

knowledge, values, and idea of existence. The assumption in this book is that the experience of recognition is the central humanizing and revelatory experience, the immediate cause of psychological and spiritual change. Recognition is thus at the heart of the literary text, both sacred and secular.[26]

Recognition goes beyond what is immediately sensed; it involves interpretation.[27] In recognition the impersonal becomes personal.[28] Schillebeeckx as well notes the importance of "the disclosure experience" as the starting point of Christology.[29] He sees the important structure of both *pneuma* and *memoria* within such experience.

The Christian experience as the local church's communal response to what Jesus actually does offer is the primary thing; the titles, although not unimportant, are secondary; and there again, even in Scripture they are interchangeable, replaceable by others, and they may die out. The saving experience persists and from time to time calls for an appropriate expression and articulation in new social and historical situations. One might call it a "disclosure" experience, a discovery event: a source experience (both for the person who had known Jesus directly and for the one who had come to know about him by way of the *memoria Jesu* and the life of the local congregation); that is to say, they have discovered in Jesus something that cannot be pinned down directly, on an empirical basis, but that to any open-minded person confronted with Jesus in a living community is going to present itself as something gratuitous, as *"given in evidence."*

It is interesting to notice the structure of this community experience, which itself links the "new life" of the local congregation, present in virtue of the Spirit, with Jesus of Nazareth.

---

[26]Diana Culbertson, *The Poetics of Revelation, Recognition and the Narrative Tradition,* Studies in American Biblical Hermeneutics, 4 (Macon, Ga.: Mercer University Press, 1989) 9.

[27]Ibid., 10–14. Also see John Hick, "Religious Faith as 'Experiencing As' " in *Talk of God,* ed. G.N.A. Vesey (New York: Macmillan, 1964) 23.

[28]Culbertson, *The Poetics of Revelation,* 12.

[29]Edward Schillebeeckx, *Jesus: An Experiment in Christology,* trans. Hubert Hoskins (New York: Seabury Press, 1979) 46, 75, 88.

> *Pneuma* and *anamnesis,* Spirit and recollection of Jesus, are
> experienced as a single reality.[30]

Culbertson also identifies a relationship between recognition
and religious experience. Not all recognition is religious experience, but "All religious experience begins with recognition,
with discovery. This discovery is neither so subjective that it cannot be reflected upon or described, nor so objective and intellec-
tually coercive that risk and loyalty are not required."[31]

As Culbertson points out, based upon her analysis of recognition experiences in literature, to describe recognition requires narrative. Recognition involves a series of experiences, is a history,
and requires a description of these experiences, namely narrative.[32]
And one can say that the disclosure or recognition within the
Scriptures requires the same—history as narrative. Hence Schillebeeckx speaks of the need for a post-critical narrative history.[33]

We can now see more clearly how the miracle narratives can
be approached at two levels—at the level of historiography and
at the level of narrative. Of the two, the latter is more significant. For indeed, one could document the factuality and details
of the actual happenings more precisely and extensively, and still
historiography would not lead to faith. But once one has come
truly to recognize Jesus as the Son of God, once one has been
enabled to make the proclamation of faith, once one has had her
or his own personal encounter with Jesus as Lord, then one can
say both that Jesus could have worked many such wonders, for
the very power of God was at work within him, and that it makes
no difference whether or not he actually did exactly what the Scriptures describe—for one has come in his or her own experiences
to acknowledge Jesus as Lord. The historiographical questions
are relativized by the faith, even though they do not lack significance. The narratives are rooted in *memoria Jesu:* Jesus
healed, cast out demons, and performed many signs. Jesus' deeds,
and the narratives about them, are invitations to faith, opportunities for recognition, not proofs of faith which then require no

[30]Ibid., 46.

[31]Culbertson, *The Poetics of Revelation,* 14.

[32]Ibid., 14–29.

[33]Schillebeeckx, *Jesus,* 77, 156.

faith or inner recognition, proclamation, and commitment to discipleship. To know Jesus is to become his disciple. As Hans Küng wrote, "What is demanded is not faith in miracles, but *faith in Jesus* and in him whom Jesus has revealed. In this sense—as again John's Gospel makes clear—the believer can dispense with miracles entirely: 'Blessed are those who have not seen and yet believe.' "[34]

There is a third level at which we can approach each of the miracle stories as well, less important for our purposes here: the level of individual and collective, personal and communal, spiritual and religious meaning which continues to nourish the faith once recognition has happened. Here we are not concerned with the broader, progressive structure, but with the details of individual narratives. For example, in the healing of the paralytic (Mark 2:1-12) we find the proclamation of forgiveness. The persistence of the hemorrhaging woman does not go unrewarded (5:25-34). The feeding of the five thousand (6:39-44) evokes the image of the Israelites being fed in the wilderness as well as Eucharist being celebrated in the community (14:22). In the story of Jesus walking on water (6:45-51), we are told not to be afraid.

The tradition of signs and wonders performed by Jesus shows us that the power of God was at work within him, a power flowing from his (hypostatic) union with God, but which is still not simply the equivalent of God's power. For God at work in Jesus always respected his human nature. Jesus' power came from within a human being whose very being was open to God. It was as a human being that Jesus performed his wonders, but as a human being in whom sin did not obstruct the power and presence and nearness of God within him and in his midst.

When discussing the power of Christ as a human being, or the power of God within Christ, or the power of the Spirit by which Jesus was led into the wilderness and in whose power he returned to the mission in Galilee, we must clarify the kind of power of which we speak.[35] *Power* is a word which has taken on many nega-

---

[34]Hans Küng, *On Being a Christian,* trans. Edward Quinn (New York: Doubleday and Co., 1976) 237; see pp. 226-38 for an excellent discussion of miracle.

[35]The kind of power that God is has been much discussed by process theology for which there are extensive bibliographies. Cf. John B. Cobb, *God and the World* (Philadelphia: Westminster Press, 1969) ch. 4; David Ray Griffin, *God, Power and Evil* (Philadelphia: Westminster Press, 1976) chs. 17-18; Bernard Loomer,

tive connotations. We associate it with coercion, force, brutality, manipulation, exploitation, domination, oppression. *Power* means getting what one wants when one wants it. We may even unconsciously associate these negative manifestations of power with the powerfulness of God. But this is not the kind of power that God is. It is the opposite of what Rollo May has called nutritive and integrative power: the power of holiness, integrity, compassion, truth, goodness, beauty, healing, learning, collaboration, non-violence.[36]

Biblically and theologically the contrast is quite clear cut: the power of sin or the power of grace, the power of evil or the power of the Spirit. The power of God is *the power of love.*[37] God does not resort to destructive or sinful manifestations of power. God's power or will is not all-coercive, but all-loving, all-merciful, freely shared: a freely chosen interdependence respectful of the other as other. If we study the mighty deeds of Christ closely, we do not find manifestations of brute or brutal force, but manifestations of love, compassion, generosity, fidelity. The power of Christ is his human and extraordinary capacity to love—a capacity rooted in his faith, hope, and union with God.

Miracle, defined as a breach of the laws of nature, is a modern word or concept. In the New Testament, Jesus' mighty deeds are not called miracles. Nor does the Vulgate translate the Greek text with the Latin word *miraculum.* The New Testament speaks rather of *dynameis* (powerful deeds), *erga* (works), or *semeia* (signs). The Synoptic *dynameis* is what C. H. Dodd has described as "a remarkable or exceptional occurrence which brought an undeniable sense of the presence and power of God."[38] The Johannine

---

"Two Conceptions of Power," *Process Studies* 6 (1976) 5–32; *Process Thought in Theology and Ecumenism,* a collection of eight essays, edited by Donald Goergen in *Listening* 14 (1979) 163–278; *Religious Experience and Process Theology,* essays edited by Harry James Cargas and Bernard Lee (New York: Paulist Press, 1976); Pierre Teilhard de Chardin, *The Future of Man* (New York: Harper and Row, 1964) esp. chs. 11–12.

[36]Cf. Rollo May, *Power and Innocence* (New York: W. W. Norton and Co., 1972); *The Courage to Create* (New York: W. W. Norton and Co., 1975). Also Paul Tillich, *The Courage to Be* (New Haven, Conn.: Yale University Press, 1952).

[37]This is a point I have developed at greater length in my *Power of Love,* esp. 234–66.

[38]C. H. Dodd, *The Founder of Christianity* (New York: The Macmillan Co., 1970) 32.

semeion suggests significatory or symbolic actions; it is their symbolic character which is highlighted.[39] In the Synoptics, the *dynameis* manifest the present or realized aspects of Jesus' eschatology; (the reign of) God is already breaking through. The New Testament "miracles" do not prove the divinity of Jesus Christ but rather a power at work that is able to defeat the power of evil. Critical analysis of the miracle stories leads to an underlying stratum of healings and exorcisms as a part of the ministry of Jesus; these are an undeniable historical nucleus. The extent of Jesus' manifestations of spiritual power may have gone beyond these; we cannot be historiographically sure, for the Gospels are not primarily historiographical records. Rather the miracle stories in the Gospels, or better the *dynameis, erga,* and *semeia,* are manifestations of power, indications of God's presence, signs that (the reign of) God has come, disclosive events, opportunities for recognition, proleptic signs of the future vindication of Christ by God: signs that we have here to do with someone sent by God for our sake, a unique messenger from God.

The Uniqueness of Jesus

In traditional Christologies from above, the question of Jesus' uniqueness was not problematic. Jesus was the *Logos* incarnate, eventually expressed in the Chalcedonian doctrine and the theology of the hypostatic union. Only Jesus is hypostatically united to God. In modern Christologies from below, Jesus' uniqueness has become a theological concern: How does Jesus differ from the prophets of Israel or later saints? Is this difference simply one of degree? Can Jesus' uniqueness be historiographically ascertained? In a Christology from below, one does not begin with Jesus' union with God, or even Jesus' uniqueness; one rather discovers it. But is Jesus' uniqueness something to which one can come from below? Is what one can come to from below adequate for the historical Christian faith? There are several possible responses to the question of Jesus' uniqueness, and they need not be mutually exclusive. The affirmation of Jesus' uniqueness is in the end a perspective of faith. Ultimately, Jesus' uniqueness is

[39]Cf. Raymond Brown, *The Gospel According to John, I-XII,* Anchor Bible 29A (New York: Doubleday and Co., 1966) 525-32.

meta-historiographical even if there are historiographical intimations of it.

Historiographically, we can talk about Jesus as a historical event, and about what God did in history through Jesus. Just as Jeremiah was not simply another Isaiah, nor John a replica of Elijah, so Jesus' vocation—what God did in history through Jesus—was unique. It is difficult to articulate the full significance of Jesus as a historical event. Understanding the historical Jesus requires going beyond historiography to theology.[40] Nevertheless, what God was doing in Jesus was new; Jesus' mission had not been accomplished by someone previously. To some degree, after Jesus, history would never be the same.

Ontologically, Jesus did not simply exemplify union with God through sanctifying grace. He was united with God hypostatically, personally—created to be the human nature of the *Logos*. He never had any ontological existence apart from God. He was an incarnation and not only a creation. However we correlate Jesus' union with God and our own union with God through grace, the mode of the former was unique: the intensity of God's presence in Jesus' human life comes from deeper within him than is the case with us. Jesus *is* God—at the ontological level. His ontological and historical uniqueness do not exclude one another.

Eschatologically, Jesus' destiny—what he became—was unique. His resurrection from the dead had a preeminence to it in the early proclamation. He was highly exalted, installed as Lord, given an ongoing function in history, in the heavens as well as on earth. He continues to function as a mediator. His personal destiny was not the same as that of Peter or Paul. Jesus' life, death, and resurrection are all intrinsically related to human history.

As a revelatory event, Jesus is a unique, normative, and unsurpassable moment in the history of revelation. This understanding has become particularly significant for Christology today. It holds together the two poles in any Christology—the historical and the eschatological, or the below and the above. In Jesus, God's self-disclosure breaks through into history. To say that Jesus as revelatory event is normative (for Christians) or unsurpassable (which does not mean that there could not be a comparable revelation, but that it would never disqualify or negate

---

[40]Goergen, *The Death and Resurrection of Jesus,* 183–203.

Jesus') does not mean that revelation is exclusively present in the Jesus event or even final with Jesus (in the sense that revelation does not continue). Yet he is a unique and supreme moment in the history of revelation. Central to Rahner's Christology is revelation as God's self-communication. Schillebeeckx speaks about Jesus as the parable of God. Peter Hodgson's Christology focuses on Jesus as uniquely God's Word—God's irrevocable self-communication.[41] Wolfhart Pannenberg has made Jesus' revelational identity with God the basis of Christology.[42] Jesus is God as self-disclosing within history: this self-disclosure is a unique moment both in human history and in the story of God.

Pneumatologically, Jesus is also a unique moment in the history of the Spirit of the world. Jesus was not who he was apart from the presence and action of the Spirit in his life. The Risen Christ gives the gift of the Spirit to his disciples and to those who believe in him. As a consequence of Jesus' life, death, and resurrection, there is an overwhelming outpouring of the Spirit. The Spirit is the Spirit of God, but also Jesus' Spirit. Just as one can no longer tell the story of God apart from Jesus (Jesus as revelatory event), so one cannot tell the story of Jesus apart from the Spirit. Jesus is intimately tied up with the very definition of God and of Spirit. Jesus is a uniquely creative advance in the history of spirit.

Soteriologically, Jesus' uniqueness is seriously scrutinized today. Yet, if one does not equate Jesus as savior, or mediator, or salvific event with the idea of Jesus as exclusive savior, one can avoid a too facile rejection of Jesus' soteriological role. The task of Christology is not so much to repeat affirmations about salvation in Christ as to break open the symbol that Christ is and unleash the salvific energy it contains. Jesus proclaimed forgiveness. Jesus freed people from false and oppressive images of God. Jesus reached out to and touched the untouchable. Jesus healed—and an extraordinary power manifested itself in him. Jesus proclaimed: God belongs to the people. Our God is a saving God who is constantly coming closer.

Anthropologically, Paul saw Jesus Christ as another *adam*. Jesus is *morphē theou*, the image of God, which is also the defi-

---

[41]Peter C. Hodgson, *Jesus, Word and Presence* (Philadelphia: Fortress Press, 1971).

[42]Pannenberg, *Jesus, God and Man*, esp. 127–33.

nition of being truly human. Schillebeeckx sees Jesus as a paradigm of what it means to be human. This need not mean that Jesus was perfect in every way, but only that there was in him a perfection of the human capacity to love. Nor does this mean idealizing him, but rather recognizing in him a supreme exemplification of what being human really means. In traditional, postbiblical theology, Jesus was both Son of God *and* son of humanity—the uniquely human one. Jesus stretches our understanding of what it means to be human. He reveals to us what being human is all about. His humanity becomes the norm for ours, rather than the other way around.

Perhaps one of the best words, although disputed, for capturing Jesus' uniqueness is *sinlessness*. Jesus' uniqueness does not consist precisely in the fact that he was human, no matter how human he was, even if he actualized his humanity to the fullest degree. Nor does it consist precisely in his divinity, for we too are divine, even though Jesus' mode of union with God was uniquely hypostatic. But his uniqueness can also be interpreted with biblical and traditional language: the Sinless One. We will turn to this in the next section of this chapter.

Finally, sacramentally, Jesus is a unique symbol. More than any of our previous approaches (none of which I would dismiss), this one seems to be very effective today. Schillebeeckx early moved post-Vatican II Catholic theology in this direction.[43] Modern Christology has focused necessary attention on the relationship between the Jesus of history and the Christ of faith, a relationship which can be more accurately understood if we speak about the Jesus of historiography and the Jesus of faith.[44] The dilemma for Teilhard de Chardin was the relationship between the Jesus of history and the Omega of evolution—a challenging issue also for anyone committed to the uniqueness of Jesus. But our question here is still different—the relationship between the Jesus of history and the symbolic Christ. Jesus is a unique and historically grounded symbol—the primordial sacrament.

The fullness or truth about who Jesus is will only be known to us when we are with the eschatological God: the time of the fullness of revelation, the day of the Lord. We will see and un-

[43]Schillebeeckx, *Christ the Sacrament of the Encounter with God.*
[44]Goergen, *The Death and Resurrection of Jesus,* 183–203.

derstand more clearly then than we can now. In that sense, Jesus is someone still to be revealed. The uniqueness of Jesus has become problematic in Christologies from below which seek to be both historiographically honest and yet in accord with Christian faith. A Christology from above did not have the same problem. Jesus' uniqueness lay in his origins from above and in the rejection of Adoptionism. It is questionable whether a Christology that remains exclusively from below can answer satisfactorily the question of Jesus' uniqueness, and in fact Christologies from below can often end up abandoning the point, for uniqueness will remain historiographically inaccessible. The singularity of being that Jesus is, indeed that any of us are, is permeated with unknowability. For Christology, Jesus' uniqueness remains a statement of faith, an invitation to *mysterium,* capable of being symbolized in a doctrine like Jesus' sinlessness but not capable of a final objectified articulation. Jesus research, even research which focuses on the unique in Jesus, cannot prove his uniqueness, nor that faith in him is justified. It can only lead us to the threshold of faith. "Jesus is Lord" remains a proclamation of faith. Faith affirms a unique relationship between Jesus and God—however that may be conceptualized or articulated.

"No one knows the Son except the Father"—such is the intimacy between the two—and, "No one knows the Father except the Son" (Matt 11:27)—Jesus had come to be a part of the self-definition of God. This is not to say that Jesus is the only son. We too are sons and daughters, and so were Mohammed and Moses before us. When Christian tradition speaks about the only-begotten Son of God (or better, uniquely begotten Son),[45] it is speaking about the eternal Word. And, since Jesus is the Word, Jesus is the uniquely begotten Son of God incarnate. Saying that Jesus is (ontologically) the only Son of God is not to say that only Jesus is son or daughter of God. Yet Jesus' relationship to God remains unique, substantive, and personal—whether we look here to the pre-existent relationship between Father and Son (Word), or to the historical relationship between the Galilean and his *abba,* or to the post-resurrection relationship between God and the one exalted to God's right hand. To know God fully is to come to know Jesus, and to know Jesus is to come to know God as *abba*

---

[45]Goergen, *The Jesus of Christian History,* 127-28.

and *imma*. They cannot be defined apart from each other. This does not deny that something comparable may be said of Gautama or Moses or Mohammed—to know God is to know God's prophets. As I have said previously, Jesus defines but does not confine God's action. But neither does God's action or presence (seemingly) outside of Jesus deny who Jesus uniquely is.

Jesus of Nazareth is the Word of God, the Word in an incarnate, kenotic mode of existence: a prophet to Israel and revelation to Gentiles, a true servant of God, raised from the dead, and exalted to share in the Lordship of heaven and earth, Son of the living God.

The Sinlessness and Freedom of Jesus

The sinlessness of Jesus is an important theological issue. For some, its denial would be tantamount to denying the divinity of Jesus. For others, its affirmation is tantamount to denying the humanity of Jesus. It suffers under the crossfire of varied Christological disputes. It involves not only the question of whether Jesus was in fact sinless, but also the question of what one means by such a statement. What is it affirming and what is it denying?

Being fully human does not necessitate being a sinner. There are those who maintain that if Jesus was sinless, then he was not one of us. Hebrews 4:15 says that Jesus was like us in all things except for sin. This is a significant exception. "If Jesus did not struggle with sin, then he cannot identify with me." But Jesus' sinlessness need not diminish the reality of his struggle, nor dislodge our affirmations of his humanity. To be human does not mean to sin. In fact, one can well argue (as Paul would) that it is sin which makes us less than human.[46] To be truly human is to be without sin. Granted, our experience of what it means to be human is often an experience of sinful humanity. But this is why we cannot use our humanity as a norm for Jesus' humanity. Jesus reveals to us what being truly human is. We cannot apply a pre-definition of humanity to Jesus anymore than we can apply to him a pre-definition of divinity.[47] Being a sinner is not es-

---

[46]Cf. Jerome Murphy-O'Connor, *Becoming Human Together,* 2nd rev. ed. (Wilmington, Del.: Michael Glazier, 1982).

[47]Goergen, *The Mission and Ministry of Jesus,* 25–45.

sential to being human, and being sinless does not destroy or diminish one's humanness: if anything, it enhances or perfects it.

Speaking of Jesus as sinless, or as a sinner, depends to a great degree upon the definition of terms.[48] What do we mean by sin? If anger is always sin, Jesus got angry. If hurting or offending someone is sin, it is hard to maintain that Jesus did not offend some of the Pharisees. If sin is insensitivity to the feelings of others, was Jesus' comparison of the Syro-Phoenician woman to a dog sensitive? Christian tradition, with its high Christology, never denied Jesus' anger, though it interpreted it as a just anger. Just what is being said about Jesus when his sinlessness is affirmed? The answer involves Jesus' relationship both to "actually sinning," and to what we call original sin and the fallen human condition.

However one understands or defines the sinlessness of Jesus, it cannot diminish the reality of his human struggle, or what we have traditionally referred to as his temptations, our interpretation of his ordeal in the wilderness.[49] Jesus is one of us particularly in his identity with the human struggle. He suffered physically, emotionally, mentally, and spiritually. His will and emotions could be pushed and pulled in different directions. This denies neither his steadfast love and fidelity nor his sinlessness.

Neither can Jesus' sinlessness negate his solidarity with sinners, as symbolically exemplified in his submission to the baptism of John. This says nothing about Jesus' sense of personal sin, nor his consciousness. It merely affirms his choice to identify himself with Israel's need for repentance and his solidarity with the people. As Joseph Fitzmyer writes, "Jesus' submission to the Baptist's washing as a sign of repentance for the remission of sins implies at least his identification of himself with sinful humanity seeking a way of righteousness given by God through John. Whether it was meant to express an awareness of sin on the part of Jesus himself is another matter."[50] No doctrine of Jesus' sinlessness can break that bond of solidarity between Jesus and the people.

---

[48]Cf. Pittenger, *Christology Reconsidered,* 45–65.

[49]Goergen, *The Mission and Ministry of Jesus,* 116–29.

[50]Joseph A. Fitzmyer, *A Christological Catechism, New Testament Answers* (New York: Paulist Press, 1982) 43.

Jesus' sinlessness does not deny that he took on the consequences of sin, that he entered into the thick of our sinful human condition. If Jesus himself was not personally a sinner, he nevertheless wrestled with the effects of sin. He was affected by the sin of the world, the human condition, passive original sin *(peccatum originale originatum);*[51] it was in fact the sin of the world that put him to death. And for Paul, death itself is a consequence of sin (Rom 5). One can too quickly interpret Jesus' sinlessness as his assumption of a pure human nature, unaffected by the history of the world, an ahistorical nature, like Adam's before the Fall. Yet the Scriptures affirm his identity with our situation (Heb 4:15); Paul writes to the Corinthians, 'For our sake he made him to be sin who knew no sin" (2 Cor 5:21a); and John says the Word became *sarx* (John 1:14). This identification of Jesus (of the Word) with our fallen humanity is clear in the Orthodox tradition and John of Damascus. For them the falsity of the Aphthartodocetists' position is not that the latter conceived of Christ's humanity as sinless but that they conceived of it as alien to the consequences of Adam's sin.[52] Jesus did not assume some kind of "ideal humanity" but the real human condition within which each of us struggles. Thus the sinlessness of Jesus does not deny Jesus' humanness, the reality of his struggle, his solidarity with sinners, and his taking on our human condition. What the sinlessness of Jesus does mean is our next question.

We must keep in mind that historically there has not been only one interpretation of Jesus' sinlessness. Here as elsewhere in Christology a certain pluralism prevails. There have been two primary opinions, or ways of focusing the question: sinlessness understood as *impeccabilitas* (impeccability, that it was not possible for Jesus to sin, *non posse peccare*) and as *impeccantia* (not actually sinning, Jesus could have sinned but did not, *posse non peccare*).

The former interpretation goes back at least to Origen in the third century, for whom Christ's union with the Logos meant his impeccability *(On First Principles* 2. 6. 5).[53] Augustine followed

[51]Cf. Piet Schoonenberg, *Man and Sin,* trans. Joseph Donceel (South Bend, Ind.: University of Notre Dame Press, 1965).

[52]Meyendorff, *Christ in Eastern Christian Thought,* 165–67.

[53]Johannes Quasten, *The Ante-Nicene Literature after Irenaeus,* vol. 2 of *Patrology* (Westminster, Md.: The Newman Press, 1965) 80.

Origen in this regard (*On the Sinful State* 2. 11. 16), and this interpretation has since been predominant. A fourth-century *Commentary on the Psalms,* however, recognizes only Christ's actual lack of sin *(impeccantia)* and not the impossibility of his sinning.[54] This was the opinion of Theodore of Mopsuestia as well: Christ was not sinless without effort, struggle; it was possible for him to sin but he did not.[55] Yet the classical Christian perspective on this question was that of *impeccabilitas,* to which medieval theology gave much attention.[56]

Each opinion can present a cogent theological argument. Christ's sinlessness understood as *impeccabilitas* is more in accord with a Christology from above; *impeccantia* ordinarily is the perspective of Christologies from below. But in a Christology that respects both methodologies, and accepts both a hypostatic union and *kenosis,* it is not easy to see how one might best understand Christ's sinlessness.

Certainly, if we look at Jesus as the Word incarnate, as hypostatically in union with God, as full of grace, the more logical opinion appears to be that Christ could not have sinned any more than God can sin. The impossibility of Jesus' sinning is simply an effect of his being the Word and of the hypostatic union.

And yet, if we accept the reality of the two natures, and want to do justice to the human nature, will, and freedom of Christ, it would seem that we must affirm the possibility of his sinning, even if he did not. What was at stake in Christ's sinning was his not being the redeemer, or not in fact making God incarnate, but that was a risk that God took: God respected human freedom and human nature at all costs. Christ was either free, and thus free to sin, or not truly free, and then the human nature of Christ played no real role in salvation.

The one opinion *(impeccantia)* seems to diminish the divinity of Christ; the other *(impeccabilitas),* his humanity. We seem to be caught in the Christological dilemma of how to affirm the reality of both natures without dismissing the reality of the union nor the reality of the *kenosis.* Christ is the Logos, and yet is also truly one of us.

[54]Grillmeier, *Christ in Christian Tradition,* 364.

[55]Johannes Quasten, *The Golden Age of Greek Patristic Literature,* vol. 3 of *Patrology* (Westminster, Md.: The Newman Press, 1966) 417.

[56]For the opinion of Aquinas, see III *Sent* 12, 1; and *ST* III, 14, 1-2.

Most modern Christology would be inclined to interpret the sinlessness of Jesus as *impeccantia* rather than *impeccabilitas.* As Schoonenberg comments, "Scripture tells us that Jesus *did not sin,* but it does not say whether he *could* sin or not."[57] Scripture's witness is certainly of prime importance; the primary references are Hebrews 4:15; 2 Corinthians 5:21; and 1 Peter 2:22.

1 Peter 2:21-22 states, "For to this you have been called, because Christ also suffered for you, leaving you an example, that you should follow in his steps. He committed no sin; no guile was found on his lips." This latter expression parallels the Gospel of John's description of Nathanael: "Jesus saw Nathanael coming to him, and said to him, 'Behold, an Israelite indeed, in whom is no guile' " (1:47). The Greek word *dolos* is used in both cases. Being without sin and without guile appear comparable, and the latter applicable beyond Jesus alone. But the Johannine tradition elsewhere lends itself to a theology of the sinlessness of the believer in imitation of the sinlessness of God's Son (1 John 3:6, 9; 5:18).[58] "No one born of God commits sin; for God's nature abides in him, and he cannot sin because he is born of God" (3:9). Sinlessness most properly describes *the* Son of God, but can also describe all those who are born from above.

2 Corinthians 5:21 ("For our sake he made him to be sin who knew no sin, so that in him we might become the righteousness of God") is an expression of the Adam/Christ contrast so central to Pauline Christology and asserts Jesus' identity with us. The sinless one, the one who knew no sin, is the earthly Jesus (unless one maintains that there is already the concept of pre-existence in Paul). He shared fully in the fallenness of humanity. The language implies a sacrifice or a sin offering. The sinless Jesus became one with our sinful human condition, so that we might become one with him and through him share in the very righteousness of God. Jesus is both sinless and one of us, sharing in the condition of fallen humanity—yet without sinning himself.

The latter is the point emphasized in Hebrews 4:15 ("one who in every respect has been tempted as we are, yet without sin"). Jesus is like us in every way, except for sin. He is the sinless one; we are the sinful ones. In Hebrews we also have the language of

---

[57]Schoonenberg, *The Christ,* 142.

[58]Cf. Raymond Brown, *The Epistles of John,* Anchor Bible 30 (Garden City, N.Y.: Doubleday and Co., 1982) 81–83 and note on 1 John 3:9c and d, 411–16.

sacrifice and sin offering ("Christ, having been offered once to bear the sins of humankind," 9:28). The sinlessness of Jesus in this case need not imply that the author of Hebrews saw Jesus as completely free of any moral offense. Jesus is the supreme high priest. On the Day of Atonement, the high priest offered a bull as a sin offering for himself, so that he might be free from sin before ministering on behalf of the people. In a similar vein, Jesus' sin offering, the crucifixion, made him sinless.[59]

The biblical references themselves do not answer all our questions about Jesus' sinlessness. Is Jesus alone sinless, or can others be so described? Does sinlessness imply moral perfection? Is Jesus sinless because of the sin offering, his death, that he offered? Do the texts imply *impeccabilitas, impeccantia,* or something else? In all the texts where Jesus' sinlessness is referred to, his relationship to us and identity with us is also stressed. Jesus' sinlessness does not make him less one of us or less in solidarity with our condition.

The question then is not whether Jesus was sinless, but rather what his sinlessness means. There are several ways to answer the question: (1) It means Jesus' fidelity, obedience, servanthood, that his human will was always to do the will of his heavenly Father. As C.F.D. Moule writes, "What Israel was meant to be in relation to God, Israel had failed to be; but Jesus had succeeded."[60] (2) Sinlessness is a symbol and a consequence of Jesus' divinity, that Jesus was one with God. Pannenberg writes, "Jesus' personal community and unity with God, his dedication to God to the point that his own freedom became identical with his divine mission and the Father's will for him, includes his freedom from all sin."[61] (3) It means that Jesus was *truly* human, an exemplification of what humanity is intended to be. Far from making Jesus less than human, his sinlessness is a symbol of a humanity achieved. As Monika Hellwig puts it, "In him we see what human life is intended to be in the image and likeness of God."[62]

[59]George Wesley Buchanan, *To the Hebrews* (Garden City, N.Y.: Doubleday and Co., 1972) 81.

[60]C.F.D. Moule, *The Origin of Christology* (Cambridge: Cambridge University Press, 1977) 151.

[61]Pannenberg, *Jesus, God and Man* 354.

[62]Monika Hellwig, *Sign of Reconciliation and Conversion,* Message of the Sacra-

To speak in a traditional vein, along the lines of a Christology from above, Christ assumes a concrete, particular human nature; but human nature has a history, and Christ's assumption of a human nature means his becoming a part of history and having a history of his own. The question is not so much about the particular human nature that Christ assumed, but about the human condition he chose to be a part of. To what degree did Christ take on our condition? The Scriptures agree: he was completely one of us.

Yet this does not mean that Christ's mode of existence in the midst of our human condition was the same as ours. Christ's condition, situation, and world was the same as ours, but his way of being there was different. His way of being in the world or mode of existence was sinless (or to use Heideggerian language, authentic);[63] *our* mode is sinful. The sinless one became sin for us: this does not mean that he adopted our sinful mode of existence, but rather that he became fully a part of our sinful condition, without losing his rootedness in the Father. The Word became *sarx;* that is, immersed itself in our concrete existential humanity, but without his freedom being destroyed. There are, in other words, two modes of taking on sin, Christ's and ours, or rather that exemplified in the last *adam* and that exemplified by the first Adam. Christ defeats sin and preserves his humanity. Adam was defeated by sin and lost his.

The sinlessness of Jesus means that he was both human and divine. His life did not contribute to the history of sin. The effect of his life was in fact to uproot the hold that sin had on the world. In the totality of his life—which does not deny the anguish, doubts, and struggles of his day-by-day existence—he was one who remained unconditionally God's, whose very being was being-towards-God. The concept of *sinner* does not help us understand Jesus, for the meaning of Jesus is that of one who did not become alienated from his own divinity. Jesus reveals sin to be what it is—alienation from one's own divinity. He remained rooted in God, as God's very own, personal human nature.

ments 4 (Wilmington, Del.: Michael Glazier, 1982) 22. For this same point, see Murphy-O'Connor, *Becoming Human Together*.

[63]For an excellent development of the contrast between authentic and inauthentic existence in Paul, along Heideggerian lines, see Murphy-O'Connor, *Becoming Human Together*.

In Jesus, divinity (grace if you will) and humanity (freedom) were united. God could not have done what was accomplished in and through Christ without the free cooperation of Jesus as a human being; and Jesus, as a human being, could not have done it without God. Kenotically, the power of God did not overwhelm the human freedom of the man Jesus. In our exploration of the meaning of Jesus' sinlessness, we are thus led to two values: Jesus' freedom and his integration (integrity).

There is no question but that one of the characteristics of Jesus, along with his association with social outcasts, his way of praying, and his obedient servanthood, was his remarkable freedom. This seems to be the way Paul understood Jesus, even if Paul had not been a disciple when Jesus was still in the flesh. For Paul, Jesus means freedom. To some degree this insight has continued throughout Christian history, even if at times the Christian Churches have felt uncomfortable with it. Ernst Käsemann comments, "The whole history of the church down to our own time reflects a like annoyance at his peculiar freedom."[64] And Rudolf Pesch observes, "The freedom of Jesus turns out to be the central christological topic in an historical and critical inquiry into Jesus, his aims and actions, his history, his effect, his person. Freedom now appears as Jesus' characteristic quality, and the one which alone makes it possible to understand in their true light phenomena such as his obedience, his doing of God's will and his acting in subordination to the divine 'must' *(dei)*."[65]

We see examples of Jesus' freedom, of Jesus himself as a liberated person, a person liberated by the Spirit of God, in his freedom to be with others, with many diverse kinds of others, from the uneducated to the scribes, from tax collectors to Zealots, from a leper to a Roman soldier, from women to Samaritans; in his relationship to God, free to address God as "Abba"; and in his sense of authority, courage, prophetic self-assurance, and willingness to speak on God's behalf. Jesus comes across as one who has been grasped by the reign of God, by God, in such a way that he has been freed, is free. His freedom is rooted in his faith. Jesus was a man of faith, a free person.

[64]Ernst Käsemann, *Jesus Means Freedom* (Philadelphia: Fortress Press, 1969) 17.

[65]Rudolf Pesch, "Jesus, a Free Man," in *Jesus Christ and Human Freedom,* ed. Edward Schillebeeckx and Bas van Iersel, Concilium 93 (New York: Herder and Herder, 1974) 57.

Yet it is one thing to recognize the freedom of Jesus, and still another to specify what it consists in. Mortimer Adler, in his extensive research on *freedom* in the history of thought, has identified four primary meanings.[66] Though different, they are not incompatible. However, the tendency in the Anglo-American tradition has been to limit freedom to free choice.

The first and ancient understanding of freedom is as power, as the capacity to do the good, as virtue. Freedom is not fundamentally choice, but the ability to do what one ought. The obstacles to such freedom are internal realities: not external circumstances, but conditions such as ignorance, passion, attachments. Freedom is a freedom from these internal realities and a freedom for seeking the good. Choices as such do not make one more free; they may only reflect one's enslavement. This is an interior or moral freedom. Only the virtuous are truly free.

A second meaning of freedom is that of self-determination, or what we call "free will." This kind of freedom—will—is possessed by all. It is not as such prevented by external circumstances or internal states. In this second meaning, all human beings are free, whether they are good or bad. It is a part of human nature, whereas according to the first meaning only the good are really free. The second freedom is the capacity to will, the capacity for voluntary in contrast to involuntary action.

A third freedom is that which derives from favorable external circumstances. If internal realities are seen as the obstacles to freedom in the first sense, external circumstances are the obstacles to freedom in this third sense. The first two meanings are actually the more classical in the West, but this third sense of freedom is the primary meaning in the Anglo-American philosophical tradition. Freedom here implies being able to choose as one pleases. Certain external realities are essential if one is to be free. Freedom is a freedom from those things that obstruct or impede my being able to do as I please. This is a freedom among alternatives and involves choices. Both the second and third freedoms pertain to choice.

Freedom can be seen as virtue, will, or choice. There is a fourth meaning which can be called "political liberty," which is the right

---

[66]Cf. Mortimer J. Adler, *The Idea of Freedm,* 2 vols. (Westport, Conn.: Greenwood Press, 1958 and 1961).

of citizens to participate in self-government and law making. One may not be politically free, and yet be free in one of the other senses, especially in one of the first two.

As stated, these freedoms are not necessarily exclusive of each other. Thomas Aquinas embraced all four of them in some form. The first meaning is that found especially in the Platonic and Stoic traditions, the second in Aristotle, the third in British and American philosophers, and in some combination or other these are the primary meanings of freedom in the history of philosophy.

One can now see that freedom is not simply one thing, and the question of the freedom of Jesus is not simple. According to the fourth meaning, Jesus was not free. He did not have political liberty. He lived in a Roman-occupied Palestine. But the applicability of the other meanings of freedom is more difficult to ascertain. If we understand the freedom of Jesus in the first sense, then the sinlessness of Jesus as *impeccabilitas* makes complete sense. Because Jesus was free, truly and completely, he necessarily chose the good. He was not able to sin, simply because he was completely free. *Impeccabilitas* does not detract from freedom or humanness—it *is* freedom and humanness, the incapacity to do evil because of one's freedom to do good. Choices, from this perspective, only manifest false freedom.

This is in fact close to the perspective of Maximus the Confessor. He distinguished between natural will *(thelēma physikon)* and the deliberative will or choice *(thelēma gnōmikon),* the latter simply being a consequence of sin.[67] Natural will, which flows from nature, conforms with divine freedom and is unable to do anything but the good. Choices do not make one more free. The capacity (through the influence of the Holy Spirit, or in the West one would say by grace) to conform oneself to God's will is freedom. The possibility of choosing between good and evil is not essential to human freedom, but an effect of sin.

Pannenberg, in spite of his Christology from below, follows this same line of thinking: "The totality of Jesus' dedication to the Father in dedication to his eschatological mission excludes any thought of a freedom of choice by the man Jesus over against God, as if there would have been for Jesus 'other possibilities' alongside his divine mission that were passed over only in his own

[67]Cf. Meyendorff, *Christ in Eastern Christian Thought,* 137–38; Pannenberg, *Jesus, God and Man,* 349–50 n. 49.

unfounded free decision.''[68] ''Apparently the choice of his mission of proclaiming the eschatological imminence of God as the beginning of salvation meant for Jesus the content of his freedom to such an extent that no other choice, no other possibility could remain open for his freedom beside it.''[69]

No matter how attractive and profound this perspective is (and it is attractive, and a profound critique of many modern concepts of freedom), I think that Jesus' sinlessness and thus freedom lay more in the direction of *impeccantia,* though I prefer a combination of both. Freedom of choice is a secondary kind of freedom, and a consequence of sin; there is a free will which is natural to humankind, but as natural and free it chooses the good. But it is precisely because freedom as choice is a consequence of sin that we attribute it to Christ—for Christ took on our sinful, human condition, and the sin-infected freedom which accompanies that.

Christ's freedom is an *impeccantia* (based on his having genuine choices to make), and an *impeccabilitas*—but the latter is something only won at the cost of pain and growth, something Jesus came to only at the end of his life, something he achieved in the course of his life, something we see when we look back later at the totality of his life. It was a freedom gained, as he achieved a humanity and humanness heretofore unknown, as he became another *adam,* as he restored to humanity its being an image of God. Pannenberg suggests, ''The thesis of a meritorious freedom of choice for Jesus' human will . . . would make his unity with God a work of his human will instead of letting that unity be something that happened to him, which he experienced as having come from God.''[70] But that is what Jesus' freedom is: meritorious, an accomplishment of Jesus' human will and God's grace. Redemption was not just a *fait accompli* in which the human Jesus only played a passive role.[71] Jesus' unity with

[68]Pannenberg, *Jesus, God and Man,* 349.

[69]Ibid., 353.

[70]Ibid., 350–51.

[71]E.g., see F. X. Durwell, *The Resurrection* (New York: Sheed and Ward, 1960) xviii, ''Christ as man was free, and the redemptive purpose was accomplished only through the loving obedience with which he freely responded as man to the divine will. The human act of love in Christ is essential to the mystery of redemption.''

God was something that happened to him (the hypostatic unity), but also something that did not remove his complete identification with our condition (the kenotic incarnation), and thus was a unity gained, preserved, as well as given. At the end of his life and struggle one can say that Jesus was incapable of sin *(impeccabilitas)* because he had become free, but that his life was a struggle to achieve that freedom. In the end sin was defeated, but not because he had not entered into battle with it. Jesus *was* free as we are free, but *became* free as we ought to be. He became fully free and truly human. In the end he was able to will only his Father's will, but that was a hard-won victory as he struggled amid the kind of freedom that we have—and showed us the way to true freedom.

Once we accept Jesus' *impeccantia* as his journey, ordeal, and struggle toward an even greater freedom, *impeccabilitas,* we must then follow this in all its implications. Jesus could have sinned but did not, could have sinned due to the freedom of choice which was his by the Word's entrance into our sinful human condition. Sin would have meant that Jesus had alienated himself from himself, that he would not have been who he was, that he was not being true to his deepest self, that he had become estranged from his own divinity—that he would not have become who he was. Had Jesus sinned, no incarnation, for, although the Word united itself hypostatically with a human nature, that union had to be continually and freely ratified throughout Jesus' life. The incarnation was only progressively realized and took a lifetime, and a death, to accomplish. As Michael Cook phrases it:

> But, Jesus' mission was not only to call *us* to respond to the Father's love. He himself had first to say *Amen* to his *Abba.* If we do not admit this, then I do not think that we can take Jesus' humanness seriously; then God is not truly working in and through his humanness but is only using it as an extrinsic instrument for the sake of something else. Hence, things could have happened differently in the earthly ministry of Jesus: his temptations were real! The question, finally is: to what extent is Jesus' humanity operative in our salvation, i.e., to what extent does his humanness truly mediate our salvation, and, cor-

respondingly, to what extent are we willing to conceive God's
risk in creating human freedom?[72]

In the end, the pursuit of Jesus' freedom and sinlessness lead
us in the same direction as the pursuit of his uniqueness: toward
an integration of human nature and divine nature. Jesus' sinlessness refers equally to both: he was one with God, hypostatically
God in the flesh; and he was one with us, fully human, and therefore without sin. The sinlessness of Jesus is not so much a symbol of his divinity and his humanity as separable realities, but a
symbol for them precisely in their unity. Jesus reveals that to be
human is to be divine. The question is not, how could Jesus be
both human and divine? but rather, how can we not be? The answer to the latter question is sin. Because he was sinless, Jesus
was both human and divine, and he reveals the nature of both.
No longer are we ruled simply by our presuppositions or precon-
ception. Jesus reveals that being human is being for God and being divine is being for others. The kind of being that we are is
structured for God. And the kind of being that God is means being totally for others. Hence Jesus is both *for* others and *in* God
(ad alios per Deum), the Human One, a Divine Person.

This integration of the human and the divine that Jesus' sinlessness symbolizes and his life actualized is the basis for the *communicatio idiomatum.* Jesus reveals in his human nature who God
is in his divine nature, and the human properties of Jesus are
properties of God as well. Jesus means freedom, compassion,
generosity, fidelity—namely, love, or the power of love. This
description of Jesus is a perfect description of God.[73]

Ultimately Jesus' sinlessness refers neither to possibility *(impeccabilitas, peccabilitas),* nor to activity *(impeccantia, peccan-
tia),* but to symbol. This is why it remains significant to Christian
faith. It is a symbol of his humanity and divinity, of his freedom
and his integration, of his uniqueness. While being human as we
are, his mode of existence was different: he was in the form of
God, a perfect image, an *adam*—all that we are intended to be.
Jesus was a symbol speaking with clarity (a dimension of the
Christ to which we must turn shortly).

[72]Michael Cook, *The Jesus of Faith, A Study in Christology* (New York: Paulist
Press, 1981) 180.

[73]Cf. Goergen, *The Power of Love.*

In Conclusion

Jesus' humanness and human experiences were no different from ours, except for his "sinlessness," which did not make him less of a human being but rather more truly human.

Although perspicacious, prophetically insightful, spiritually and religiously sensitive, and biblically wise, he was not omniscient. God was present to him (he *was* God's presence) in accord with human nature and in the midst of the existential, historical human condition. "God's knowledge" was not simply covered with human clothing. Rather, God, or better God's Word, came to be in a new incarnate mode of existence—as one of us.

Although Jesus worked marvelous deeds, deeds of power, and although God's power was at work in him, he was not omnipotent in the way that we ordinarily associate with God's transcendent mode of being. God's power was both contained and released from within God's incarnate mode of existence, a particular human nature. God was both revealed and concealed through Jesus' true humanity. Jesus' *human* nature was God's incarnate mode of presence. Jesus was both God's human nature and a truly human nature or being.

Christian faith, shortly after the resurrection, came in varied ways to affirm Jesus' uniqueness within the human race—clearly a meta-historiographical conviction or judgment. Jesus' followers, however, simply saw in him a pre-eminence, leaving open the question of how it may be best to try to articulate, interpret, or understand that uniqueness.

I have attempted here to "capture," or "signify," or "symbolize" that uniqueness by retaining the affirmation of Jesus' sinlessness (again a meta-historiographical statement), a sinlessness best characterized as Jesus' absolute freedom and integration.

Jesus both was free, and became free: his freedom was something that needed to be reaffirmed, regained, reowned at every stage of his life and human growth. It was not to be taken for granted, as given to him once and for all. Jesus became absolutely free (free not to sin) because of his solidarity, unity (hypostatic union) with God. Jesus became what/who he was. His freedom was the actualization, integration, manifestation of his (hypostatic) union with God.

Jesus' (hypostatic) unity with God was a unique bestowal of grace. It was the grace of union, a most intense and unsurpassable grace. The effect of this unique grace was Jesus' freedom and thus sinlessness. But, as with all of us, just as grace is operative, so we must be co-operative. Grace and nature work together. Grace does not destroy nature but perfects it. It is grace that makes us free. Jesus' (hypostatic) unity with God is the supreme instance of grace, nature, and freedom at one with each other.

Through grace we necessarily choose the good freely.[74]

True freedom is a paradox. It is both the capacity to sin and the inability to sin.

Jesus was truly human, truly free, necessarily sinless.

Jesus' freedom and sinlessness are visible only in an act of faith. Like the resurrection of Jesus, they are meta-historiographical historical facts: affirmations of faith that seek to be understood or interpreted theologically.

Jesus' sinlessness and absolute freedom (his uniqueness) were both a point of contact, solidarity, identity with humanity and a point of separation, difference, pain. Jesus felt what not being a sinner meant, felt the impact and implications of his freedom, felt what it was like to be different. Jesus was both "at home" with humanity and "a stranger" in our midst. He felt this strangeness that he embraced freely.

So often it is our sinfulness (forms of false power) that connects us with each other, that is the basis of in-group solidarity. And yet there was no way in which Jesus could be connected with us in these false ways, no way in which he could have sinned, not even in order to be more one of us. He felt both this connectedness and disconnectedness with us. He felt it painfully, a pain uniquely his—the pain of being divine.

We ordinarily do not think of God as experiencing pain, or as having feelings. We have traditionally spoken of God as impassible and immutable. Yet the God of the Scriptures acts, feels, responds. Certainly to speak of God as feeling is to speak analogously, as it is to speak of God as thinking. To speak of God at all is a risk, yet we must do so—to do justice to our human experiences of God and to do justice to God as self-communicating. We speak about God as love, about God as happy, of the wisdom of God, and of the joy or compassion or generosity or fidelity of God, and so we can likewise speak analogously of the

[74]Ibid., 192–213.

pain of God.[75] In fact we can speak of God's capacity for pain and suffering as infinite. This is what is revealed in the cross: the pain of God, the pain from loving, the non-indifference of God, how much God cares.[76] The revelation of a God who cares (Immanuel) is what the incarnation is all about.

[75]Cf. Gerald Vann, *The Pain of Christ and the Sorrow of God* (Oxford: Black-friars Pub., 1947) esp. ch. 7, "The Sorrow of God," 59–75.

[76]Cf. Goergen, *The Power of Love, 192–213.*

6

The Historiographical Jesus
and the Symbolic Christ

Mary Douglas has given us cause for concern: "One of the gravest problems of our day is the lack of commitment to common symbols. If this were all, there would be little to say. If it were merely a matter of our fragmentation into small groups, each committed to its proper symbolic forms, the case would be simple to understand. But more mysterious is a wide-spread, explicit rejection of rituals as such."[1]

At the same time that symbol and ritual have become problematic for us at the levels of culture and life, however, they have become the object of reflective scrutiny. Susanne Langer sees symbolism as the key to a new philosophical epoch, the generative idea in epistemology, a notion fundamental to any conception of a mental life that is characteristically human. "Symbolization is the essential act of mind; and mind takes in more than what is commonly called thought. Only certain products of the symbol-making brain can be used according to the canons of discursive reasoning. In every mind there is an enormous store of other symbolic material, which is put to different uses or perhaps even to no use at all—a mere result of spontaneous brain activity, a reserve fund of conceptions, a surplus of mental wealth."[2]

[1]Mary Douglas, *Natural Symbols, Explorations in Cosmology* (London: Barrie and Jenkins, 1973) 19.

[2]Susanne K. Langer, *Philosophy in a New Key* (Cambridge: Harvard University Press, 1963) 41.

Ernst Cassirer's philosophy of human culture made symbol the clue to specifically human reality, the distinctive mark of human life. The human person is not confined to sense data or sense knowledge. The ability to symbolize makes another kind of knowledge possible—of which language, myth, art, religion, science, and history are all but varied forms. For Cassirer, specifically human knowledge is symbolic knowledge.[3]

By way of example, one can contrast the world of art and the world of science. Both are human, cultural, symbolic forms of knowing. "Heraclitus' saying that the sun is new every day is true for the sun of the artist if not for the sun of the scientist."[4] Science is an abbreviation of reality, art an intensification; science depends upon acts of objectification, art upon acts of contemplation. Art too is knowledge, but a specific kind of knowledge. "The conceptual interpretation of science does not preclude the intuitive interpretation of art. . . . It is a characteristic of the nature of man that he is not limited to one specific and single approach to reality but can choose his point of view and so pass from one aspect of things to another."[5]

In volume 2 of this series I spoke about two interrelated, specifically human kinds of knowledge: objective and personal.[6] According to Michael Polanyi both are forms of personal knowledge. Yet the historiographer and the poet place different value on the sense of objectivity and on the personal element. However different, both are forms of symbolic knowledge.

According to Cassirer, the varied symbolic forms that constitute human life cannot be reduced to one another, but neither are they a disparate aggregate. They all manifest the fundamental task of harmonizing two indispensable forces, a conservative tendency toward stabilization and a rejuvenating tendency toward renovation and originality. The varied symbolic forms complement each other; they are interdependent.

---

[3]Cf. Ernst Cassirer, *An Essay on Man, An Introduction to a Philosophy of Human Culture* (New Haven: Yale University Press, 1944). Also his more extensive treatment, *The Philosophy of Symbolic Forms,* 3 vols. (New Haven: Yale University Press, 1953-1957).

[4]Cassirer, *An Essay on Man,* 144.

[5]Ibid., 170.

[6]Goergen, *The Death and Resurrection of Jesus,* 183-203.

Among symbols (signals, signs), a first distinction is made with respect to animal communication and human communication. Human communication is distinctive. We cannot reduce it to being of the same order as the forms of communication among other animals. We distinguish between the signals by which other animals communicate and the symbols which form the basis of human communication. This is basic to the distinction between anthroposemiotics and zoosemiotics.[7]

Within the world of human culture, I myself distinguish three kinds of symbols or ways in which signs and symbols function: (1) simple signs, whether natural or conventional; (2) tensive symbols, whether personal, social, or archetypal; and (3) metapersonal symbolic realities. Our concern will primarily be with the last, but we must clarify the others first.

We can begin to grasp the difference between the simple sign and the tensive symbol by reference to Philip Wheelwright's distinction between two kinds of language, block or steno language and fluid or tensive language.[8] Wheelwright's distinction does not refer to language in an exclusively verbal sense, but includes nonverbal signs and symbols as well, such as images or gestures. And there is no clear cut, categorical division between the two; they differ not so much in kind as in degree. Wheelwright's distinction can also be contrasted with my previous distinction between objective and personal knowledge—two kinds of knowledge manifesting themselves in two kinds of language.

Steno language is exact, limiting, precise, restrictive, representational. It diminishes the connotative richness of language. A steno meaning can be shared or understood in almost exactly the same way by a very large group, in theory by all people who use the same language. Examples would include words like *tree,* or *chien,* or *circle,* or a mathematical symbol, or a particular gesture. "Scientific" and "logical" language are steno by intent, not simply as a result of habit, for they consciously seek to eliminate ambiguity as far as possible; they seek precision. Steno language is the appropriate vehicle for objective knowledge. If steno lan-

[7]Cf. John Deely, *Introducing Semiotic, Its History and Doctrine* (Bloomington, Ind.: Indiana University Press, 1982).

[8]Cf. Philip Wheelwright, *Metaphor and Reality* (Bloomington, Ind.: Indiana University Press, 1962); and *The Burning Fountain, A Study in the Language of Symbolism* (Bloomington, Ind.: Indiana University Press, 1954).

guage is taken as the model for all language, however, the result is a semantic form of positivism.

Tensive language is more fluid, open, "poetic," rich, and presentational rather than representational. Tensive language can suggest more than one meaning simultaneously (plurisignification). It is more suited to express the unique. "Non-poetic language is not adapted to the unique; its natural reference is to ideas and perceptions that are publicly and easily shared."[9] "Poetic" language contrasts with "scientific" language. Images and metaphors are the ingredients or units of tensive language.

All language, of course, is symbolic; it functions as a system of signs. These signs, however, can be simple signs or tensive symbols, or to use Wheelwright's designations, steno language or tensive language. A sign or symbol can never be considered by itself alone. It "is employed to *mean,* to *intend,* to *stand proxy for,* something beyond itself."[10] What a simple sign, or steno or "scientific" or "logical" language means or intends, however, stands in contrast to what a tensive symbol or tensive language expresses. A public exactitude and an uncompromising identity of reference is the nature of steno language—its strength and its weakness we might add. Tensive language does not seek the same kind of exactness. One might say that it is exact in a different way. Its strength is that it draws upon multiple associations, often subconsciously interrelated. Tensive language taps a "stored up potential of semantic energy."[11]

The same word or reality may function in both ways. Consider the flag, or the cross. Each can function as a steno symbol or tensive symbol; each can denote a particular country or citizenship, or particular faith or religious practice, but each can also connote a wide variety of other associations.

---

[9]Wheelwright, *Metaphor and Reality,* 50.

[10]Ibid., 29.

[11]Ibid., 94; see 92–98. Expressions such as *sign, symbol,* and *referent* provoke much debate today in linguistic and semantic theory. I make my own use of the expressions clear in the text. For further discussion, see F. W. Dillistone, *The Power of Symbols in Religion and Culture* (New York: Crossroad, 1986); Loretta Dornisch, *Faith and Philosophy in the Writings of Paul Ricoeur* (Lewiston: The Edwin Mellen Press, 1990); Christopher Norris, *The Context of Faculties: Deconstruction, Philosophy, and Theory* (New York: Methuen, 1985).

Wheelwright contrasts steno and tensive, representational and presentational language. This is akin to Susanne Langer's distinction between discursive and presentational symbolic forms. Objective knowledge, steno language, and discursive forms, while not exact synonyms, do share much in common; as do personal knowledge, tensive language, and presentational forms. As Langer observes, the form that language takes "requires us to string out our ideas even though their objects rest one within the other; as pieces of clothing that are actually worn one over the other have to be strung side by side on the clothesline. This property of verbal symbolism is known as *discursiveness;* by reason of it, only thoughts which can be arranged on this peculiar order can be spoken at all."[12] Yet it would be a mistake to limit thought, intuition, experience only to that which can be expressed by discursive forms. Poetry is the use of language to express what is inexpressible discursively. There are things in the world of our experience for which discursive forms of expression are ill-suited.

For example, visual forms—lines, colors, shapes—are not discursive. "The laws that govern this sort of articulation are altogether different from the laws of syntax that govern language. . . . They [visual forms] do not present their constituents successively, but simultaneously, so the relations determining visual structure are grasped in one act of vision."[13] Georgia O'Keeffe once wrote: "The meaning of a word—to me—is not as exact as the meaning of a color. Colors and shapes make a more definite statement than words."[14]

There can be no dictionary for the meaning of a line or a shade of color, no fixed meaning for them. "There are different media of graphic representation, but their respective elements cannot be brought into one-to-one correlation with each other, as in language: *'Chien'* = 'dog,' *'moi'* = 'me,' etc. There is no standard key for translating sculpture into painting, or drawing into inkwash because their equivalence rests on their common *total reference,* not on bit-for-bit equivalences of parts such as underlie a

[12]Langer, *Philosophy in a New Key,* 81; see 79–102.

[13]Ibid., 93.

[14]Georgia O'Keeffe, *Georgia O'Keeffe* (New York: Viking Press, 1976). Also see Laurie Lisle, *Portrait of an Artist, a Biography of Georgia O'Keeffe* (New York: Washington Square Press, 1980).

literal translation."[15] Although there may not be in fact such a thing as one-to-one correspondence, there are equivalencies. Discursive language, like steno language, implies these proximate equivalencies; its foundation is denotation. Tensive language lives by connotation. Language tends to be discursive, although poetic and religious language are not necessarily so. Religious language, particularly mystical language, is more like art and music which are presentational rather than representational or discursive. Here we do well to recall Cassirer's observation that in all symbolic forms there are two tendencies: a conservative tendency toward stability and a rejuvenating tendency toward originality.

A simple sign is a symbolic form that is based upon some equivalence between the sign and the concept to which it refers. *This* indicates or means *that*. It is denotative. A tensive symbol is connotative, involves a plurality of significations, and communicates that to which it refers less discursively. It is a symbol at a fuller and richer level.[16]

Simple signs can be further classed as natural or conventional; tensive symbols can be so classed as well but it is less helpful to do so. Signification is a process by which something refers someone to something else. It is the nature of a sign to bring to mind something other than itself. A natural sign is a reality which, by its very nature, signifies something else. A cloud suggests the possibility of rain; smoke implies fire; a groan signifies pain. Animals other than human beings may read many of the natural signs.

[15]Langer, *Philosophy in a New Key,* 96. See the references in n. 11 above as well.

[16]Although I refer to Langer, Cassirer, Wheelwright, and others, my own classifications or distinctions are not to be simply identified with theirs; their insights simply help me to clarify my own preferred way of speaking. Langer, for example, distinguishes two aspects of meaning, logical (*it* means) and psychological (*I* mean). Her primary concern is with logical meaning which she discusses in terms of a distinction between sign and symbol. Symbolization can mean either denotation or connotation. Thus, for Langer, the three most common meanings of logical meaning are signification, denotation, and connotation. My own approach at this point is between what I call simple signs and tensive symbols. My simple sign has similarities to her use of the word "sign," but also to some aspects of her "denotation." My tensive symbol has similarities to some aspects of her "connotation" as well as what she calls "psychological meaning." Thus I do not want my own usage to be identified with anyone else's as such.

A conventional sign is one devised by human convention and deliberation. It is decided that something will stand for something else. Such human conventions are common and rest upon an agreed upon system. Traffic signals and signs are consequent upon human decisions by which they come to signify something. Much of human life is made up of conventional signs. Alphabets, language, mathematical symbols, even customs, rituals, and traditions all involve conventional signs.

Upon closer scrutiny, classifications such as these break down. Even natural signs must often be learned and cannot be abstracted from social experience. They admit a variety of meanings. Smoke may denote fire, but its concrete meaning can vary from culture to culture: a method of signaling and communication among navite Americans, proclaiming the progress of a papal election, coming from the windows of a farmyard barn, not to mention cigarette smoke or that of a charcoal grill. The dividing line between a natural and conventional sign is not always clear cut. Yet natural signs more directly and immediately refer someone to that which they signify.

A simple sign involves a relationship in which *this* means or signifies *that*. This is true of both natural and conventional signs. Smoke is a natural sign signifying fire. A whistle is an arbitrary or conventional sign signifying that the race is to begin. This does not mean that signs cannot be misinterpreted. "The misinterpretation of signs is the simplest form of *mistake.*"[17] A bell could mean someone at the front door, the back door, the telephone, your telephone, my telephone. It is not that the sign signifies more than one thing, but that one may misinterpret the one thing signified. *I* have made a mistake.

Tensive symbols can be classified as personal, social, and archetypal, based upon their comprehensiveness or breadth of appeal. A personal tensive symbol is one that has tensive meaning for a particular individual; it communicates personal meaning. A particular image or tree or setting or poem or proverb may evoke associations from my childhood; it means many things to me personally. *Remsen,* as a word or simple sign, denotes a particular town in western Iowa. As a personal tensive symbol, it connotes much more: it is where I was born and raised. As one

[17]Langer, *Philosophy in a New Key,* 59.

enters the town today, a billboard reads, "Welcome to Remsen, Not a Town, but a Way of Life." In other words, not simply a sign, but a tensive and personal symbol. In a similar fashion, a dream or its images may have personal meaning and significance. A word, an image, an aspect of nature, a work of art, or a particular profession could be personally symbolic for someone.

A social or corporate tensive symbol bears significance and meaning for a group—members of a community, a family, a race, a nation, a sexually distinctive group, a religious body—for example, the flag, school song, Notre Dame de Paris, Bible, football, cemetery, White House.

An archetype is a relatively universal tensive symbol; it conveys meaning to a large portion, if not all, of humankind. Archetypal symbols occur over and over in widely diverse cultures that are not directly historically connected. The sea, the sky, the earth, mother, mother earth, the phallus, blood, water, light, the circle, the number three—all move us in the direction of archetypal symbolism. Philip Wheelwright writes, "Of all archetypal symbols there is probably none more widespread and more immediately understandable than *light,* as symbolizing certain mental and spiritual qualities."[18] Water also, with its power to cleanse as well as to sustain life, has functioned as an archetypal religious symbol. The major transitions in life, the "rites of passage," also have an archetypal character, suggesting a cycle of death and rebirth. The circle archetype manifests itself in the images of the wheel, the halo, the lotus flower. Archetypes as symbols help us to enter into a deeper level of reality. Reality is not structured in order to be communicated or experienced by steno language or simple signs alone. There is more to reality than what just meets the eye. "Tensive symbols may perhaps offer hints about the nature of things which straightforward techniques must either ignore or distort. If reality is largely fluid and half paradoxical, steel nets are not the best instruments for taking samples of it."[19]

Every theology or philosophy has its presuppositions, implicit assumptions, perhaps an unclarified intuition. My own perspective is to see reality as having depth. Teilhard de Chardin, with his own brand of phenomenology, arrived at this same perspec-

---

[18]Wheelwright, *Metaphor and Reality,* 116.

[19]Ibid., 128.

tive on reality on the basis of his study of evolution and the human phenomenon. The world has two dimensions for Teilhard, the without and the within. Both always go together, and in fact unfold together.[20] Complexification at the level of the without is accompanied by an interiorization or centration at the level of the within.

Philosophy and theology have often spoken of layers to reality, or seen some realities as more real than others, and even spoken of reality in terms of this world and another world. There is no need to speak in this fashion, however, and we do so less and less. There is only one world, this world, but there is more to this world than that which meets the eye. There is the whole world of the within as well as the worlds yet to come. But all are part of one world which is continually in the process of giving birth.

Seeing reality as having depth, as comprising both a without and a within, abandons a Platonic perspective which sees the really real as another world of ideal forms. There is no other world than this one. Reality as comprising increasingly deeper and deeper vistas is not simply Aristotelian either, however. Granted that this world is the really real world, the within is as real as the without and the within lies like an abyss before us.

The image of a well gives us a feeling for depth. We see an onion as having layers which can be successively peeled away. There is more than what lies on the surface. There is a whole world inside the atom, and this is even more true of a living organism, especially if we consider the more advanced forms of animal life. A human person is a highly complex reality, but one whose within is as advanced as its without, if not more so. Even when we think we know a person, there is more there. The depth of a human person seems inexhaustible.

A universe that has depth cannot be known by empirical methods alone. Such a universe has to reveal its depth, its secrets, its innermost being. There is more there than that which meets the eye, or the microscope, or the telescope, although these instruments are not to be dismissed as insignificant by any means. But it is important not only that we probe further, but that reality respond, or even initiate.

[20]Especially see Teilhard de Chardin, *The Phenomenon of Man.* The bibliography on Teilhard is extensive. See Donald Goergen, *Personality-in-Process and Teilhard de Chardin,* unp. doctoral diss., 1971, University Microfilms.

Sometimes reality does just that: it opens itself up or lets itself out or unconceals itself. Shakespeare writes a sonnet. The world evolves and new forms of life emerge. Someone has a psychic breakdown, and what had previously lay hidden finds itself exposed. A woman gives birth.

It is not just a question of material depth, such as with subatomic energy, nor even of psychic depth, whether animal or human. For a religious person there is more to human interiority than *psyche* alone. There is *pneuma* or spirit as well. Not only psychology, but also pneumatology, as well as biology, are necessary if we are to understand the whole of the human person.

But these are only examples. Our point is simply that created reality is so structured that it has two sides to it, an outside and an inside, extension and depth. It also has a third dimension to it: time. It's not as if it simply is or isn't. It comes to be and takes its time. It comes to be by way of birth and continues to be constituted at the levels of the without and the within by growth. Created realities are not born finished. They truly are what they will become. The dimensions of spatiality, becoming, and depth are constitutive of being. I am a social being; I have a history; my inner self is my ground. Not all of reality is communicable by simple sign or steno language, nor even by tensive symbols or language. Yet archetypal tensive symbols are profoundly communicative and revelatory.

In Jungian psychology, archetypal symbols are associated with the collective unconscious. One of the major breakthroughs in modern psychology was the discovery of the unconscious. Jung postulated in addition to one's personal unconscious a collective unconscious as well, distinguishable from the personal unconscious, a portion of the psyche which we all share in common and which is linked to the history of the species, whose content comprises primordial images or archetypes. It is impossible to define the collective unconscious as such, but it expresses itself when the archetypes appear, for example in dreams.[21]

[21] For Jung's own discussion of archetypes and the collective unconscious, see C. G. Jung, *Collected Works* (New York: Pantheon Books, for the Bollingen Foundation) esp. vol. 9, part 1 (1959), but also vols. 7 (1953, new edition 1966) and 9, part 2 (1959), trans. R.F.C. Hull. Cf. Frieda Fordham, *An Introduction to Jung's Psychology* (London: Penguin Books, 1966); and Calvin Hall and Vernon Nordby, *A Primer of Jungian Psychology* (New York: New American Library, 1973).

Archetypes are unconscious. Although Jung refers to them at times as primordial images, they are not fully developed pictures. They are more like images or forms without content.[22] They do not correspond as such to the actual manifestations or exemplifications of the archetypes as produced in a particular culture or particular person's life. One's personal mother or father, or one's images or experiences of them, are to be distinguished from the archetypal mother or father which we all possess. Jung explains:

> Again and again I encounter the mistaken notion that an archetype is determined in regard to its content, in other words that it is a kind of unconscious idea (if such an expression be admissable). It is necessary to point out once more that archetypes are not determined as regards their content, but only as regards their form, and then only to a very limited degree. A primordial image is determined as to its content only when it has become conscious and is therefore filled out with the material of conscious experience.[23]

Archetypes are universal; we all inherit them. There is no limit to their number, although some exert more influence than others.

In addition to archetypal images of the good mother or father, of a goddess or god, there is the archetype of the bad mother or father as well, a witch (in its negative connotation) or a devil. The old wise man (or hero or savior) and the earth mother are other significant archetypes. Some archetypes refer to nature—sun, moon, water, wind—or to geometric shapes—the square, or circle. The four most significant archetypes for Jung are the persona, the shadow, the anima and animus, and the self.

Archetypes, or archetypal images, express themselves through symbols: this is the only way we come to know them. For example, a child of some sort is often a symbol of the self. So also are the images of Christ and of Buddha. Jung's understanding of the symbolization through which the unconscious expresses itself differs from that of Freud. For Freud, symbolization conceals or disguises a wish or instinct that seeks fulfillment, such as the sexual or aggressive impulses that manifest themselves in dreams. In ad-

---

[22] Jung, *Collected Works,* vol. 9, part 1, 48.
[23] Ibid., 79.

dition to this, for Jung, symbols express or are manifestations of the archetypes, even if they only represent them imperfectly. The symbol is not a sign that means something everybody knows. Rather, it represents an attempt to elucidate something that still belongs to the domain of the unknown or something that is yet to be.

Although I am not using "archetypal symbol" in a specifically Jungian sense, Jung helps us to appreciate its character. Tensive symbols can be personal, social and collective, or relatively universal and archetypal. This last does not mean that the meaning is the same for all, but that the symbol functions tensively for all those for whom the symbol has meaning.

Although our examples have been few, anything can become symbolic. Nature readily lends itself toward acquiring symbolic significance. Consider the stone or rock in a Japanese garden, at Stonehenge and Avebury, or for Jacob in Genesis 28:10-22. Animals can be symbolic, as in Paleolithic cave paintings, the signs of the zodiac, the early Christian symbol of the fish as well as the animal symbols for three of the evangelists (the lion for Mark, ox for Luke, and eagle for John). Geometric forms can be symbolic, such as the triangle, or a number such as three. The circle is one of the most universal symbols of wholeness: mandalas, the lotus, the halos of the saints, the Gothic rose windows. The story of the Gothic cathedral in the West shows how architecture itself is symbolic.[24]

A study of symbolism takes one readily from nature to art, for art is a supreme revelation of the symbolic world. Aniela Jaffe writes, "The artist has at all times been the instrument and spokesman of the spirit of his age. His work can be only partly understood in terms of his personal psychology."[25] A distinction in art between a "sensory" style (a more direct reproduction of the sub-

---

[24]Cf. Louis Charpentier, *The Mysteries of Chartres Cathedral*, trans. Ronald Fraser (Wellingborough, Eng.: Thorsons Publishers, 1980); Georges Duby, *The Age of the Cathedrals, Art and Society, 980-1420*, trans. Eleanor Levieux and Barbara Thompson (Chicago: University of Chicago Press, 1981); George Henderson, *Gothic* (London: Penguin Books, 1978); Edwin Panofsky, *Gothic, Architecture and Scholasticism* (New York: New American Library, 1976); Otto von Simson, *The Gothic Cathedral* (New York: Harper and Row, 1962).

[25]See the excellent essay, "Symbolism in the Visual Arts," in *Man and His Symbols*, ed. C. G. Jung (New York: Dell Pub. Co., 1976) 285.

ject) and an "imaginative" style (presenting the fantasy or experience of the artist) permeates art history,[26] and is a parallel to Cassirer's two indispensable tendencies manifest in all of human culture, the tendencies toward conservation and toward renovation.[27] But whatever our theories may be, we can come to a better understanding of symbolism by turning to the world of art, beauty, and aesthetics.

Art is not simply a matter of personal taste. To consider it as such reflects the tendency to privatize the world of meaning, the world of beauty and mystery, the world of aesthetics and religion, all that cannot be reduced to objective knowledge alone. "The judgement that makes the aesthetic experience what it is should be distinguished from the judgements which express our special tastes by affirming our preferences. Taste is not the inner organization of aesthetic perception but merely something which sharpens or dulls it."[28] Art is rightly called beautiful if it meets the criteria for aesthetic objects, if it has the power to communicate with us, if it embodies the meaningful in the sensuous.[29] Art is a world that opens us out to another world, or other realities in our world, or other dimensions of our world. Art takes us out of ourselves and beyond ourselves. Although Plato saw the poet and artist as twice removed from the really real, he did see beauty as an epiphany of the really real in our world. Art, literature, music open us to reality, can draw us more deeply into it, and allow us to experience it as beautiful.

In aesthetics, especially since the eighteenth century, a distinction has been drawn between two kinds of aesthetic experience: the beautiful and the sublime.[30] "The sublime points to a tran-

[26]Ibid., 278-85.

[27]Ernst Cassirer, *An Essay on Man,* 222-28.

[28]Aidan Nichols, *The Art of God Incarnate, Theology and Image in Christian Tradition* (New York: Paulist Press, 1980) 92.

[29]Cf. ibid., 89-104. See Mikel Dufrenne, *The Phenomenology of Aesthetic Experience,* trans. Edward Casey et al. (Evanston: Northwestern University Press, 1973). I make no effort or pretense here to develop or defend any particular aesthetic theory, something which a theologian needs eventually to do. I recognize the varied philosophies of art, especially since Baumgarten (1714-1762), the founder of aesthetics in the eighteenth century. See Leo Tolstoy, *What Is Art,* trans. Aylmer Maude (London: Oxford University Press, 1969).

[30]Cf. esp. Karsten Harries, *The Meaning of Modern Art* (Evanston, Ill.: North-

scendence beyond appearances. It allows man to look through the finite into the infinite. The finite becomes the veil of the infinite. This infinite can be identified with a numinous reality transcending man. The positive sublime can thus be defined as the epiphany of the numinous.''[31] The sublime puts us in touch with the numinous, the transcendent, the *mysterium tremendum et fascinans* of Rudolf Otto's description.[32] The sublime in art seems to demand a sense of immensity, which nature provides with its mountains, oceans, deserts, and forests but which can also be conveyed in a Gothic cathedral. Some works of sculpture are doors to the sublime, such as Michelangelo's *David,* as are liturgy, iconography, and at times a human person—one who manifests wisdom, age, and suffering. Not all that is beautiful is sublime.

This is a helpful distinction. With it we can better appreciate the history and theology of Christian iconography. Yet traditionally the sublime would have been subsumed under the category of the beautiful. For Dionysius the Areopagite, "Beauty" is one of the names for God.

> But the super-essential Beautiful is called Beauty because of the beauty communicated by it to all beautiful things in accordance with their nature, and because it is the cause of the harmony and splendor in all things, flashing forth upon them like light the beautifying beams of its fontal Ray. . . . It is called the Beautiful because it is altogether beautiful and more than beautiful, and is eternally and changelessly beautiful. . . .[33]

The Orthodox see iconography as theology, as akin to liturgy, and rooted in Christology. Theology can be expressed in words (what we ordinarily think of as theology) or in images (sacred art and the icons): "The ways of iconography, as means of expressing what regards the Deity, are here the same as the ways of the-

---

western University Press, 1968) 36–45. Also, Edmund Burke, *A Philosophical Enquiry into the Origin of Our Ideas of the Sublime and the Beautiful* (London: Routledge and Kegan Paul, 1958).

[31]Harries, *The Meaning of Modern Art,* 45.

[32]Rudolf Otto, *The Idea of the Holy,* trans. John W. Harvey, 2nd ed. (London: Oxford University Press, 1958).

[33]Dionysius the Areopagite, *The Divine Names,* ch. 4, trans. the editors of the Shrine of Wisdom (Fintry Brook, Eng.: The Shrine of Wisdom, 1957) 34–35.

ology. The task of both alike is to express that which cannot be expressed by human means, since such expression will always be imperfect and insufficient."[34]

In Orthodoxy, the icon is inspired, religious, sacred, not secondary to but on a plane with liturgy and Scripture: "The mystery enacted and the mystery depicted are one, both inwardly in their meaning and outwardly in the symbolism which expresses their meaning."[35] Both in liturgy and in iconography one is giving expression to one's faith in the mutual interpenetration of the divine and the human, in the participation of the one in the other, in the doctrine of salvation as deification, as ultimately rooted in and revealed by the Christological doctrine of the incarnation: "Thus the icon is not a representation of the Deity, but an indication of the participation of a given person in Divine life."[36]

We cannot separate the history of theology from the history of art. We need an aesthetics sensitive to theology, and a theology sensitive to aesthetics: the reality of symbolism undergirds both of them. This is the foundation for Aidan Nichols's *Art of God Incarnate* which is an effort to develop "an aesthetic theology," or a theology which takes clues from and is modelled on aesthetics. Art may be more appropriate for expressing the significance and uniqueness of Jesus than philosophical theology, "not because of any *a priori* superiority of art over against conceptual thought, but because art is more appropriate for an epoch in which the divine is known to have presented itself through the material, the contingent, and the particular. Precisely because we know that, we also know that it will be easier to *depict* [italics mine] God in Christ than to conceptualize the incarnation."[37]

Theology, which in its own self-understanding is rooted in symbol, finds a close affinity with art, music, and poetry, and is drawn in that direction in order to understand itself better. Art forces theology to clarify its own use and understanding of symbol.

I have thus far clarified only two kinds of symbols and language: the simple sign and the tensive symbol. Now I must pro-

[34]Leonid Ouspensky, "The Meaning and Language of Icons," in Leonid Ouspensky and Vladimir Lossky, *The Meaning of Icons* (New York: St. Vladimir's Seminary Press, 1982) 48.

[35]Ibid., 31.

[36]Ibid., 36.

[37]Nichols, *The Art of God Incarnate,* 86.

ceed to an understanding of the third kind, the metapersonal symbolic reality, the most important for Christology.

Metapersonal Symbolic Reality

A metapersonal symbolic reality (1) is an extra-mental public object (it has existence outside any particular individual's psychic life; it is a reality), (2) which draws me as a whole person toward it or into it (which I experience personally), and (3) which also draws me beyond it into a reality in which the symbol itself participates (I participate in the reality in which it participates; it functions as mediation, or mediates or communicates a further or deeper level of reality to me). As with other kinds of symbols, the metapersonal symbol may be nature (e.g., the desert) or a product of human construction (e.g., liturgy). Its being an extra-mental public object simply means that it cannot be reduced to any one individual's psychic experience. It has existence beyond and communicates meaning to more than an individual. It is real. To some degree, this is true of simple signs as well and of the "object" of objective knowledge; but "objectification" is not desired nor valued in this kind of symbolic knowledge. The experience does not lead to objective knowledge nor lend itself to objectification, although it is possible to have objective knowledge of a desert or of liturgy. On the other hand, not all tensive symbols are extra-mental; many are images which have their primary existence in the psychic life of an individual or group. A metapersonal symbol is clearly encountered as a reality distinct from oneself.

This kind of symbol is a reality that draws me into it (it is active, takes initiative). This distinguishes it from a simple sign which is outside me and remains outside me and I outside it (although there may be a minimal degree of indwelling in that it conveys some meaning to me). This symbolic experience cannot be conveyed by objective knowledge; objectification destroys or terminates the experience. Yet it is not personal knowledge either, though experienced personally; for personal knowledge implies something becoming or being a part of me. Here I am becoming part of it. It is not "my" meaning or dream or even "ours." A metapersonal symbolic reality exists beyond or outside all of us. Again, this fact does not rule out having personal knowledge as well of a particular desert or liturgy. A particular tree or place along the sea may have personal meaning for me or us; it is my tree, or our place. It is possible to know metapersonal symbols objectively and personally (although that is not to know them with their full symbolic significance). It is not just a question of a person's way of experiencing or knowing, however. Simple signs and tensive symbols are not metapersonal symbols; metapersonal symbols have a reality of their own, although they can be experienced or known in other ways than as metapersonally symbolic.

A metapersonal symbol is a real transcendental; it exists, and it takes someone beyond it. It primarily functions as a mediation of the transcendent. Its very nature is to be a symbol. Its reality is a symbolic reality. In order to appreciate the character of a metapersonal symbol, one must be conscious of the fact that symbol and reality are not mutually exclusive. Something is not "merely" a symbol. As Aidan Kavanagh expresses it, "Symbol is reality at its most intense degree of being expressed."[38] A symbol is a particular kind of reality in which reality discloses itself to us rather than being grasped at by us.

A symbol is reality, and reality is symbolic. Where the symbolic character of reality breaks through most strongly, there we have a metapersonal or transcendental symbol.

The very nature of a symbolic reality is to mediate more of reality, or to lure me into something bigger, more, other than itself alone—except that one cannot simply say "other." For the symbol *is* that other as well. Avery Dulles uses the expression "a single interlocked reality" to describe what underlies symbolic mediation: "Symbols do not necessarily point to things strictly other than themselves. Although there must be at least a formal distinction between the symbol and what it points to, the symbol and the symbolized may constitute 'a single interlocked reality.'"[39] A metapersonal symbol contains as well as mediates the reality it signifies.

The very nature of symbolic reality is to communicate that which it mediates, that which it *really is*. There is a mutual interpenetration between the symbol, *qua* symbol, and the reality sym-

[38]Aidan Kavanagh, *Elements of Rite: A Handbook of Liturgical Style* (New York: Pueblo Pub. Co., 1982) 103.

[39]Avery Dulles, *Models of Revelation* (Garden City, N.Y.: Doubleday, 1983) 266–67; also see 131–54.

bolized. Karl Rahner's theology of symbol makes a similar point. A symbol in its deepest sense, a metapersonal symbolic reality as I have called it, mediates the real presence of something that is more than it is and yet something that it also is; and it draws others into a participation in that in which it participates, what Rudolf Otto calls the numinous.[40] Karl Rahner writes, "Our task will be to look for the highest and most primordial manner in which one reality can represent another. . . . And we call this supreme and primal representation, in which one reality renders another present . . . a symbol: the representation which allows the other 'to be there.' "[41]

A metapersonal symbol is not representative in simply an indicative, or conventional, or even tensive way. The symbol is to some degree the reality it communicates, while that reality always transcends, is more than, this symbol alone. Rahner continues:

> In a real theology of the symbol, based on the fundamental truths of Christianity, a symbol is not something separate from the symbolized (or different, but really or mentally united with the symbolized by a mere process of addition), which indicates the object but does not contain it. On the contrary, the symbol is the reality, constituted by the thing symbolized as an inner moment of itself, which reveals and proclaims the thing symbolized, and is itself full of the thing symbolized, being its concrete form of existence.[42]

In order to grasp better the character of a metapersonal symbolic reality, we can consider examples: the desert, liturgy, a human person. One can know a desert objectively (perhaps as a geographer or geologist), or personally (as someone who narrates a personal and particular experience of it), but also symbolically (as it mediates the presence of transcendence).

The wilderness was formative in Israelite and Judaean history, and thus contributed to the birth of monotheism and faith in God as personal. It also played a formative role in the life and experience of Jesus. "It is no whim of history that the birth of the

---

[40]See Otto, *The Idea of the Holy*, 5-7.

[41]Karl Rahner, "The Theology of the Symbol," trans. Kevin Smyth, in *Theological Investigations* 4 (Baltimore: Helicon Press, 1966) 225.

[42]Ibid., 251.

first monotheistic faith took place in a desert, or that it was followed there by the other two great religions, Christianity and Islam.''[43] The experience of nature at its purest can only be narrated; the desert or wilderness is something very simple, yet multifaceted; something uncontrollable, unpredictable, and surprising; something that contains a sense or hint of the presence of transcendence; something, that for all its awfulness and capacity to evoke fear, is awesome and beautiful. "Its varied colors, its fantastic shapes, its breathtaking vastness and staggering heights, its solemn silence, especially this stillness—these delight the senses, overwhelm them, can lead only to a beauty that one cannot grasp. Its uncontaminated and sometimes unthinkable purity can easily lead to the description from Deuteronomy 1:19—'that great and terrible wilderness.' ''[44]

To use an earlier distinction from aesthetic theory, we are perhaps talking here about the desert not so much as beautiful but as sublime.[45] Its immensity, its purity, its sublimity is what enables this particular reality to be a symbol, to have a revelatory power, to mediate the divine presence. To experience this sublime kind of beauty is to be taken outside of oneself. It is not, as in a personal experience or personal knowledge, that I feel that something or someone has become a part of me, affecting the totality of me, but rather that I am becoming a part of it, or stand in awe because of the way I have been drawn into that which will always transcend me, will never be "mine."

The reality of the desert and of the desert experience includes its reality as symbol. There is no separating the real from the symbolic. It is simply a symbolic reality. Such a symbol opens up a symbolic knowledge and consciousness which as such is not objective/discursive or personal/intuitive but participative/transcendent. But:

> A symbol is not only a way of knowing which draws me ever deeper into sharing its reality; a symbol is a reality that always refers me beyond itself. The reality of the symbol is unconfined.

[43]Michael Evenari, Leslie Shanan, and Naphtali Tadmor, *The Negev: The Challenge of a Desert* (Cambridge: Harvard University Press, 1971) 9.

[44]Donald J. Goergen, "The Desert as Reality and Symbol," *Spirituality Today* 34 (1982) 73.

[45]Also see Otto, *The Idea of the Holy,* 50–71.

> To participate is to go deeper into reality. As symbol it is not
> just "this water," "this height," "this desert," but this desert
> partaking of and manifesting a beauty in which it too partici-
> pates and which is essential to it. Beauty is not confined by
> "place" but revealed "within" it. Nature and symbol mediate
> reality to us and allow us to share in it.[46]

A particular reality may function symbolically at several levels.
For example, the Sinai as a simple sign simply denotes a particular geographical region. The Sinai also, however, and probably
more often, functions as a tensive symbol, connoting and symbolizing a rich and wide range of meaning and associations, particularly for the Jewish people. But finally, and most importantly
from a religious point of view, the Sinai as a metapersonal symbolic reality is a place where originally some Hebrew people actually encountered God, or sensed the transcendent presence, and
where people today can still so experience the immanence of the
Transcendent One.

Another example of a metapersonal symbolic reality is liturgy,
a product of human culture and religion rather than nature, yet
a symbolic action. Not anything and everything can function as
a metapersonal symbol—not any and every aspect or piece of nature, nor all ritual. Not every religious experience implies a
metapersonal symbol. A metapersonal symbol is a reality that by
its nature has the capacity to mediate the numinous.

Liturgy, solemnly celebrated, mediates the divine presence. In
Orthodoxy a theology of liturgy cannot be separated from the
beautiful and sublime. God is beauty, and liturgy a reflection of
and participation in that great and terrible beauty. Liturgy draws
me out of myself and into it. It does not become a part of me,
like personal meditation; rather I become a part of it. Liturgy
implies a we and a Thou. Liturgy takes me into it as a social action and beyond it as a symbolic action.

Like the desert, liturgy can function symbolically in varied ways.
A particular gesture may be a simple sign. Particular actions, images, expressions, rituals, songs, words, movements are tensive
symbols, social in nature, perhaps even archetypal. Individual elements contain a wide range of associations, whether good or bad.
In the experience of the liturgical action itself, the ingredients are

---

[46]Donald J. Goergen, "The Desert as Reality and Symbol," 76.

not to be objectified and analyzed. This does not mean they have no cognitive significance. The whole liturgy, however, is a metapersonal symbol in which God once again reaches out and embraces God's people who worship in awe in God's presence. Liturgy is multifaceted, and this self-communication of the numinous is but one facet, but the facet that makes it a symbolic reality in the fullest sense. Scripture is filled with tensive language. The lectionary itself is a tensive symbol. But liturgy as a whole is more than all the tensive symbols combined. For Christians, the primary metapersonal symbol is the ecclesial action of the Eucharist.

Our third example may be the most difficult to articulate: a human person may also be a metapersonal symbol. Although there is more depth to every human person than that which meets the eye, and although in theory every human person can be a metapersonal symbol mediating a sense of divine presence, not all people actually are metapersonally symbolic.

One cannot delineate a list of qualities or criteria for someone to be so symbolic: rather, when one is in the presence of such a person, one knows it. There is more there than the person alone. A certain quality, for example, compassion; or wisdom, that comes from age; or familiarity with suffering in one's own experience—whatever it is, a person can be experienced as a symbolic presence. One almost hesitates to choose examples. We cannot canonize such people apart from the perspective of other people who have sensed or recognized the presence of transcendence. Can we suggest Gandhi, Heschel, Sadat, Oscar Romero or not? To be such a symbolic presence or reality does not take fame. Many of us may have recognized the presence in people we have met whose names will not make history. Yet this does not imply that everyone is such a symbolic reality.

A human person, like nature and art and liturgy, can be a symbol in several ways. A particular person may be a personal, tensive symbol for me, or a social, tensive symbol for a group. I can, of course, know a person objectively (by reading data on a resume), even psychoanalytically. But I can also know a person personally, as a person, with personal knowledge. I can love that someone, or be in love. Someone may even be the occasion for a religious experience, a conversion, in my life. But all these are still personal knowledge and not symbolic knowledge at its fullest.

As a metapersonal symbol, a person mediates a transcendent, spiritual presence, into which I am drawn, which to some degree that person is. To know a person symbolically in this sense is to know that person metapersonally (not impersonally, but suprapersonally).

To articulate his own experience of the divine as present in the world, Teilhard de Chardin coined the word *diaphany*—that which shines through.[47] Teilhard will probably go down in the history of twentieth-century spirtuality as the mystic of the divine omnipresence, the divine milieu, the cosmic and Christic sense.

God can come to be known in varied ways: objectively (in which case we know about God), personally (in which case we have met God), or symbolically (in which case we are drawn into the very life of God).

There are three primary kinds of symbol: the simple sign, the tensive symbol, and the metapersonal symbolic reality. We can correlate with this three primary kinds of knowledge: objective, personal, and symbolic knowledge proper. We discussed objective and personal knowledge in volume 2. There we saw that even objective knowledge is to some degree personal, yet we reserved the name "objective" for that way of knowing in which objectification is considered its primary value. Both objective and personal knowledge are also symbolic; yet we reserve "symbolic" for that way of knowing in which neither the objective nor the personal but rather the transcendental is the most valued aspect. A metapersonal symbol correlates with a special kind of knowledge of symbolic consciousness: transcendental or symbolic knowledge proper.

Symbolic or transcendental knowledge shares with objective knowledge the fact that one is talking about a reality outside of oneself. A symbol is a reality outside the human person; it transcends the human person, is other than the person. Yet that reality is not strictly speaking an object; there is something very personal about it. It communicates with a person and is experiential. But it is a personal experience of a "beyond me." In that sense it can be described as ultrapersonal, suprapersonal, or transpersonal. But to describe symbolic knowledge in terms of per-

47See Teilhard de Chardin, *The Divine Milieu,* 108–12; in the paperback edition, 128–32.

sonal knowledge does not do justice to its most dominant characteristic. Although objective knowledge and personal knowledge are distinct, we did not define or describe them in terms of each other, nor as opposites. We did not call them objective and non-objective, or personal and non-personal. Similarly, symbolic knowledge is not opposed to but complements the other two ways of knowing. This knowledge is participation to an even stronger degree in that which is known, namely, the symbol and what it symbolizes or mediates. All knowledge, as Polanyi pointed out, involves a form of indwelling. In symbolic knowledge one is literally taken outside of oneself into the other.

In objective knowledge, to some degree, I "get outside of myself." In personal knowledge such a distanciation from the self is not desirable. In personal knowledge I prefer to get further "inside myself," at my experience, intuition, or insight. It is "me" or some aspect of me that I am attempting to articulate and formalize. So it would be folly to distance myself from that interior reality. Rather I have to go more deeply inside myself. Symbolic knowledge also includes me, and I do not leave myself behind in order to know. Yet symbolic knowledge is not a going deeper into me; it is I being drawn deeply outside of myself, not in the manner of objectification but rather in the manner of participation. I find it easiest to distinguish symbolic knowledge and personal knowledge by saying that with personal knowledge the knowledge is mine, is a part of me, but in symbolic knowledge I am a part of it. I am part of, personally experiencing, something which transcends me, which is other than me, which includes me. It is as if I am taken up in the grip of what I thought I could grasp. What I am drawn into is not an object but a symbol. Symbolic or transcendental knowledge flows from a consciousness or awareness that is effected through the mediation of a metapersonal symbolic reality, even if that awareness, to use an expression from Polanyi, is tacit.

Although I am using "symbolic knowledge proper" in a more restricted way than does Avery Dulles in his discussion of symbolic communication, nevertheless his description is apt. "Symbolism gives not speculative but participatory knowledge—knowledge, that is to say, of a self-involving type. A symbol is never a sheer object. It speaks of us only insofar as it lures us to situate ourselves mentally within the universe of meaning and value which it opens up to us. . . . Symbol introduces us into realms of awareness not normally accessible to discursive thought."[48] Likewise, although mystical experience and mystical knowledge is not necessarily symbolic knowledge proper (it may be personal knowledge of God), Thomas O'Meara's comment is also appropriate: "The experiences, messages, and stories of mystical experience in the dark night do not tend to objectification, for authentic mystical experience terminates not in information but in ineffability."[49]

Symbolic realities, symbolic consciousness, symbolic knowledge, symbolic language, while not exactly synonymous, are closely related. David Tracy, whose starting point is the development of a fundamental theology and the categories of limit-situations and limit-questions, categories that we find at the boundaries of our common, human, everyday, existential experience, which categories can be called an at least implicitly religious horizon or dimension to life, raises the problem of language as well. In my own terms, symbolic knowledge cannot be expressed readily in analytical, conceptual, discursive, or steno language: hence the problem of language in contemporary theology. As David Tracy notes:

> In terms of the language we employ for such experiences [limit experiences], the analysis may also manifest that at a certain point the language of conceptual analysis begins to falter. Instead, the human spirit begins to search for metaphors expressive of the experience (abyss, chasm, limit) and for narratives capable of expanding and structuring these metaphors (parables, myths, poems). . . . In a word, the language initially most appropriate for expressing that experience is symbolic as distinct from strictly conceptual. . . . Symbolic language may find further though partial expression in the conceptual language of metaphysics—especially the analogical language of metaphysics. However helpful a later metaphysical language

[48]Dulles, *Models of Revelation,* 136–37.

[49]Thomas F. O'Meara, "Toward a Subjective Theology of Revelation," *Theological Studies* 36 (1975) 427.

may be, all authentic limit-language seems to be initially and irretrievably a symbolic and a metaphorical one.[50]

All language is, of course, symbolic. Language is a system of signs. But just as there are three levels or kinds of symbolic knowledge (objective, personal, symbolic proper) and symbolic realities (simple sign, tensive symbol, and metapersonal symbolic reality), so there are different kinds of symbolic language.[51] Myth remains one of the more immediate ways in which the deepest and richest levels of symbolic consciousness express themselves in language. We see the problem: metapersonal symbols and properly symbolic knowledge, to the degree that they are expressible at all, require properly symbolic language—the language of mystery and beauty.

Jesus of Nazareth, the earthly, historical Jesus, was a metapersonal symbolic reality: our discussion of symbol has been leading us toward an appreciation of this statement. Jesus was someone in whom (the reign of) God was present and through whom it manifested itself. Jesus was the presence of that reign, a mediator of that divine presence, a diaphany of God. In him and through him people, and history itself, came into contact with (the reign of) God, with eschatological reality, with God's very self.

When we speak of Jesus as a symbol, we can do so at various levels. As a simple sign, the word *Jesus* simply denotes a particular, concrete, historical individual. In his lifetime, the word often functioned in that way—as a simple sign. But the word *Jesus* was and is more than a simple sign; it also functions as a tensive symbol, for it connotes much more than a particular individual. In his lifetime, Jesus was a symbol that functioned differently for his mother, for his disciples, for the crowds who followed him,

---

[50]David Tracy, *Blessed Rage for Order: The New Pluralism in Theology* (New York: The Seabury Press, 1975) 107–08.

[51]See vol. 3 of this series, Goergen, *The Jesus of Christian History,* where I discuss philosophical language, mystical language, and pastoral language or the language of proclamation. Philosophical language is more often steno language as that expression is used in this volume. It values precision. Both mystical language and the language of proclamation are more often tensive language. They are more experiential, personal, or rhetorical. Symbolic knowledge proper, as used in this volume, is more often expressed in the language of myth.

for the Pharisees, for the Sadducean elite, for Pilate. And Jesus as a tensive symbol is not confined by his earthly, historical existence alone. As the Christ, Jesus is a tensive symbol to an even greater extent.

As a tensive symbol, Jesus of Nazareth, or Jesus Christ, can be seen as symbolic in personal, corporate, and archetypal ways. Jesus was a personal tensive symbol for his mother—her son; for Peter, for James, for John, for Martha, for Mary Magdalene—a symbol of hope, or of friendship. Jesus has remained a personal tensive symbol throughout history: for Peter after the resurrection, for Paul, for Julian of Norwich, for Dorothy Day. But after the resurrection, Jesus Christ (even the change of name is symbolic) becomes even more a social or corporate tensive symbol—a symbol that will "mean" or symbolize different things for Christians and for Jews, for Christians of the second century and Christians of the fourth century, for the early Johannine community and the Church of Matthew, in India and in Latin America. As the name of Jesus, and the movement which takes that name, becomes more and more a social symbol, there is no separating the reality of Jesus from a community for whom Jesus embodies a particular meaning. They perhaps are bound together by that common meaning and symbol; it may be the basis of a particular corporate identity; we have an *ecclesia*. Jesus functions as both a personal and corporate symbol. So does the symbol of the cross, perhaps the most basic tensive symbol in the Christian symbol system, one whose complete meaning can never be fully and conceptually unravelled, so rich is it with associations that steno language can never reveal its meaning.

Jesus, or Jesus Christ, is also an archetypal symbol in the Jungian sense. For Jung, in fact, Jesus functioned as a symbol for the archetype of the self.[52] For Jung, regardless of Jesus' historical existence, he embodies a myth and exemplifies the archetype of the self. (The Antichrist corresponds to the shadow of the self.) "Christ is our nearest analogy of the self and its meaning."[53] For Christians, Christ *is* the image of the self. To speak of Jesus Christ as an archetypal symbol does not as such deny the historical ac-

---

[52]See esp. "Christ, a Symbol of the Self," in Jung, *Collected Works,* vol. 9, part 2, 36–71.

[53]Ibid., 44.

tuality of Christ nor the appropriateness of metaphysical or theological interpretations of the Christ image.[54] Yet metaphysics and theology cannot deny that Christ also functions psychologically, at the level of archetypes, in the collective unconscious.

As historical, as we have stated, Jesus was also symbolic, and not only tensively: he was in his very being a symbolic reality, metapersonal and transcendent—a reality in whom history and eschatology came together as we would say today. This is what we mean when we say that Jesus is an image of the invisible God (Col 1:15). Jesus still, as Lord and Christ, continues to function as a metapersonal symbol. In his eschatological existence, however, he is related differently to our histories. But Jesus has left us the Eucharist as a primary, tangible, metapersonal symbol of himself, in which he remains really present among us.

Jesus, as a symbol, causes us to pause and reflect upon the relationship between symbolic reality and historical reality, between the symbolic Jesus and the historical Jesus, just as we did when reflecting upon the Jesus of historiography and the Jesus of faith. It has become common parlance in contemporary Christology to talk about the Jesus of history and the Christ of the Churches or the Christ of faith. The seeming dichotomy between the two (as if in an almost incipiently Nestorian way Jesus and the Risen Christ are two different persons rather than one and the same) has been a fundamental concern and problem for Christology today. For someone like Teilhard de Chardin, the issue was different: what is the relationship between the Jesus of history and the Omega of evolution, between the historical Jesus and Christ-Omega? For all orthodox Christology, the Christ is always this Jesus: there is only one Jesus Christ, as expressed in that name, where it is not torn apart or separated. Jesus of Nazareth and the risen Jesus are one person, and one can properly speak about the historical Jesus Christ, or the risen Jesus Christ, or the confessed Jesus Christ, or even the symbolic Jesus Christ, but in all of these there is but one Jesus Christ. Our question now is about the relationship between the historical Jesus and the symbolic Christ.

[54]Ibid., 67–68.

The Symbolic Christ

There is more to the Jesus of history than symbolism alone. There is his personal life, experiences, struggle, anguish, faith, hope, joy, message, relationships, pain, and death. There is also more to the symbolic Jesus than his history alone. He is even "more" in history than he historically (or historiographically) was. He *is* this more, this surplus, already in history, and even more so as raised from the dead. Again, the Jesus of history is more than the Jesus of historiography; yet there is but one Jesus. Jesus is more than his historical existence, both in terms of his own personal eschatological continuation and in terms of his significance, especially ecclesial significance: what he comes to symbolize and continues to embody and mediate. Yet as a real symbol, as a symbolic reality, he must be rooted in history, must be or have been historical. There can be a distinction but no ultimate separation between Jesus as historical reality and Jesus as symbolic reality.[55] As historical, Jesus is also already symbol, and as symbol, Jesus cannot be non-historical. As a tensive symbol, Jesus could be "only symbol." But as a metapersonal symbol, Jesus must have had real, historical existence. It was this historical Jesus who is first of all the symbolic Christ.

The universal significance of Christ today is at the symbolic level. Neither the historiographical Jesus nor the Churches' Jesus alone can solve the question of Christ's universality. Symbol and art, however, teach us that the universal is always found in or communicated by the particular (here there is no scandal of par-

[55]I sense such a split between the Jesus of history and the symbolic Christ in David Tracy's Christological proposals. For example, see *Blessed Rage for Order,* 214–18. I accept his distinction between the two ways by which possibilities may become facts (actualization and symbolic representation), but I do not think that the distinction is an adequate grounding for Christology. The symbolic Christ is not what the Christ title symbolically represents but also its actualization in the Jesus of history. Tracy admits "that the representational reality present in the office of Messiah may be found in words, deeds, and destiny of Jesus of Nazareth" (216); yet he also discusses the new quest for the historical Jesus and historical-psychological reconstruction as unnecessary. Granted the almost insuperable difficulties of this task, Jesus' own actualization of human possibilities and not only the re-presentative factual character of Christological symbolic language is significant to Christology; otherwise one severs the symbolic Christ from the historical Jesus. Cf. Edward Schillebeeckx, *Interim Report on the Books, Jesus and Christ* (New York: Crossroad, 1981) 28.

ticularity). The unfortunate dichotomy in contemporary Christology between "Jesus" and "the Christ" is itself symbolic of a disturbing split in the modern consciousness. And the arguments over which is more important, historiography or faith, Jesus or the Christ, Christology from below or from above, too readily resembles modern power politics. Can we do without Jesus? without objective, historiographical knowledge of Jesus? Can we dismiss two thousand years of Christian reflection and experience? Can we detach ourselves from our personal knowledge of the Risen Lord? So likewise, we cannot tear the historical Jesus and the symbolic Jesus apart. They are one and the same person. Every metapersonal symbolic reality is both concrete and metahistoriographical, rooted both in and beyond history. And so with the symbolic Christ: he is both "in history" and "from God." He is both in history and more than history, thus not wholly accessible by historiography alone, nor a "mere symbol" lacking in reality. He is a historical symbolic reality—both historical and symbolic, both symbolic and real. Even the historical Jesus expressed his own consciousness and faith by means of symbolic language and actions.

The task facing contemporary Christology is how to break open the symbol that Jesus Christ is, how to unveil his significance for us today, how to resymbolize (more than reconceptualize or demythologize) all that the Christ event once symbolized, indeed, how to answer the question: where do we find Jesus Christ today? For there is more to Jesus than Jesus alone, narrowly, individually conceived. There is a social dimension to the historical Jesus and to the symbolic Christ. Not only his humanity, and not only his divinity, but also his sociality is constitutive of who Jesus is. He is always the one who is with-us and for-us. He can only be defined in relationship to us, as *pro me.* Jesus Christ, the symbol, stands as a mediator between us and the really real, the eschatologically real. As symbol, Christ is social. He is not who he is by himself alone, but only in relationship to God and to others.

Christ stands before us and behind us as a tensive symbol of salvation, of another *Adam,* of the gift of the Spirit, of a friend of sinners and of disciples, of the reign of God. Thus Christology means more and becomes more than the person of Christ: it becomes soteriology, anthropology, pneumatology, sociology, ecclesiology, and theology. In Jesus we are faced with a new understanding of existence (Christology as soteriology, anthropology, pneumatology), a call to discipleship (Christology as sociology and ecclesiology), and a new image of God (Christology as theology and doxology).

The Jesus of history is the Christ (at least for Christians); but *Christ* is a more extensive, inclusive, tensive, wider concept. We too are in Christ and are Christ. The word *Jesus* may be a simple sign or steno language, but Christ talk is always tensive. As Christ, Jesus is intrinsically relational and social. This society of Jesus' presence, this relational network, this body in its fuller, corporate sense is intrinsic to who Jesus is. Jesus is not who he is by himself alone.

The philosophy and theology of symbolism is beginning to play a foundational role for Christology. A symbolic Christology is one that gives significance to an interpretation of Jesus as a symbolic form or symbolic reality. Of course, symbolic Christologies vary, from those in which Jesus Christ may be only a tensive symbol (symbolizing, pointing to, evoking, but not really being that which he symbolizes) to those in which Jesus is a symbolic reality (participating in, communicating, mediating that which he symbolizes). And among the latter, there are different degrees in which Jesus is thought to participate in that which is symbolized. In and of itself, a symbolic Christology does not deny the doctrine of the hypostatic union. Interpreted along the lines of Thomas Aquinas, the hypostatic union means that the very being or *esse* of Christ is the eternal *esse* of the Logos, that the humanity of Christ is but the fully human nature of the Logos, that God created the human nature of Christ specifically for this Logos, in order that the humanity of Christ might be the means by which the Logos makes its full appearance on earth and in history. This simply means that the hypostatic union is the supreme exemplification of what a symbolic reality is, a symbolic reality par excellence. A more profound symbol there could not be. Jesus Christ is the symbol of God.

The importance of the category of symbol for doing Christology is being more and more recognized. It was a basic category in Paul Tillich's Christology.[56] Karl Rahner found it highly suggestive:

[56]See Paul Tillich, *Systematic Theology,* vol. 2 (Chicago: University of Chicago Press, 1957).

> All discussion of the object and meaning of devotion to the heart
> of Jesus should take place in the perspective of a theology of
> symbolic reality. Such a theology has not yet been written, and
> the foregoing considerations do not replace it. Their only aim
> was to show . . . that such a theology of Christian symbolism
> could and should be written because reality in general and above
> all, Christian reality is essentially and from its origin a reality
> to whose self-constitution the "symbol" necessarily belongs.[57]

For Rahner, the Logos incarnate is the symbol of the Father. A
symbol, strictly speaking, is the self-realization of a being in the
other, in which the symbol remains distinct from what is symbolized, yet is constituted by what is symbolized, and where what
is symbolized expresses itself.

> If a theology of symbolic realities is to be written, Christology,
> the doctrine of the incarnation of the Word, will obviously form
> the central chapter. . . . The incarnate Word is the absolute
> symbol of God in the world, filled as nothing else can be with
> what is symbolized. He is not merely the presence and revela-
> tion of what God is in himself. He is also the expressive pres-
> ence of what—or rather, who—God wished to be, in free grace,
> to the world, in such a way that this divine attitude, once so
> expressed, can never be reversed, but is and remains final and
> unsurpassable.[58]

It is through symbolic realities (symbolization) that God communicates God's self to creatures.

Among modern Catholic theologians, the one who is most suggestive along these lines is Edward Schillebeeckx, from his early
theology in which Christ was the primordial sacrament to his more
recent theology in which Christ is parable of God and paradigm
of humanity. (Catholic theology of the sacraments has been a help
toward the reconstruction of a Christology in which Jesus is sacrament or symbol.)

Early in his theological career, Schillebeeckx manifested an in-
terest in Christology with his well-known *Christ the Sacrament*

---

[57]Rahner, "The Theology of the Symbol," 249–50.
[58]Ibid., 237; see 234–45.

of the Encounter with God.[59] His theology and method have changed between *Christ the Sacrament* (original Dutch edition, 1959) and his present project, the trilogy of *Jesus: An Experiment in Christology* (Dutch edition, 1974), *Christ: The Experience of Jesus as Lord* (Dutch edition, 1977), and *Church: The Human Story of God* (Dutch edition, 1989). Yet, throughout his theological development, there is continuity in the way Jesus Christ is conceived in sacramental, parabolic, paradigmatic, and symbolic ways.

In his more recent, explicitly Christological work, *praxis* and *orthopraxis* have become a prominent Schillebeeckx theme and concern: the implications of his "experiment" in Christology for being a Christian in our world. Equally important is his stress on human experience. Schillebeeckx describes his intention behind *Jesus* as disclosing as adequately as possible the history of Christian origins.[60] The task requires an investigation into Christian *experience,* the early Christian movement and its experience of Jesus.

It is experience that underlies the origins of Christianity; there is no revelation without experience. There is also an interpretative element: how the experience was expressed. The first expressions of the original experience Schillebeeckx calls "first order" affirmations. More explicit expressions, following further reflections, are "second order" affirmations. The term "second order" does not imply "less significant." "Thus a christology . . . is the account of a particular experience of encounter which identifies what it *experiences,* i.e., which gives a name to what it experiences."[61]

The New Testament is an interpretation of the early experiences of Jesus, a tradition of Christian experiences, or a Christian tradition of experience: the (interpreted) experiences that lie at the origins of Christianity. Christology, in order that it might speak to our day and not remain simply a historical investigation, needs

---

[59]For a Schillebeeckx bibliography, see *The Schillebeeckx Reader,* ed. Robert Schreiter (New York: Crossroad, 1984) 297–321. Also see *The Praxis of Christian Experience: An Introduction to the Theology of Edward Schillebeeckx,* ed. Robert Schreiter and Mary Catherine Hilkert (San Francisco: Harper and Row, 1989).

[60]Schillebeeckx, *Christ,* 23.

[61]Schillebeeckx, *Interim Report,* 14. See also 10–19, 50–63.

to bridge the gap between "then" and "now." Experience is once again the clue, for the two sources in doing Christology are the tradition (which is the expression of interpreted experience) and present-day experiences. Christianity is, at its core, an experience, then and now: experience is the hermeneutical key for Schillebeeckx (both for historical reconstruction and for contemporary relevance).

Yet, though Schillebeeckx's major contribution to Christological discussion is most visible in his most recent hermeneutical project, understanding Jesus as symbol has remained a recurring suggestion from him since the beginning. Nor was experience absent from his earlier theological concerns. Jesus Christ was a sacrament *of encounter.* In the earlier work, Christ was the primordial sacrament (*the* sacrament), the Church was the sacrament of the Risen Christ, and "the seven sacraments" were ecclesial acts of the Church, and therefore symbolic actions which shared in the saving work of the Risen Christ. "A sacrament is a divine bestowal of salvation in an outwardly perceptible form which makes the bestowal manifest; a bestowal of salvation in historical visibility."[62] This describes first of all, of course, Jesus Christ.

Every authentic sacrament involves "a personal encounter with the living God."[63] Jesus is the sacrament, or if one wishes, the paradigm of this personal encounter. But, given the resurrection and eschatological existence of Christ, the Eucharist functions now as that focal sacrament. The Eucharist is a symbolic, ecclesial action of the Risen Christ.

> Christ's visible and efficacious presence in the Church calls to mind the image of a stone thrown into a pond, making ripples spread out in continuous concentric circles. The ripples flow in all directions from the one central point. This point is the Church, the visible presence of Christ's grace on earth, and from it all movement can be seen to flow. The sacrament of the Eucharist is situated at the heart of this central point—the Eucharist is the focal point of Christ's real presence among us.[64]

[62]Schillebeeckx, *Christ the Sacrament,* 15; also see 13–17, 47–57, 62–64, 78–82.

[63]Ibid., 164.

[64]Ibid., 267.

Sacramentality remains a theme throughout all of Schillebeeckx's theology.

Whereas in *Christ the Sacrament* Jesus Christ was the primordial sacrament, in Schillebeeckx's later works Jesus is parable, paradigm, and symbol. In *Jesus,* Jesus is a parable of God and a paradigm of what it is to be truly human: "The assessment of a person *qua* person cannot be a matter of scientific and theoretical analysis. . . . listen to the Jesus story in such a way as to recognize in it the parable of God himself and so too the paradigm of the human character of our being-as-men. . . ."[65] Jesus is a sacrament and a parable of God: "the life story of the man Jesus as a story of God."[66] In his interpretation of the Fourth Gospel in *Christ,* Schillebeeckx returns to the concept of sacrament: "He [Jesus] is what he *gives,* says John finally; to put it in modern terms: he is the primal sacrament of God."[67] In his *Interim Report* on the first two volumes of his trilogy, he writes: "Throughout the Bible, the coming of the kingdom of God is the coming of God as salvation for human beings. Jesus Christ is the great symbol of this God, and not of any other god: 'The image of the invisible God' " (Col 1:15).[68]

Schillebeeckx's sacramental theology and Christology are also theologies of creation. It is material realities that are sacrament and symbol. Christology, or a theology of Jesus, is a theology of creation, for Jesus is an intensification of what creation is intended to be, concentrated creation, a specific way of making belief in creation more precise.[69]

The exploration into Christology in the end makes us aware of symbolic consciousness and symbolic realism. In such a world, typology deserves some reconsideration.[70] Both typological exegesis and the structure of prophecy-fulfillment are rooted in a sym-

---

[65]Schillebeeckx, *Jesus,* 650.

[66]Ibid., 80.

[67]Schillebeeckx, *Christ,* 396.

[68]Schillebeeckx, *Interim Report,* 105–06; see also 129–32.

[69]Ibid., 126–28; also see *Christ the Sacrament,* 12.

[70]We must keep in mind that typological exegesis is distinct from allegorical exegesis. Suggestive insights into typology can be found in John Marsh, *The Gospel of Saint John,* Pelican New Testament Commentaries (London: Penguin Books, 1968) 17–20, 56–59; and Nichols, *The Art of God Incarnate,* 84.

bolic world, which is what an investigation into the meaning of the Christ event discloses our world as being—a world of symbols only fathomable to symbolic ways of knowing. This does not mean that any type or prophecy finds its complete meaning, an exclusive meaning, in events to come. It simply means that types or prophecies contain a surplus of meaning beyond their immediate historical contexts. The brazen serpent in the desert or an Isaian prophecy has meaning both in and beyond its immediate historical context. They were also symbols of things to come. So is Jesus likewise a symbol of more to come. This was the basic content of his life and message: there is more to come. God is on the way. God is here. Jesus is both historical event and eschatological reality. Jesus himself becomes the One to come. He embodied eschatological reality, prefigured it, and will be with it when it comes. He is Immanuel, a prophecy of surplus meaning that speaks to all times. We can rephrase the Baptizer's question: Are you he who is to come, or shall we wait for more? And Jesus' response: Both.

In Conclusion

I have distinguished three kinds of knowledge: objective, personal, and symbolic. All knowledge is symbolic and all knowledge is personal, yet the distinctions can still be maintained. The different kinds of knowledge are symbolic in different ways or personal to different degrees. Objective knowledge attempts to objectify what it seeks to understand, sees this objectification as desirable even if not totally achievable, and thus values putting emotional distance between the knower and the known. Personal knowledge both requires and desires an experiential involvement, presence, or affinity between the knower and known. The person neither seeks nor desires distantiation. Symbolic knowledge proper is metapersonal, transcendental, and seeks to express the experience of being drawn into a reality or mystery in which one is no longer the knower or the subject but rather is disclosed as being witness, guest rather than host. Religious knowledge can be all three: objective knowledge of religion or religions (the history or phenomenology of religion), personal religious knowledge (human experiences of God, religious experiences, spiritual life, an experiential knowledge of one's own tradition of faith), and symbolic religious knowledge (such as one might encounter in ritual, myth, or symbol proper). Christology can also be concerned with all three kinds of knowledge, e.g., a historiographical knowledge of Jesus, a personal faith in Jesus as Lord, Christ, or Savior, and a symbolic knowledge of Jesus, the metapersonal embodiment and sacrament of God.

One cannot know Jesus truly or fully without all three kinds of knowledge: the portraits that scholarly biblical research give us, the personal experiences of Jesus as salvific, and being apprehended by the symbolic Christ. To emphasize one form of knowing Jesus to the exclusion of the others risks grave distortion: a Jesus who does not save, a Jesus created according to our own preferences, or a Jesus separated from Word, sacrament, and community.

Ultimately we need to recognize that true knowledge of Jesus is symbolic knowledge, properly speaking. Jesus *is* metapersonal symbolic reality. That says most profoundly who he is. Jesus *is* a symbol, perhaps *the* symbol, reality at its most real breaking through. Jesus is the really real disclosing or revealing itself, the Christ, the symbolic Christ. With Jesus Christ, as with all metapersonal symbolic realities, we find ourselves in the grip, in the presence, of what we thought we would grasp. We are in the presence of mystery, the *mysterium Christi,* the paschal mystery, the symbolic Christ.

Ultimately, the best way to understand or interpret Jesus is as symbol. This in no way disparages or makes unnecessary our historiographical knowledge of Jesus. Indeed, such knowledge helps us both to unpack the symbol of Jesus and to communicate the Jesus symbol to our period of history. Nor does this make less significant our personal experiences of Jesus. The symbolic Christ must also be personally meaningful. Yet, to understand Jesus fully, wholly, we must realize that Jesus is first and foremost a symbol, that is, a metapersonal symbolic reality through whom the transcendent is, has been, and will be made present and active. In Jesus, as in every symbol, earth and heaven come together—as is the case in the Fourth Gospel. It takes more than historiography to understand history; it takes theology as well. Theology's proper concern is symbolic reality. Theological knowledge is symbolic knowledge: an invitation to encounter mystery.

Christologists of the twentieth century have grown up with the dilemma of contrast between the historical Jesus and the Christ of faith. Developmentally, the dilemma was probably necessary even if falsely posed. The contrast rather is between the historiographical Jesus and the symbolic Christ who are not in opposition to each other. There is more to Jesus, even the earthly Jesus, than the historiographical Jesus alone. But at the same time, concern for the symbolic Christ, the Christ for yesterday, today, and forever, does not disallow the value of historiographical accessibility. Symbolic knowledge does not regard objective knowledge as an enemy, unless objective knowledge itself makes itself out to be such. There is but *one* Jesus Christ: the Jesus of history, the symbolic Christ. Even in history Jesus functioned primarily as symbol. Symbols are historical realities even if not all historical realities are symbolic realities. Ultimately our concern must be not the historiographers' Christ, nor the Church's Christ, but the symbolic Christ.

Ritual is the enactment or reenactment of a myth. Myth is a symbol in narrative form. Behind or underneath or within both ritual and myth is a symbolic reality. Christian ritual and the Christ myth (or narrative), through sacrament and word, make the symbolic Christ present. Both in history and today the same symbolic Christ, Jesus Christ, is present. Jesus Christ mediates God's presence, is God as present. In Jesus, (the reign of) God is made manifest. In Jesus, the symbolic Christ, God is with us. Jesus Christ is Son of God, son of Mary, Immanuel.

7

Christology and Pneumatology

Just as Christology is inseparable from soteriology, indeed, in one sense is soteriology, so Christology is inseparable from pneumatology, and again, in one sense, is pneumatology. Jesus' life and mission are completely interwoven with that of the Spirit.

One of the best attested, most accepted facts in the life of Jesus is his baptism by John. All of the accounts of the baptism associate it with the Spirit (Mark 1:10; Matt 3:16; Luke 3:22; John 1:32-33). In volume 1 of this series I spoke of the baptism as the first publicly accessible religious experience in the life of Jesus. James D. G. Dunn has written, *"Jesus' baptism by John was probably the occasion for an experience of God which had epochal significance for Jesus,* even though that significance may only have been fully grasped after some reflection by Jesus. The most striking elements of this experience were *Spirit and sonship.*"[1] Jesus' baptism seems to have been an experience of the Spirit and an empowerment by the Spirit. Shortly thereafter, the Spirit drives or leads Jesus into the wilderness (Mark 1:12; Matt 4:1; Luke 4:1)—the occasion for another experience, an ordeal that puts Jesus' sonship to the test, a time during which he may have come to know God as *Abba/Imma.*[2] As we saw in volume 2 the Christological moment, the moment at which Jesus is understood to have become the Christ, shifts or varies. Although in Matthew and Luke Jesus becomes son at the time of his baptism through the

---

[1] James D. G. Dunn, *Jesus and the Spirit* (London: SCM Press, 1975) 65.

[2] Goergen, *The Mission and Ministry of Jesus,* 129-45, 278-81.

power of the Spirit, in their infancy narratives Jesus becomes son at conception, which takes place through the power of the Holy Spirit (Matt 1:18, 20; Luke 1:35). Jesus' sonship and mission are inseparable from the working of the Holy Spirit.

"And Jesus returned in the power of the Spirit into Galilee" (Luke 4:14). Although each of the Synoptics has its own theology of the Spirit, for all of them Jesus' life is inseparable from the Spirit. The Spirit is power, the power of God, and Jesus is conscious of that power at work within him—in his healings, exorcisms, and in the authority with which he taught. One of his best-attested sayings is his interpretation of the exorcisms: "But if it is by the Spirit of God that I cast out demons, then (the reign of) God has come upon you" (Matt 12:28; Luke 11:20 has "finger of God" rather than "Spirit"; also see Mark 3:28-30). In volume 1, I situated Jesus in the prophetic and charismatic traditions of ancient Israel.[3]

Jesus was empowered by the Spirit in his ministry to others and conscious of the Spirit at work in his ministry. Jesus was a man of the Shema, of faith and prayer.[4] Prayer was the source from which Jesus gained his strength. His prayer and consciousness of sonship were based in his experience of God as *Abba/Imma*. This too is rooted in the life of the Spirit within him. Prayer and mission were but two sides of a coin. "As he found God in prayer as Father, so he found God in mission as power."[5] Jesus' life and mission were completely interwoven with the life of the Spirit.

After the crucifixion, Jesus gives his disciples the gift of the Spirit. In John 20:21-23, this takes place on the occasion of an appearance-experience. In Luke, the occasion is Pentecost (Acts 2:1-4). Again, although the accounts vary, the post-resurrection events are an experience both of Jesus and of the Spirit. Particularly in Paul, but also in Luke (Acts 16:7), the Spirit *is* Jesus. The Spirit plays a major role in the life of Jesus. Jesus is inseparable from the Spirit. So in the early Church, Jesus and Spirit are still tightly woven together. The Spirit is particularly important in the writings of Paul, Luke, and John.

---

[3]See ibid., 109–204; and Dunn, *Jesus and the Spirit,* 41–92.

[4]Goergen, *The Mission and Ministry of Jesus,* 129–45.

[5]Dunn, *Jesus and the Spirit,* 90. Also see Jesus' twofold solidarity with God and with the people in Goergen, *The Mission and Ministry of Jesus,* 109–281.

In the theology of Paul, the Spirit and the risen Jesus Christ are barely distinguishable.[6] Practically speaking, they are one. In Romans 8, Paul distinguishes those who walk according to the flesh and those who walk according to the Spirit. "But you are not in the flesh, you are in the Spirit, if in fact the Spirit of God dwells in you. Anyone who does not have the Spirit of Christ does not belong to him" (Rom 8:9). Is there any difference for Paul between being "in Christ" and "in the Spirit"? God's Spirit can be identified as Christ's Spirit. As Romans 8 continues, it is the Spirit who makes us also to be sons and daughters of God, enables us to pray as Jesus taught us, crying out "Abba," and makes us co-heirs with Christ (Rom 8:14-17). In Galatians 4:6-7, it is the Spirit of God's Son who accomplishes all of this.

Although the Spirit and Christ are not simply equated (they are distinguishable), they are nevertheless intimately related. Since the Christ event, and since the resurrection, practically speaking, they are one and the same. "Therefore I want you to understand that no one speaking by the Spirit of God ever says 'Jesus be cursed!' and no one can say 'Jesus is Lord' except by the Holy Spirit" (1 Cor 12:3). Although there is an entire prior history to the activity of the Spirit of which Paul is quite aware, after Jesus, for Paul, practically speaking, Jesus and the Spirit are one. They have put their mark on each other. "For by one Spirit we were all baptized into one body . . . and all were made to drink of one Spirit" (1 Cor 12:13). Although there is no "body of the Holy Spirit," there would be no body of Christ if it were not for the work of the Spirit. According to Dunn, all the New Testament writers see the gift of the Spirit as the one essential element of Christian initiation.[7] No Spirit, no body of Christ. The shared experience of the Spirit was the basis for the unity of early Christian communities.

The Spirit of God has practically identified itself with Christ; it is thus also the Spirit of Christ. "Now the Lord is the Spirit, and where the Spirit of the Lord is, there is freedom. And we all, with unveiled face, beholding the glory of the Lord, are be-

[6]Yves Congar, *I Believe in the Holy Spirit,* vol. 1: *Revelation and Experience of the Spirit,* trans. David Smith (New York: The Seabury Press, 1983) 37-39. Also Dunn, *Jesus and the Spirit,* 318-26.

[7]Dunn, *Jesus and the Spirit,* 6, 159-65. Also see James D. G. Dunn, *Baptism in the Holy Spirit* (London: SCM Press, 1970).

ing changed into his likeness, from one degree of glory to another; for this comes from the Lord who is the Spirit" (2 Cor 3:17-18; also see Phil 1:19). Given their intimate relationship, at times almost interchangeability, and the way in which they have mutually put their mark on each other, Dunn has made the interesting suggestion that Paul's hymn to love (1 Cor 13:4-7) and the fruit of the Spirit (Gal 5:22) are "character sketches" of Jesus and of what it means to put on Christ.[8]

Luke does not give a theology of the Spirit as developed as Paul's, certainly not of the effects of the Spirit in Christian life, yet the Spirit is everywhere felt and abundantly present. In the Gospel, the Spirit plays a crucial role in the life and ministry of Jesus, in his conception (Luke 1:35), during the visit to Elizabeth (1:41-42), in the prophecy of Simeon (2:25-32), on the occasion of Jesus' baptism (3:21-22), during the wilderness experience (4:1-2), and the return to Galilee (4:14). The healings and exorcisms are manifestations of the gift and power of the Spirit. Jesus is clearly a man of the Spirit, whose life is bound up with the life of the Spirit.

In the Acts of the Apostles, the Spirit becomes the central figure in the coming to be and building up of the community. This book is really an account of the acts of God, or rather, the acts of the Spirit. If the Gospel is a Jesus book, then Acts is a Spirit book, and they belong side by side.

The whole setting for the Book of Acts and the emergence of the post-resurrection Jesus movement is the Jerusalem Pentecost (2:1-47), a work of the Holy Spirit. But the Jerusalem experience is simply the first of many "Pentecosts" in the Book of Acts. The Spirit acts in the pentecosts in Samaria (8:14-17) and in Ephesus (19:1-7). The Spirit continues to act through Peter (4:8; 8:14-17; 10:44-48; 11:15-17) and Paul (9:17-18; 13:9; 19:1-7). For Luke, Jesus' baptism and Christian baptism are a baptism of the Holy Spirit (Luke 2:16; Acts 1:5; 11:16; 19:1-6). The Spirit and Jesus are not identified in Luke, nor even as seemingly one as in Paul, yet their stories and activities interpenetrate and are inseparable: "This Jesus God raised up, and of that we are all witnesses. Being therefore exalted at the right hand of God, and having received

---

[8]Dunn, *Jesus and the Spirit,* 321.

from the Father the promise of the Holy Spirit, he has poured out this which you see and hear" (Acts 2:32-33).

In the Fourth Gospel we again find a foundational role played by the Spirit both in the life of Jesus and in the community of disciples. Jesus has the gift of the Spirit. "And John bore witness, 'I saw the Spirit descend as a dove from heaven, and it remained on him' " (John 1:32). Notice that the Johannine theologian says not only "descended" but also "remained." The union of Jesus with the Spirit continues throughout Jesus' life and ministry. The Spirit is central to the Johannine Jesus' theology, as in the discussion with Nicodemus (3:5-8). Jesus is baptized with the Holy Spirit (1:33) and is the one who gives the Spirit. "As yet the Spirit had not been given, because Jesus was not yet glorified" (7:39b). And on Easter evening, the "Johannine Pentecost": "And when he had said this, he breathed on them, and said to them, 'Receive the Holy Spirit' " (20:22).

As in Paul, Jesus and the Spirit are distinguishable but closely identified. Paul's "Spirit of Jesus" is the Johannine "other Paraclete." The theology of "the Paraclete" is peculiar to the Fourth Gospel; it is developed in five texts in the farewell discourse (14:16-17; 14:26; 15:26-27; 16:7-11; 16:13-15). The Paraclete, that is, the Comforter, the Advocate, is described as "another" (14:16). Clearly Jesus is the first Paraclete, and the activities of the two cannot be understood apart from each other.

Both the Son and the Paraclete come from the Father (3:16; 5:37; 7:29; 8:18; 12:45; 14:16; 14:26). Both teach (14:26). Both are truth (1:17; 14:6; 16:13; 18:37). The Advocate will be sent by Jesus and by the Father (14:16, 26; 15:26; 16:7), in Jesus' name (14:26), and will bear witness to Jesus (15:26) and glorify him (16:14). The work of the Father, the Son, and the Spirit are in harmony. The Son does the work of the Father who sent him (e.g., 5:19-47; 10:25-30; 12:44-50) and the Paraclete or Spirit continues the work of the Son (16:12-15). "As the incarnate Logos 'exegeted' . . . the Father (John 1:18), so the Spirit exegetes Jesus."[9]

We have seen the Spirit as intimately interwoven into both the life of Jesus and the experience of the early Christians: they are inextricable. The story of the Spirit of God, however, pre-exists the story of Jesus, as does the activity of the Word. Jesus is simply

[9]Ibid., 356.

one part of the history of the Spirit, even if so crucial a part that they become inseparable.

In the Hebrew Scriptures, the word *ruah* (*pneuma* in Greek) occurs 378 times; it means breath, air, wind, or soul. It can denote quite simply the breath or the wind, but also the life-force, and even (about one-third of the times that it occurs) the breath of the Lord or power by which God acts *(ruah Yahweh)*. The breath (or Breath) of the Lord is, of course, holy. It is the Holy Breath.[10]

The Breath of the Lord is seen as especially active in the charismatic history of Israel: with the "judges," the prophets, and in wisdom. After the occupation of Canaan by Joshua, and before the institution of the monarchy, leadership in Israel rested with the "judges," charismatic leaders and warriors upon whom the Breath of the Lord came, such as Othniel (Judg 3:10), Gideon (6:34), Jephthal (11:29), and Samson (13:25; 14:6; 14:19). Likewise the Holy Breath was with Samuel, Saul, and David (1 Sam 10:6; 11:6; 16:13).

During the period of the monarchy, the Spirit or Breath of the Lord was particularly associated with prophecy. The gift of the Spirit was the gift of prophecy. The prophetic *word* was attributed to the *spirit,* especially during the exilic, post-exilic, and early Jewish periods (e.g., Ezek 2:2; 11:5; Isa 48:16; 61:1; Zech 7:12; 2 Chr 24:20). The Deutero-Isaian servant was to be a person of the Spirit (Isa 42:1). Joel 3:1-2 linked the Spirit in eschatological times with all peoples. In prophecy, the Word of the Lord and the Spirit of the Lord were closely intertwined.

In Wisdom literature, wisdom is closely linked and almost identified with the Spirit. Wisdom possesses a spirit (Wis 7:22), is a spirit (1:6), and acts in the form of a spirit (7:7). Wisdom is one expression of the Holy Breath or Holy Spirit (see Wis 7:22–9:18). Some of the Fathers of the Church regarded Wisdom as prefiguring, not the Word, but the Holy Spirit.[11]

Wisdom, word, and spirit were not personalized in any way as distinct from God or within God in Israelite and Judaean history. They were ways of talking about God. They were God, but God as acting, reaching out, leaning toward us, God in communication with creation.

[10] Yves Congar, *I Believe in the Holy Spirit,* 1:3–14.

[11] C. Larcher, *Études sur le Livre de la Sagesse* (Paris, 1969) 329–414.

God as Triune

One cannot do Christology without encountering pneumatology. Christ and the Spirit simply go together. But this continues to raise questions for us. Who do we say that Jesus is? Who is Christ? And what of the Spirit of God? Who is the Spirit? The Jesus phenomenon leads us to talk in a certain way about God. God-talk cannot be separated from Christ and the Spirit. Thus we can see, even in Christology from below, that we are led in the direction of the threefold unity of God. One of the implications of Christology and pneumatology is that they affect our image and language of God. Christian monotheism is a Trinitarian monotheism. But what does this mean?

I do not intend here to develop a theology of the threefold unity as such nor to pursue the history of the doctrine. But I can put in my own words how I have come to express this superabundant unity that God is. For Christology and pneumatology imply Trinity.

My preferred image or word for God, as God, is *Abyss*. Before any sophisticated reflection takes place which might talk about God as pure actuality or being itself or the ground of being, God is present to me as an incomprehensible and unfathomable abyss. God simply is. And God is always more than I can conceive or imagine. God is without end. There is no defining God because God is not delineated. God's being is an abyss of being, a neverending depth.

This image or word is compatible with the experiences that underlie apophatic theology as well as with rational theology which affirms that God is more unlike anything we know than like anything we might think. To our intellects God is an abyss of intelligible incomprehensibility.

This starting point helps us to keep in perspective what or who it is that we are dealing with. It keeps us on the right road. The image of course is quite common in mystical theology. For Gregory of Nyssa, the spiritual pilgrimage is a journey into the chasm of the unknowability of God.[12] Catherine of Siena frequently spoke of God as an abyss—an abyss of charity, an abyss

---

[12]Cf. Jean Danielou, *Platonisme et théologie mystique; essai sur la doctrine spirituelle de Saint Grégoire de Nysse* (Paris: Aubier, Editions Montaigne, 1944).

of providence, an abyss of wisdom, or just an abyss.[13] She had this in common with her Dominican brothers to the north. For both Eckhart and Tauler God is *Abgrund* (abyss, without ground), and the *Grund* of our souls flows into or out of this *Abgrund*.[14] In modern theology, one can quickly make a connection with Karl Rahner's "holy mystery."[15]

God is mystery because God is without a ground, is self-grounded. There is no other in terms of which we can understand or explain God. God is God, and there is no going further. When we come to God we find ourselves in the grip of what we thought we could grasp. We find ourselves in the mysticity and mystery of a neverending abyss. This abyss at first has no face. It simply is.

But there is more to God than this abyss alone. God is also Word and Spirit. The Word is not the Abyss as such, but the Word is God, and likewise the Spirit is God, even if not the Abyss. The Word and Spirit come from out of the Abyss, however. The Word and Spirit are not always easily distinguishable, and in fact were fairly indistinguishable prior to the Christ event. Yet, from all eternity, in the fullness and richness of God's being, God is Abyss, Word, and Spirit. Irenaeus spoke of Word and Spirit as two hands of God. They are, but they are fully God. What then can we say of the Eternal Word and the Holy Breath?

The mysterious infinitude that is God has led the Judeo-Christian tradition to affirm strongly two aspects of God: God's totally other and unutterable transcendence and God's unfathomable and absolute nearness. The language of transcendence and the language of immanence are both valid God-talk. God is totally other only if we add "and also totally present," and God

---

[13]Catherine of Siena, *The Dialogue*, trans. Suzanne Noffke, Classics of Western Spirituality (New York: Paulist Press, 1980) e.g., 325, 365; *The Prayers of Catherine of Siena*, ed. Suzanne Noffke (New York: Paulist Press, 1983) 64. Cf. Goergen, *The Jesus of Christian History*, 180–200.

[14]John Tauler, *Spiritual Conferences*, trans. and ed. Eric Colledge and Sister M. Jane, O.P. (Rockford, Ill.: Tan Books and Pub., 1978) esp. 88, 118–19, 124–25, 186, 195, 203, 254. Also see Tauler, *Sermons*. Also see Champellion, "La place de termes 'gemeute' et 'grunt' dans le vocabulaire de Tauler," in *La mystique rhenane*, colloque de Strasbourg (Paris: Presses Universitaires de France, 1963) 179–92. See ch. 2 n. 21 (p. 38 above).

[15]Karl Rahner, *Foundations of Christian Faith: An Introduction to the Idea of Christianity*, trans. William V. Dych (New York: The Seabury Press, 1978) 44–89.

is totally present only if we add "and also totally other." "Abyss" attempts to convey God's transcendence; "Word" and "Spirit" characterize God in the mode of immanence. If God were only Abyss, one could not capture God's closeness and nearness and presentness. And if God were only Word and Spirit one could not capture the undelimited otherness of God. Either God is put at a distance from us, or God is created in our own image and according to our fancy—unless we make the effort to find language to express the full reality.

Both Word and Spirit then denote God in the mode of immanence—God as leaning toward, reaching out, in touch with and touching our lives and our history. If God were not Word and Spirit, there would be no contact with God, in fact there would be no creation to be in contact with God. There would be only the abysmal God. But as Word and Spirit God can be described as self-communicating, self-giving, self-revealing, as coming, as near, present and close.

Nothing has yet been said to make us describe this threefold unity of God in personal terms. Insofar as God in the mode of immanence is in contact with us in a personal and interpersonal way, we can and must describe God as person. But this says nothing about a tripersonal unity. Indeed, at this point, it is better for us not to use personal language. God is triune—Abyss, Word, Spirit—in God's very innermost self, but Abyss, Word, and Spirit are not "persons" in any modern sense of the term. This has been made clear in contemporary theology, both Catholic and Protestant. In the theologies of Barth, Rahner, and Schoonenberg, God is one God, one divine nature, but three hypostases, and this latter expression is better translated as "modes of subsistence." Even for Thomas Aquinas, *hypostasis* in the theology of the Trinity is best translated as "subsistent relationship."[16] The relationship among these three modes of subsistence need not be our concern here, except to say that the Word and Spirit come from out of the Abyss or are sent forth by the Abyss. What is clear is that the Abyss, Word, and Spirit are God, fully and truly God, and yet distinguishable from each other—one God in three divine modes of subsistence.

---

[16]Yves Congar, *I Believe in the Holy Spirit,* vol. 3: *The River of the Water of Life Flows in the East and in the West,* trans. David Smith (New York: The Seabury Press, 1983) 81. See Thomas Aquinas, *ST,* I, q. 29, a. 4.

This may not be easy to see, and indeed is impossible to express adequately, but can nevertheless be acceptable if we refrain from personalizing these three modes of subsistence for a while. Let us use an analogy (a very weak one, as all analogies for speaking about God are), the analogy of space (weak because we conceive space as limited whereas God is unlimited). If we confine ourselves to a certain amount of space, say the space of the room I am sitting in, our language for this space speaks of various dimensions, such as length, breadth, and depth. Now the length is clearly not the breadth nor the depth and yet all refer to the one common space. This space can exist as depth or as breadth or as length. So is God as three subsistent modes or relationships. The Word is not the Abyss or the Spirit and yet is defined by its relationship to both. The Word comes from out of the Abyss, is all that the Abyss is, but *as* Word.

> For this reason I bow my knees before the Father, from whom every family in heaven and on earth is named, that according to the riches of his glory he may grant you to be strengthened with might through his Spirit in the inner person, and that Christ may dwell in your hearts through faith; that you, being rooted and grounded in love, may have power to comprehend with all the saints what is the breadth and length and height and depth, and to know the love of Christ which surpasses knowledge, that you may be filled with all the fullness of God.
>
> Ephesians 3:14-19

> Can you find out the deep things of God?
> Can you find out the limit of the Almighty?
> It is higher than heaven—what can you do?
> Deeper than Sheol—what can you know?
> Its measure is longer than the earth, and broader than the sea.
>
> Job 11:7-9

> Then the Lord answered Job out of the whirlwind:
> "Who is this that darkens counsel by words of knowledge?
> Gird up your loins like a man,
> I will question you, and you shall declare to me.
> Where were you when I laid the foundation of the earth?
> Tell me, if you have understanding.
> Who determined its measurements—surely you know!
> Or who stretched the line upon it?

On what were its bases sunk, or who laid its cornerstone,
when the morning stars sang together,
and all the sons of God shouted for joy?"

Job 38:1-7

Then Job answered the Lord:
"I know that thou canst do all things,
and that no purpose of thine can be thwarted.
'Who is this that hides counsel without knowledge?'
Therefore I have uttered what I did not understand,
things too wonderful for me,
which I did not know.
'Hear and I will speak;
I will question you, and you declare to me,'
but now my eye sees thee,
therefore I despise myself, and repent in dust and ashes."

Job 42:1-6

O the depth of the riches and wisdom and knowledge of God!
How unsearchable are his judgements
and how inscrutable his ways!
"For who has known the mind of the Lord,
or who has been his counselor?"
"Or who has given a gift to him that he might be repaid?"
For from him and through him and to him are all things.
To him be glory for ever. Amen.

Romans 11:33-36

We have said something that helps us to distinguish the Word and the Spirit from the Abyss, but we need to say something further about their distinctiveness from each other, since both are modes of subsistence by which God is immanent to creation.

If we refer back momentarily to the analogy with the length, breadth, and depth of space, keeping in mind that there is one common nature (as space), we can still see that the three *hypostases* are distinct. The Abyss is the vast, endless depth from which both Word and Spirit come. The Abyss has never been without the Word and Spirit, and yet there is a relationship of origin. The Abyss is the eternal origin. To use traditional Trinitarian language, the Abyss is *genitor* but *ingenitus;* the Abyss *begets* the Word. Speaking the language of tradition again (and theologies of the Trinity are simply a search for a somewhat adequate language or way of speaking about the Christian experience of God), the Spirit is distinct from the Word in terms of origin in that the Spirit comes from the Abyss *through the Word*. The Spirit is not begotten by the Abyss, but nevertheless *proceeds* from the Abyss through the Word. The Abyss is still *principaliter* the source of the Spirit, but the Spirit does not proceed from the Abyss apart from the Word. In fact, in many Hebrew texts, one would have a difficult time distinguishing Word and Spirit because they are so closely allied. So there are two different modes of coming from the Abyss manifest in the generation of the Word and the Spirit. The Spirit is the Spirit of the Word as well as proceeding from the Abyss.

But this language may obscure our point. The Word and Spirit are distinct not only in their origins but also as breadth and length are distinct. The Word is the length of God, God going forth to the ends of the earth. The Word is active in creation and human history. The primary function of the Word is that it speaks God, reveals God, discloses and communicates from out of the Abyss what God is. Were it not for the Word, God would remain totally unknown, *totally* other, utterly distant, unbridgeable mystery. But because God is both Abyss and Word, God both transcends everything and anything we say about God and yet is present to our understanding. For God is revealed by the Word in and through creation and the history of salvation and revelation.

The Spirit is the breadth of all that there is. The Spirit too is a going forth *(ad extra)* from God, but it does not so much reveal God as fill all with God. The Word creates; the Spirit recreates. The Word reveals; the Spirit transforms. It is the Spirit that lies at the depths of my soul and permeates the breadth of God's creation. The Spirit is groaning from within creation (Rom 8:18-25) and praying from within my own innermost self (Rom 8:14-16; Gal 4:6-7).

Granted, to speak of length, breadth, and depth may be strange, weak, and inadequate language, but it does reflect our struggle to express our experience and understanding of God. God is eternally transcendent (Abyss) and also drawing near and reaching out (Word and Spirit), self-communicating (Word) and self-giving (Spirit), giving the Gift (Spirit) of God's very own self to us. It is through the Word and in the Spirit that we become one with God.

It is of help to me not to personalize the threefold oneness or triunity of God immediately. But now we are more easily able to do so. The Abyss is *Abba/Imma,* the origin of the Word, of the uniquely begotten Son, and the Spirit is of course the Holy Breath, the Spirit of Jesus.

The Son is the incarnate Word, or the Word incarnate is the Son, Jesus Christ, our Lord. Here, with Schoonenberg, and in accord with New Testament language, I would prefer not to speak of the eternal Word as Son. Son means the crucified and risen one, the eternal Word incarnate. But the Son *is* that Word, and that Word has become this Son, and the Son is the full and unsurpassable expression of all that the Word is, so by way of extrapolation backwards one can call God's Word Son insofar as that Word is directed or destined to be Son. But, more precisely, when the Word became flesh, the Word *became* Son. Now we can speak of the Word as a person not only in the traditional sense of *hypostasis* (subsistent relationship, mode of subsistence) but also in the currently understood sense of *person.* The Word became a person and we can relate personally to the Word, the Word incarnate, Jesus Christ, Son of the Living God, who was crucified for our sake and raised from the dead. The Word not only acts in history but has a history. But prior to the incarnation, it is better to say God acts, for there is only one actor, one consciousness and freedom, one divine nature, one God. This God, Abyss, Word, and Spirit, *becomes* three persons. This threefold unity becomes a tripersonal unity, still one God, but now Father, Son, Spirit.

For indeed, all New Testament texts that speak of the relationship between the Spirit and Son are concerned with the economy of salvation, the economic Trinity.[17] We call God Father/Mother, or address the Abyss that God absolutely is in a personal and intimate way, only because of the Word incarnate. We only know the Father because of the Son. And likewise we call Jesus Christ the uniquely begotten Son because, in the history of salvation, Jesus was son, came to this particular filial consciousness as obedient servant, and learned his sonship in the school of suffering. Indeed he became the perfect son of the almighty but all-merciful, compassionate, and ever-present Abba.

[17]Congar, *I Believe in the Holy Spirit,* 3:49.

And so with the Holy Spirit: however the relationship between Word and Spirit in the immanent Trinity be expressed, in the economy of salvation, the Spirit becomes the Spirit of Jesus as well as of the Father—simply because the Father and Son are one. So the Spirit is stamped with the seal of Christ. The Spirit too is not only *hypostasis,* an eternal and divine mode of subsistence, but also a person in our sense, for the Spirit has become Jesus' very own Spirit, the Spirit of the Risen Christ released at Jesus' glorification and present in the world and building up the Church. This selfsame Spirit is the soul of the world and the Church, the Gift, the Paraclete. Although we have not always addressed the Spirit as personally as we have the Father and Jesus Christ, the Son, we nevertheless have done so on occasion: "Veni Creator Spiritus."

Now to say that the Son *is* the eternal Word and the Holy Spirit in the formula of Christian baptism *is* the eternal Breath is not to say that there is not more to the Word and Breath than Jesus Christ and the Spirit of the Risen Lord. The Word that Jesus is and the Spirit that Jesus gives both have a pre-history prior to the Christ event. Nor can we say that their ongoing activity in the Church and among Christian people need exclude their presence elsewhere, although both Word and Spirit are now and forever intimately tied up with Christ. The Word will always be the Word that became Jesus Christ and the Spirit will always and everywhere be the Spirit of Christ, even if the body of Christ cannot contain them. Christ and the Church cannot confine, although they do define, the Word and Spirit. The Word subsists completely and unsurpassably in Jesus Christ, but not exclusively so, and likewise with the Spirit's presence to the Church. For Christian people there is one God, who brought our ancestors out of the land of Egypt and who later raised up prophets and sages from their midst, whose very own innermost being is as Abyss, Word, and Spirit—three divine hypostases or modes of subsistence which have been revealed through the Christian experience of Father, the Father of our Lord Jesus Christ, and Son, the Word incarnate, and the Holy Spirit, the Breath that comes from the Father through the Son—our God from all eternity and revealed in the economy of salvation as the Father, "the Father of glory" (Eph 1:17), the Word/Son, "the reflection of his glory" (Heb 1:3), and the Spirit, "the Spirit of glory" (1 Pet 4:14).

A Christian theology of God is a theology of this Trinity: a theology of God, Yahweh, Abba, as well as a theology of Jesus and a pneumatology. There is no Christology without pneumatology, and for Christians no pneumatology without Christology. Jesus Christ is intimately, inseparably, linked to Word and Spirit. There is more to the story of Jesus than Spirit, and more to the story of the Spirit than Jesus, but for Christians they are still inseparable from each other. Jesus is both the Word incarnate and the one anointed by the Spirit, raised from the dead by the Spirit, and who gives us the Spirit as Gift. Thus pneumatology not only enhances one's Christology but is essential to it.[18]

Pneumatology, East and West

One of the criticisms by the East (Orthodoxy) of the West is that Latin and Catholic Christianity has lacked an adequate theology of the Spirit. In the East, the close connection between the doctrine of incarnation (Christology) and deification (pneumatology) necessitate a theology of the Spirit. In the West the connection between Christology and ecclesiology, especially when the Church is principally defined as the body of Christ and experienced in institutional and structured form, can leave the Spirit out of the picture. It is to the credit of Yves Congar to have given us a pneumatology and restored the link between pneumatology and ecclesiology. Not: God-Christ-Church-sacraments, but God-Christ-Spirit-Church—a truly Trinitarian-grounded ecclesiology. Even here, however, we must resist a Christian pneumatology's becoming exclusively ecclesiocentric. The Spirit is unleashed on the world.

However inadequate it may have been, Vatican II attempted to remedy the theological vacuum left by an undeveloped theology of the Spirit. At least there are intimations of a pneumatological consciousness in the conciliar documents: there are at least 258 references to the Spirit on which one can build. The pneumatology of the council is Christocentric; the Spirit is the Spirit of Christ. It is also very much related to the renewal of ecclesiology. The council's definition of the Church is not limited to its

---

[18]Congar, *I Believe in the Holy Spirit,* 1:156–57. Congar's own pneumatology is ecclesiocentric and needs to be developed further in the direction of the Spirit's presence in the world and in other religions of the world.

being the body of Christ. The church is the people of God and the temple of the Spirit. Reconstructing ecclesiology was one of the major achievements of the council. Rahner held that the most valuable contribution of the council was its theology of the local Church.[19] Congar himself maintained that the council's most significant contribution was reversing the order of the second and third chapters of *Lumen gentium,* the Constitution on the Church, and thus placing the Church as the people of God before a consideration of the Church as hierarchically structured. M.-D. Chenu spoke about the theological shift to "signs of the times" and the consequent understanding of Church as *présence au monde,* and that the world became a constitutive part of the understanding of the Church in *Gaudium et spes* (Constitution on the Church in the Modern World), as a Copernican revolution in ecclesiology.[20] Whether a pneumatology was theologically developed or not (and such would not be the work of a council), the presence of the Spirit made itself felt. Epicleses (invocations to the Holy Spirit) were introduced into the new Eucharistic Prayers. There was no epiclesis in the pre-conciliar Roman Canon.[21]

One can see that the council laid the basis for a post-conciliar theological task—the construction of a theology of the Spirit. Post-Vatican II theologians have undertaken the task with great seriousness. The role of the Spirit in Christology is a path being explored. Congar, Schillebeeckx, and Schoonenberg have all provided contributions toward a pneumatology.

One of Congar's lifelong interests has been ecumenism and one of the theological differences between the East and the West has been the theology of the Spirit, symbolized in the addition of the *filioque* to the Nicene-Constantinopolitan Creed in the West. Congar is of the firm conviction that the *filioque* ought to be suppressed, not because it is false teaching as understood in the West but because suppression would be an appropriate ecumenical gesture.

The Greek Fathers were very aware of the inexpressible character of the mystery of the Trinity. An apophatism lies in their back-

---

[19]Karl Rahner, "The New Image of the Church," in *Theological Investigations* 10, trans. David Bourke (New York: The Seabury Press, 1977) 3–29.

[20]Marie-Dominique Chenu, *La "Doctrine Sociale" de l' Eglise comme ideologie* (Paris: Les Editions du Cerf, 1979).

[21]Congar, *I Believe in the Holy Spirit,* 1:170.

ground. From their perspective, Western approaches to the Trinity appear to say too much and to be too rational.

For the Greeks, the Father alone is the absolute source, the originating principle within the Trinity: the monarchy of the Father. The Father is the "source" *(pēgē)*, the "beginning" *(archē)*, the one who is without any other source *(anarchos)*. "The Father is the principle of the goodness and the divinity that we contemplate in the Son and the Spirit."[22] To the Greeks, the Western *filioque* (the Spirit thus proceeding from the Father *and* the Son) compromises the absolute monarchy of the Father. As Congar points out, however, the West is committed to the monarchy of the Father. There is a difference of theology between East and West but not a difference in faith. The East has relied heavily on John 15:26 and the West on John 16:14-15 and 20:22.

The Son and the Spirit, whose source equally is the Father, are distinguished in the East by two different modes of coming to be, two modes of origination. The Greeks are reluctant to say much more about these inexpressible modes than what has been revealed. The Son comes from the Father by "begetting." The Father is the unbegotten one and the eternal Son the only-begotten one. This is an eternal begetting: begotten, not created. The Spirit comes from the Father by "proceeding" *(ekporeusis)*. John 15:26 describes the mode of coming to be of the Spirit alone. The distinction between Son and Spirit in the East is based on these two modes of origin, not as in the West on their character as "relations" as well. More than that there are two distinct modes of coming from the Father ought not be said. "The Father is the source by begetting and procession of all the good hidden in that source itself."[23]

Although there is but one source of the divine triune life, this does not mean that there is no relationship or dependency between the Spirit and the Son. Biblically, the Spirit is the Spirit of Christ, as well as the one who proceeds from the Father. Although there will be theological differences among the Orthodox themselves, both past and present, one can still say that an acceptable formula could be that "the Spirit proceeds from the Father *through* the Son." "From the Father, through the Son, in the Spirit" is in fact the classical way of talking about the life of the Trinity.

[22]Gregory Nazianzen, *Orat.* 2, 38. In Migne, *Patrologia Graeca*, 35:445.

[23]John Damascene, *De fide orthod.* I, 12. In Migne, *Patrologia Graeca*, 94:848.

This relationship between the Spirit and the Son is present in Athanasius and Basil the Great, and even more clear in Gregory of Nyssa, Cyril of Alexandria, John Damascene, and Maximus the Confessor.[24] The expression "through the Son" for the East both indicates a relationship between the Spirit and Son and preserves the one source or cause, the monarchy of the Father. However, "and the Son" *(filioque)* goes too far. Congar attempts to show that the Western *filioque,* properly understood, has the meaning of "through the Son."

At this point one must clearly distinguish between the teaching or theology of the *filioque* and the inclusion of the *filioque* in the Creed. Congar insists that the *filioque* of the Latin West, properly understood, is orthodox, non-heretical, and ought to be admitted as such by the East, but this by no means implies that it belongs in the Creed. This distinction was apparent to Pope Leo III at the time of Charlemagne. Charlemagne pushed for the inclusion of the *filioque* in the Creed. Pope Leo refused. Although he agreed with the teaching of the *filioque,* he engraved the text of the Creed without it in both Greek and Latin and had them hung in St. Peter's (A.D. 810). The *filioque* seems to have been added to the Creed in Gaul and Spain during the last decade of the sixth century (and added in good faith, thinking that it came from Nicaea-Constantinople), but the Creed with the *filioque* was not introduced into the Mass in Rome until 1014.[25]

Two important facts should be kept in mind. The Catholic West should recall that the Council of Constantinople's teaching on the Spirit said nothing about the Son's role in the Spirit's procession from the Father. The Spirit is "Lord, giver of life, who proceeds from the Father, who is adored and glorified with the Father and the Son, who has spoken through the prophets." The *filioque* is a Western interpolation into a Creed of the universal Church. The Orthodox East should recall that the West was teaching the *filioque* at a time when East and West were still in communion with each other. The East did not consider the West heretical in that regard.

Another difference between the theologies of the Trinity of East and West lies in the emphasis the West places on the divine na-

[24]Congar, *I Believe in the Holy Spirit,* 3:24–56.

[25]Ibid., 54, 57, 129.

ture as a starting point for its theology of the unity in the Trinity. But we need not pursue that here. The starting point among the Orthodox is the three hypostases, the divine Persons. The basis of the unity in God for the East is not so much one common divine nature but the Father, as well as the *perichoresis* or *circumincession.*[26]

Congar maintains that the faith of the West is fundamentally the same as the faith of the East with respect to the Trinity, but that the theology of the West developed along different lines with a different vocabulary. In the East, the Father is the absolute origin of the Son and Spirit, who are distinct by two modes of coming to be. Likewise, *filioque* properly implies: from the Father *through* the Son, certainly not from the Father *and* the Son as from two principles or sources.

For Anselm, in the West, only the Father is *genitor* and *ingenitus.* The Son is *genitus* and the Spirit *procedens.* Although his theology is distinctly Western, he does not refer to the Son as *procedens,* the word the Greeks reserve for the mode of coming to be of the Spirit *(ekporeusis). Procedere* is not generalized yet to refer to both the coming to be of the Son and of the Spirit. Thomas Aquinas later speaks of two processions but distinguishes the modes of coming to be as a begetting of the Son and a spiration of the Spirit.[27] Bonaventure's theology of the Trinity comes closer to that of the East than many others do. The Father is clearly the absolute source, *auctor,* the only *auctor,* the *plenitudo fontalis.*[28]

The source of the specifically Latin theology of the Trinity is Augustine. His *De Trinitate* is not the first treatise on the Trinity in the West, yet it is formative of Western theology. Does his theology stand in opposition to the faith of the East? How does he understand the *filioque?*

For Augustine, the Father is the absolute source of both the Son and the Spirit. He expresses this, however, with his phrase, *"principaliter a Patre."* "The Father is the principle of all divinity or, to be more precise, of the deity, because he does not take his origin from anything else. He has no one from whom he has

[26]Ibid., 72–78.

[27]Thomas Aquinas, *ST,* I, 27–43.

[28]Congar, *I Believe in the Holy Spirit,* 3:109–14, 135–36.

his being or from whom he proceeds, but it is by him that the Son is begotten and from him that the Holy Spirit proceeds."[29] And, "It is not in vain that God the Father is called the one by whom the Word is begotten and from whom the Holy Spirit principally proceeds. I have added *principaliter,* 'principally,' because the Holy Spirit also proceeds from the Son. But it is the Father who gave it to him."[30] One can see that the translation and interpretation of Augustine's *principaliter* is crucial.

Augustine affirms that the Spirit proceeds from the Son, although *principaliter a Patre.* Is this more than "through the Son"? Augustine is here clearly conscious of Scripture and the text of John 20:22. "I cannot see what he could otherwise have meant when, breathing on the faces of the disciples, the Lord declared, Receive the Holy Spirit." The Spirit clearly in some way is related to the Son as well as to the Father.

The *filioque* did not originate with Augustine, but it is clearly able to express his faith. The Father is the absolute source, and the Spirit is the Spirit of the Father (Matt 10:28; John 15:26). But it is also clear that the Spirit is the Spirit of the Son (Gal 4:6; John 14:26; 20:22; Luke 6:19). Although the Spirit is said to be from the Father (John 15:26), he also in some way "proceeds" from the Son. Augustine protects the origin *a Patre* by his *principaliter.* He is attempting to be faithful to Scripture on both counts. Scripture testifies that the Spirit is also from the Son, but *principaliter* from the Father.

Augustine's understanding and orthodoxy here are rooted in his commentary on the Gospel of John. The Father communicates everything to the Son except fatherhood. All that the Son has comes from the Father. Then the proceeding of the Spirit from the Son is ultimately, absolutely, *principaliter* from the Father, but from the Father through the Son. For Augustine the *filioque* has the clear sense of *per Filium.*[31]

Wherein then lies the problem? Social, political, and religious factors contributed to the split between East and West. The West was eventually insufficiently careful in respecting the expression

---

[29]Augustine, *De Trinitate* IV, 20, 29. In Migne, *Patrologia Latina,* 42:908.

[30]Ibid., XV, 17, 29. In Migne, *Patrologia Latina,* 42:1081. And 26, 47. In Migne, *Patrologia Latina,* 42:1095.

[31]Congar, *I Believe in the Holy Spirit,* 3:85–87.

of the faith in the East. This is clear by the addition of the *filio-que* to the Creed. Another part of the problem is the problem of language. Doing theology to a great degree is a search for language to express and respect mystery. In translating languages, which are expressions of different cultures as well, there may be no absolute equivalents. In our case here, the Latin *procedere* is not an exact equivalent of the Greek *ekporeuomai*. As in the difficulties between Antioch and Alexandria, so here. What is needed to express the faith in the West may appear to be heretical in the East. *Procedere* has a wider and less precise usage, and in the West was easily able to refer to both the begetting of the Son and the proceeding of the Spirit. And the East's sense of *a Patre solo* was expressed in the West as *a Patre principaliter.*

This is not to deny other theological differences (as distinct from a different faith). For instance, we find in Augustine the emphasis on the mutual opposition of the relationships which plays a significant role in Western theology. Father, Son, and Spirit are relational terms. The Father is Father only by relationship to the Son, and the Son is Son only by relationship to the Father. The Spirit who proceeds from the Father is still not the Son. Thus Spirit and Son are distinct because they are different relationships. This theological approach is more difficult when one comes to the Spirit. Father and Son are correlative and constitute a relationship by definition. For the Spirit, Augustine turns to the word Gift, and the Father and Son are the Giver. "In order to have a reciprocal correspondence in this case, we must speak of gift of the giver or the giver of the gift."[32]

Another characteristic of Augustine's theology of the Trinity is his search to find images for it in the human world, such as the psychological images in his triadology, for example *amans, amatus, amor;* or *memoria, intelligentia, voluntas.* All of this was to assist believers in their understanding, to aid people in the faith *(fides quarens intellectum).*

Two extremes or dangers are present in the *filioque* discussion: first, in the West, to discuss the *filioque* as if it were a question of words only, which is offensive to the East; second, in the East, to exaggerate its significance, when in fact it was taught in the West and accepted as non-heretical in the East when East and

---

[32]Augustine, *De Trinitate* V, 12, 13.

West were still in communion. Maximus the Confessor himself saw the *filioque* in the sense of *dia tou huiou* and thus regarded it as unobjectionable.[33] Congar has made an important contribution toward this discussion.[34] He sees the two formulae as distinct but complementary.

According to Congar, the Roman Catholic Church should suppress the *filioque* in the Creed, return to the original form of the article on the Holy Spirit, and reintroduce this normative form into its liturgy. The formula of the Greeks has its advantages. It would be an ecumenically significant gesture. The Old Catholics and Anglicans have agreed to suppress the *filioque*. Many Catholic theologians favor its suppression. The formula has not been obligatory for two centuries for Eastern Rite Catholics.

Even if the *filioque* ought to be withdrawn from the Creed, it ought to be accepted as a legitimate, non-heretical understanding of the faith of the Church. The language in which the Church expressed itself for centuries cannot be repudiated. This does not mean that one has to accept the Fourth Lateran Council and the Second Council of Lyons as "ecumenical" in the strict sense. What is implied rather is that the Greek expression and the Latin expression of the Trinitarian faith are complementary, representing two different approaches. This does not mean the two expressions are synonymous nor of equal value. Indeed the Greek one is more ancient and representative of the universal faith. Congar writes:

> What we have to aim at and what can, in fact, be reached is a recognition both of the unity of faith on both sides of Catholicity and of the legitimate difference between the two dogmatic expressions of this mystery. Each expression is consistent in itself, and each is impossible in the categories and vocabulary of the other side. In the course of two centuries of discussion, neither side has succeeded in convincing the other or in persuading it to accept its point of view. There is no chance that this goal will be reached in the future. In fact, we may say quite unambiguously that this is not a goal to be pursued.[35]

[33]Congar, *I Believe in the Holy Spirit*, 3:214.
[34]Ibid., 213–14. Cf. all three volumes of *I Believe in the Holy Spirit*.
[35]Ibid., 3:201.

Theology in the West, in the light of Vatican II, and as an ecumenical obligation, carries the burden of developing a more adequate pneumatology. Has the *filioque* led to a subordination of pneumatology to Christology, to the relative absence of pneumatology from ecclesiology, to the subordination of the charismatic role of the Spirit in the Church to the more institutionalized and historical structures of the Church, to a difficulty of accepting and validating renewal from below, to a failure to recognize the unity and diversity that flow from life in the Spirit? What has been the cause of an underdeveloped pneumatology in the West? The need for theological work in this area is clear.

Congar's pneumatology relates the Spirit to the life of the Church, the sacraments, and personal holiness. Its limitation is that it neglects a fuller testament of the Spirit in relation to a theology of the world as a whole, both in the call to justice and in the history of religion.[36]

For Congar, the Church is the fruit of two divine missions, those of the Son and the Spirit. The Spirit is truly a "co-instituting principle" of Church. The Church is instituted and developed as much by the Spirit as by Christ. The Spirit makes the Church one, catholic, apostolic, and holy. The Spirit is the source or principle of both the unity and the diversity of the Church.

The Spirit makes the Church catholic in space (i.e., in the world) and in time (i.e., in history). The Spirit is at work in the world and in history. The Church is not only the people of God, but the peoples of God. In continuity with Pope John XXIII, the Second Vatican Council, and the theology of his own confrere, Chenu, Congar points to "the signs of the times" as basic to the relationship between the Church and the world.

The Spirit makes the Church apostolic, keeps it faithful to the apostolic faith, but "Church" here means the people and not only the hierarchy. Congar retrieves the words of Pope Paul VI: "The lay person is, like the bishop, a successor of the Apostles."[37]

The Spirit is the source of the Church's holiness. This does not negate the sin and sinfulness in the Church as well *(simul iustus et peccator)*, which the Church is often hesitant to admit. We can "grieve" the Spirit (Eph 4:30) or "quench" it (1 Thess 5:19) or

[36]Congar only deals with these in his reference to signs of the times, *I Believe in the Holy Spirit*, 2:31, 219–24.

[37]Congar, *I Believe in the Holy Spirit*, 2:49. Cf. *The Pope Speaks* (1968) 253.

"resist" it (Acts 7:51). Yet the Spirit remains the co-instituting principle in the life of God's people(s).

Ecclesiology is inseparable from pneumatology. Congar attempts to remedy earlier approaches to ecclesiology in which systematic thought primarily worked within a scheme of God-Christ-Church as its dogmatic outline. With Congar this must be revised: Christ-Holy Spirit-Church. Ecclesiology is a function of pneumatology and not the other way around.

Sacraments are the ecclesial acts of the Church, the actions of the *ecclesia congregata,* and here more than anywhere we can see the effect of Vatican II in the life of Christians and of the Church, in the renewal of the liturgy and the revision of liturgical rites, and in the emergence of a renewed pneumatology. Liturgy and sacraments are a function of pneumatology. The classical Roman theology of the sacraments since the Middle Ages has been deficient when it comes to pneumatology but the post-Vatican II liturgical revisions exemplify a revised pneumatology and the growing consciousness of its importance. Thus liturgical theology in the West today is finding itself less removed from the liturgical life of the East. In going to its roots, liturgy in the West finds its connectedness with the East—one of Congar's foundational ecumenical concerns.

One of the most obvious areas for exploring current Catholic theology of the Spirit is in the revised rites of Christian initiation. Confirmation is one of the sacraments of Christian initiation, linked to baptism and Eucharist. Today we affirm the unity of these three stages of initiation. Confirmation is more a completion or further stage of baptism than a different sacrament as such. Christian baptism is already baptism in the Spirit. Confirmation then is not the sacrament of the Spirit. The Spirit is given and present in all the stages of Christian initation. The Spirit is essential both to baptism and to Eucharist. In confirmation, the Spirit already given in baptism is liturgically "sealed." The new rite of confirmation expresses it thus: "Receive the seal of the gift of the Spirit." This formula is an early formula of the Byzantine Rite, and its use reflects the coming closer together of East and West.

This same movement of West toward East and toward a more clearly conscious pneumatology is reflected in the inclusion of an explicit epiclesis (an invocation for the sending of the Spirit) in the Eucharistic Prayers. There was no explicit epiclesis involving the Holy Spirit in the Roman Rite since the time of Gregory the Great; the old Roman Canon lacked one. The new Eucharistic Prayers all contain an epiclesis before the account of the institution and after. The significance of the epiclesis is related to the controversy over the precise moment of consecration or transformation. The Catholic West since the Middle Ages emphasized the words of institution to the exclusion of other elements, and thus failed to recognize the unity of the anaphora or Eucharistic Prayer as a whole and the possibility of a more gradual rather than instantaneous transformation of the bread and wine. The lack of an explicit epiclesis does not imply that the West was not convinced that the Holy Spirit played a role equal to that of the consecrating function of the words of institution. Yet the neglect of the epiclesis had its effects. Sacramental theology follows upon liturgical practice.

The question of the epiclesis is not only a question of the Eucharist but of the theology of priesthood as well. The controversy over the moment of consecration is concerned equally with the agent of consecration, whether it be the priest and words of institution or the Holy Spirit invoked in the epiclesis. Again we note a difference in the theologies of East and West. In the West, since the twelfth century, the sacrament of ordination is conceived as the power to consecrate the Eucharist, the power of orders, with the priest acting *in persona Christi*. But this is a one-sided emphasis on the words of institution and a faulty Christology disconnected from pneumatology. The priest acts both *in persona Christi* and *in persona ecclesiae*.[38] The ordained minister presides but the community co-celebrates the Eucharist. In the East, the epiclesis is spoken in the plural. The whole *ecclesia* invokes the Spirit, who is called upon to make effective the words of Christ cited by the priest. The action of the Spirit is essential to the Eucharistic action.

Note some of the contrasts between the different emphasis on the Holy Spirit and on the ordained minister in Eastern and Western rites.[39]

[38]Cf. David Power, "Representing Christ in Community and Sacrament," in *Being A Priest Today,* ed. Donald J. Goergen (Collegeville, Minn.: The Liturgical Press, 1992) 97–123.

[39]Congar, *I Believe in the Holy Spirit,* 3:240.

	Eastern Rite	*Western Rite*
Baptism	"N. is baptized."	"I baptize you."
Anointing with chrism or confirmation	"the seal of the gift of the Spirit"	The renewed rite has the Eastern form.
Eucharist	epiclesis	words of institution
Penance	"May God forgive you"; "Heal your servant."	"I absolve you." But the renewed form is Trinitarian and an implicit epiclesis.

Ecclesiology, sacramentology, and the theology of the Christian life are chapters in pneumatology. The Spirit acts in the Church, in the sacraments, and in our own personal lives.[40]

The Spirit is the Gift par excellence. As Gift, the Spirit is promised in its fullness only eschatologically, but is possessed already as the guarantee of that which is to come (Eph 1:13-14). This eschatological emphasis is manifest in several of the Fathers who retain the reading of Luke 11:2 found in a number of manuscripts: "May thy Holy Spirit come upon us and purify us" rather than "Thy kingdom come" (Gregory of Nyssa, Evagrius, Maximus the Confessor). *Gift* is Congar's preferred name for the Holy Spirit in his personal meditation on the third *hypostasis*. Here he is in good company—Acts 2:38; 8:20; 10:45; Basil the Great; Hilary of Poitiers; Augustine; Thomas Aquinas; and many others.

A theology of the Holy Spirit emphasizes not only the presence but also the indwelling of God. We become temples of the Holy Spirit (1 Cor 3:16; 6:19; Gal 4:6; Rom 8:9-11; John 14:16-17; 1 John 4:12-13). Depending upon one's theology of the Trinity, this indwelling may or may not be seen as an appropriation to the Holy Spirit of what in fact is the indwelling of the Trinity.

The Spirit is the principle of our sanctification and deification. The Spirit makes the members of Christ's body holy. The incarnation itself is a work of the Holy Spirit. Through the power and gift of the Spirit we also become daughters and sons of God.

---

[40]Ibid., 2:3-146; 3:217-74.

It is the Holy Spirit who makes life in Christ real, personal, and inward. Here one must examine one's "theology of spirituality." Such a theology is really pneumatology. In Christian life, *spiritual* does not mean the opposite of material (its connotation since Cartesian dualism). Christian spirituality rather means "animated by the Holy Spirit." The spirit in spirituality is not the nonmaterial or even the interior life but the Holy Spirit.

The Holy Spirit is the principle of both personal and ecclesial renewal, revival, and conversion. Sectarian evangelism ought not be seen as having a monopoly on these realities or this language. They are traditional and are manifest throughout the history of the Church. Congar would consider the ecumenical movement as a work of the Spirit, and we can consider other movements in the same vein. A theology of the Spirit in our personal lives includes the gifts of the Spirit. The biblical basis for these gifts is Isaiah 11:1-2 (Septuagint). The Holy Spirit teaches us and helps us to pray (Luke 11:13; Rom 8:15, 26; Gal 4:6; Eph 6:18). The Spirit who dwells in our hearts (Rom 5:5) prays from within us.

The work of the Spirit within us is always *ad Patrem:* to the Father, through the Son, in the Spirit. This expresses the classical sense of the relationship within the Trinity, as well as being the structure of the Church's liturgy. The Spirit reveals and leads us to the Son, who reveals and leads us to the Father, the unbegotten source of life.

The Spirit brings true freedom. Much of Christian life is a struggle between two spirits, between the flesh and the Spirit (Gal 5:16-18, 25; 6:7-8; Rom 8:5-11). Yet it is the Spirit and only the Spirit who makes us truly free (2 Cor 3:17; Gal 5:13, 18; Rom 8:2, 14). One might say that true freedom is itself a gift of the Spirit. And it is the Spirit who compels or frees the Church to go beyond itself.

We can see the richness of Congar's pneumatology. I have indicated only its broad outlines. At least we see the paramount significance of pneumatology. Theology suffers when pneumatology is relegated to a forgotten shelf. Every Christology must be a pneumatological Christology. For Congar, the Spirit is the co-instituting principle of the Church, an essential agent in sacramental and liturgical life, and the source of personal holiness and renewal. The weakness of his pneumatology is that he does not explore to the same degree the Spirit at work in the world, in the contemporary thirst for justice, and in the history of religion. He only points in these directions.

In Conclusion

The story of the earthly Jesus comes to a close with the death and resurrection of Jesus and the gift of the Spirit. The mission of the Risen Christ is completely interwoven with the mission of the Spirit. The Spirit has become the Spirit of the Risen Christ as well as the Spirit of God. The Spirit is Christ's gift and is even known as Gift. Jesus had to die before the other Advocate could come. The resurrection becomes more complete with the coming of the Spirit.

There is no Easter without Pentecost and vice versa. They form an inseparable whole. Jesus and the Spirit can be distinguished but not separated. Jesus is a work of the Spirit and the gift of the Spirit is a consequence of the work of Jesus. Christology and pneumatology cannot be severed from each other. The Spirit is the gift of Jesus par excellence, essential to the Jesus story, the culmination of Jesus' mission. Christology culminates in and necessitates pneumatology.

It is not a question of whether to have a Spirit Christology or a Logos Christology; we must have both. Jesus Christ cannot be adequately understood apart from a theology of the Word and a theology of the Spirit. Jesus is both Word enfleshed and anointed by the Spirit.

The Jesus story in one way is but a chapter in the story of the Word and but a chapter in the story of the Spirit. Jesus cannot be understood apart from Word and Spirit and vice versa. Jesus *is* the Word even if there is more to the Word than Jesus alone. Jesus plants his seal on the Word. Ever since Jesus, the Word is always and remains the Word that became enfleshed in Jesus. And the Spirit *is* the Spirit of the risen Jesus, even if there is more to the work of the Spirit than Jesus alone. Jesus also plants his seal on the Spirit. Wherever the Spirit is active, it is still the Spirit of the Risen Christ. And whatever the works of the Word, they were and are the works of the Word that became self-identified with Jesus Christ.

Thus no one comes to the Father (the Father of our Lord Jesus Christ) except through the Son and in the Holy Spirit. The Spirit enables us to recognize who Jesus truly is; Jesus enables us to recognize who God truly is. Both Christology and pneumatology (neither of which can be brought to completion apart from the other) remain in the end theology: they open up the mystery of God. Like Jesus himself who preached God, so Christology and pneumatology return us to God.

As I said in volume 1, Christology is an invitation to an encounter.[41] We do not come to Christology with a pre-knowledge of God. Rather we come to knowledge of God through Jesus Christ. Christology precedes the theology of God.

The Spirit is the Spirit of God, the Holy Spirit, and the Spirit of the Risen Christ. The Spirit has been unleashed by Christ on both Church and world. The theology of this Church and the theology of the world are continuing chapters in the theology of the Spirit.

[41]Goergen, *The Mission and Ministry of Jesus,* 25.

8

Son of God, Son of Mary, Immanuel

As I have indicated previously, any Christology needs to be ecclesially, professionally, and socially responsible.[1] Yet no one Christology can ever be considered definitive by itself alone. Every Christology is limited in the face of the *mysterium Christi* which it attempts to articulate and to which it is accountable.

There is no one single starting point for Christology; it will depend upon those for whom the Christology is intended. There is no Christology in itself apart from those to whom it is intended to speak.

For the purposes of evangelization, one might choose to begin with the resurrection of Jesus and the proclamation of the Risen Christ. The resurrection urges a decision of faith, and the Risen Christ is Jesus alive. However, for Christians already catechized, profound understanding may be reached by beginning with the incarnation, a theology of Jesus that begins from above. On the other hand, in a secular society and post-Christian culture, a better starting point may be the earthly Jesus whose power to reach and speak to people even apart from faith remains astounding. In the end, any Christology needs to be attentive to all facets of the Jesus story. Wherever one steps into that story, one will eventually need to give attention to every part of it.

Given the crisis of faith today and the need to bring people to the truth of faith, I suggest we begin with the resurrection of Jesus. However, I began this series with Jesus research and the earthly

[1]Goergen, *The Mission and Ministry of Jesus,* 20.

250

Jesus. And the greater portion of this particular volume has been a theology of the incarnation. We must now attempt to put these facets of the mystery together.

The Risen Christ

Jesus, raised from the dead, is at the heart of the early preaching and the core of Pauline theology.[2]

However one approaches the resurrection, it forces the question: do *you* believe in Jesus as raised from the dead? That question must be answered before going further. The answer requires faith. If the answer is yes, it means that one can never know Jesus fully apart from faith. The only real Jesus is a Jesus of faith. One comes to the very important awareness that there is always more to Jesus than the historiographical Jesus alone. The resurrection was a historical but meta-historiographical event. Thus the full truth about Jesus is meta-historiographical.

How do we articulate or express our faith in Jesus as alive? The early Christian proclamation of this experiential and personal knowledge was: God has made him both Lord and Christ (Acts 2:36). In other words, Jesus is the Christ. Who do you say that Jesus is? The Christ. The Risen Christ. The first Christians believed that the resurrection of Jesus from the dead gave witness to the fact that Jesus was the Christ of God. A theology of Jesus became a Christology.

This now raises a very significant meta-historiographical or theological question. What do we mean by "the Christ"? What content are we to give it? The answers to that question make us realize the truth of the insight that there is one Jesus but many Christologies. Who do we say that the Christ is? Faith in the resurrection of Jesus necessitates the Christological inquiry. Jesus is the Risen Christ, but who is the Risen Christ? Who or what is the Christ of God whom we identify as being Jesus?

The Word Incarnate

In the New Testament itself there are varied answers to this question. Matthew, Mark, Luke, John, and Paul all respond

---

[2]Goergen, *The Death and Resurrection of Jesus,* 88–111, 117–79. Also see the first chapter of this volume.

differently, though not incompatibly. One of the most profound, poetic, and influential responses is that of the Fourth Gospel: the Christ is God's very own Word incarnate.[3]

This is clearly not the only response in the New Testament. In fact, I have suggested that it is uniquely Johannine. Once the Johannine Christians came to this theology of Jesus, however, it could not be ignored. It was one New Testament theology among several, yet it required that Christian faith take a stand with respect to it. In fact it became extremely significant for the historic Christian faith and tradition. Many Christologies became theologies of the incarnation.[4]

To deny the incarnation is to pursue a path other than that of the New Testament as a whole. Christian tradition attempted to be faithful to the whole of the New Testament, or rather it took the whole of the New Testament to be faithful to the Christian tradition.

There is no question but that the incarnation raised a host of theological issues. One cannot avoid them, however, by dismissing the truth of the incarnation.

We realize today that any theology of the incarnation must do justice to the humanity of Jesus. A theology of the incarnation requires both a theology of the Word (a theology of God, of the prior actuality of God), a clear concern and strength of the Alexandrian tradition, and a theology of the human (a theological anthropology), a clear concern and strength of the Antiochene tradition.

Christian tradition recognized that one does not rationally explain the incarnation. The incarnation is historical but meta-historiographical, intelligible but meta-rational. Hence the varied ways of grappling with it in mystical theology, philosophical theology, and pastoral theology.[5] For Luther, the "how" question was not even theologically appropriate. Yet Lutheran theology in the end was not able to avoid the difficulties a theology of the incarnation raised.[6] Mystical language, philosophical language, and pastoral language all had their contribution to make.

---

[3]Goergen, *The Jesus of Christian History*, 9–35.

[4]Cf. ibid.

[5]Ibid., 166–256.

[6]Ibid., 232–56.

In the end no theology does full justice to the mystery that the incarnation suggests. Yet it has tremendous implications for theology. Is Christianity incarnational or not? The answer to that question says something about who our God and who the God of Jesus Christ is. Christology wrestles not only with the Christ of God but also with the God of Jesus Christ, God incarnate, the God who became enfleshed as a first-century Galilean Jew.

The Prophet and Sage from Nazareth

Jesus of Nazareth was God's Word incarnate. But what was God's Word incarnate precisely like? The incarnation meant the spatio-temporal delimitation of God's Word geographically and historically. Although there is more to Jesus than the Jesus of historiography, nevertheless historiography remains our primary access to the biblical, historical Jesus Christ.

God's Word was enfleshed as Jesus, that is, as a Jewish prophet, a Palestinian teacher of wisdom, and a servant in solidarity with victims even unto and in his death.[7]

Whatever the precise details of Jesus' self-awareness, he played and was seen to play a prophetic role. He was like the prophets of old—God-conscious and socially conscious (and not self-conscious). Jesus did not preach or teach much about himself. He primarily rather proclaimed God (not the reign of God, for the reign of God *is* God).[8] It was a particular human experience of God out of which Jesus preached and a particular experiential understanding of God that Jesus proclaimed. In Jesus we meet God, and we meet the God of Jesus. Who is this God whom Jesus preached?

As prophet and preacher, Jesus' starting point was always God and God's word. But Jesus knew God's love for the people, the *am ha-aretz,* and that God's word was always addressed to a particular people in particular circumstances in a particular period of history. Jesus spoke God's word to this people. One could not be radically God-conscious without being socially conscious because Jesus' God was radically socially conscious. A loving,

---

[7]Cf. Goergen, *The Mission and Ministry of Jesus,* 109–281; and *The Death and Resurrection of Jesus,* 11–70.

[8]Goergen, *The Mission and Ministry of Jesus,* 220–29.

challenging, compassionate, confronting, generous, just, faithful, holy, and living God was the gospel Jesus preached.

Jesus' wisdom, his parables and proverbs, stories and sayings,
disclosed a God who loves people, who freely chooses to be for
and with people, who is self-defined and self-communicated as
One-who-is-with-us, who can no longer be defined apart from us,
who is clearly seen as with and for those from whom societies
readily distance themselves: the poor, the stranger, the foreigner,
the widow, women, orphans, children, the handicapped, the uneducated, the alienated, the religiously marginal, the untouchable,
the unclean, sinners, those without social or religious status, the
lost, the forgotten, the invisible, those without voice, without
hope, who are suffering, persecuted, victimized, abused, dismissed, oppressed, tortured. God's love is a profoundly and truly
human love.

Jesus preached not only in word but especially in deed. Through
his symbolic and prophetic actions, healings, exorcisms, associations, friendships, meals, and journeys, Jesus made God present,
felt, tangible. He proclaimed that God belongs to people and that
nothing can come between God and God's beloved ones. In the
most symbolic and prophetic action of all, Jesus' freely accepted,
tragic death by public crucifixion, he remained in solidarity with
the victims of the world until the end—revealing God's very own
social, political, economic, cultural, and religious word or critique
of any society's unacceptable acceptance of marginalization and
victimization. Jesus was a faithful servant of God even unto death
and society was revealed as unwilling or unable to love as God
loves—humanely.

The Crucified Savior

The most significant fact about Jesus is not that he was Son
of God in a unique way, nor that he was raised from the dead,
but rather that his life and mission were salvific for us. *Savior
(sōtēr)* is not a word frequently applied to Jesus in the New Testament but nevertheless it conveys his significance through the centuries, even if the salvation that comes from Jesus may have been
understood in a variety of ways (forgiveness of sin, resurrection
from death, deification, liberation, justification, sanctification,
revelation).

The tensive symbol par excellence of Jesus' life, mission, and ministry is certainly the cross. His death captures in a compact form the meaning and salvific significance of his life; his death cannot be adequately interpreted or understood apart from his life and vice versa.

In Jesus' solidarity with the outcasts of this world even unto death on the cross, in his martyrdom giving witness to a hope and justice beyond this world, in his obediential and filial servanthood to the God who alone is king, in his vicarious and redemptive suffering on behalf of humankind, and in his suffering as revelatory of the pain of God, his death became corporately and even universally significant beyond his own self. In his death, Jesus is supremely revealed as "for us" and God is revealed as "with us." In Jesus, God is with us (Immanuel).

We are saved through Jesus, God's rejected mediator, even if salvation is not confined to Jesus and the Jesus movement alone. Through Jesus, God breaks through in an unsurpassable way into our midst. God is truly with us. The full implications of this cannot be grasped by objective knowledge alone, nor even communicated adequately in tensive language, but can only be experienced symbolically as God's presence in Christ. That experience is salvific.

Jesus becomes for those who follow him the Way, the Truth, and the Life. He opens for us a door to God and to humanness. He teaches us through word and deed the truth about God and tells the truth about ourselves and humanity. Through Jesus we are saved, since the way to being truly and fully human is revealed and restored by his disclosing to us the living and true God. We come to true humanity only through solidarity with the wretched of the earth and we come to true solidarity with people only through union, intimacy, solidarity with the God of people. Jesus remains for us the one who talks to us about God, in whom (the reign of) God is revealed and made present, and through whom all forms of idolatry can and must be set aside. Jesus finally empowers us to be what he calls us and challenges us to be— truly human—with the gift of the Holy Spirit, his very own Spirit, in whom we too become daughters and sons of God, capable through suffering of becoming the images and likenesses of God that we were created to be—mirrors of the God of love, compassion, justice, generosity, and fidelity. Through Jesus we are brought into the heart of the *mysterium Dei*. We are saved.

Imitatio Dei
Discipleship

To recognize Jesus for who he is, to know Jesus in truth, is to become his disciple. Jesus in history invited others to follow him, and the Risen Jesus continues to do so today. To know Jesus is to confess him as Lord and Christ.

But what does it mean to follow Jesus? What does it mean to be in our culture and our period of history what Jesus was in his? Discipleship, or patterning our lives after that of Jesus, is to do what he did, namely, to pattern our lives after that of God. Jesus' mission and ministry were an *imitatio Dei.*

Jesus personally experienced God. He preached God. His *praxis* was the *praxis* of God. He made God's power and presence effective and near. He molded and modeled his life after that of God. He spent time with God. He took counsel from God. He struggled with God. He was intimate with God. He knew God like a son knows his father. He loved God with his whole heart, his whole soul, and all his strength.

And, like God, Jesus loved his neighbor. Like God, Jesus was there for them—for the widow, the women, the orphan, the children, the stranger, the strange, the foreigner, the despised, the outcast, the poor, the sick, the uneducated, the untouchable, the invisible, the lost, the forgotten, those in need of hope, those who needed to be challenged, those who needed to be healed, or awakened, or valued. Jesus belonged to the people as much as he belonged to God.

Jesus was God's. But Jesus was also the people's. And there was no dichotomy or tension between the two, because God belongs to the people and people belong to God. God loves people—not possessively but intensely, not exclusively but inclusively. God's love is faithful but challenging, compassionate but disturbing, generous but demanding, tender but strong, seeking justice but also forgiving.

Jesus sought to embody God in his life. He was the embodiment of God. He participated in the very life of God. He felt the feelings of God. He made God tangible and visible and real. God's Spirit was his very own Spirit, so interwoven was Jesus with the Spirit of God. Jesus was God's Word, God's prophet, and God's wisdom.

Jesus was both Son of God and son of Mary. He was Immanuel. Through him, God is with us.

Our discipleship, our *imitatio Christi*, our participation in the *mysterium Christi*, our membership in the body of the Risen Christ must also then embody the *praxis* of God, must become an *imitatio Dei* in our culture and our period of history, must render the living and true God tangible and visible and real. Our lives must also be an invitation to an encounter with God. God's Spirit must be our very own. We come to God, through Christ, in the Spirit.

Our stance must always be *ad Deum,* or rather *per Deum ad mundum.* We belong to others.

Bibliography

Abelson, J. *The Immanence of God in Rabbinical Literature.* New York: Hermon Press, 1912/1969.

Adam, Karl. *The Christ of Faith: The Christology of the Church.* New York: Pantheon Books, 1957.

Adler, Mortimer J. *The Idea of Freedom.* 2 vols. Westport, Conn.: Greenwood Press, 1958, 1961.

Aldwinckle, Russell F. *More Than Man: A Study in Christology.* Grand Rapids, Mich.: William B. Eerdmans Publishing Co., 1976.

Ancelet-Hustache, Jeanne. *Master Eckhart and the Rhineland Mystics.* New York: Harper Torchbooks, 1957.

Arintero, John G. *The Mystical Evolution in the Development and Vitality of the Church.* 2 vols. Trans. Jordan Aumann. St. Louis: B. Herder Book Co., 1949.

_____. *Stages in Prayer.* Trans. Kathleen Pond. London: Blackfriars Publications, 1957.

Aulen, Gustaf. *Christus Victor: An Historical Study of the Three Main Types of the Idea of the Atonement.* New York: The Macmillan Co., 1969.

_____. *Jesus in Contemporary Historical Research.* Trans. I. H. Hjelm. Philadelphia: Fortress Press, 1976.

Aumann, Jordan. *Spiritual Theology.* Huntington, Ind.: Our Sunday Visitor, 1980.

Baillie, D. M. *God Was in Christ: An Essay on Incarnation and Atonement.* New York: Charles Scribner's Sons, 1948.

Barth, Karl. *Christ and Adam: Man and Humanity in Romans 5.* Trans. T. A. Smail. New York: The Macmillan Co., 1968.

_____. *The Humanity of God.* Richmond: John Knox Press, 1970.

Beare, F. W. *Commentary on the Epistle to the Philippians.* London: Adam and Charles Black, 1969.

Bell, G.K.A., and D. A. Deissmann, eds. *Mysterium Christi.* London: Longmans, Green and Co., 1970.

Boers, Hendrikus. *Who Was Jesus? The Historical Jesus and the Synoptic Gospels.* San Francisco: Harper and Row, 1989.

Boff, Leonardo. *Jesus Christ Liberator: A Critical Christology for Our Time.* Maryknoll, N.Y.: Orbis Books, 1978.

Bonhoeffer, Dietrich. *Christ the Center.* Trans. John Bowden. New York: Harper and Row, 1960.

_____. *Letters and Papers from Prison.* Trans. Reginald Fuller. New York: The Macmillan Co., 1966.

Borg, Marcus J. *Conflict, Holiness and Politics in the Teachings of Jesus.* New York: Edwin Mellen Press, 1984.

_____. "A Temperate Case for a Non-Eschatological Jesus." In *Forum,* vol. 2, no. 3 (September 1986). Bonner, Mont.: Polebridge Press, 81–102.

_____. *Jesus: A New Vision.* San Francisco: Harper and Row, 1987.

Borowitz, Eugene B. *Contemporary Christologies: A Jewish Response.* New York: Paulist Press, 1980.

Bouyer, Louis. *The Eternal Son.* Trans. Simone Inkel and John F. Laughlin. Huntington, Ind.: Our Sunday Visitor, Inc., 1978.

Bravo, Francesco. *Christ in the Thought of Teilhard de Chardin.* Trans. C. B. Larme. Notre Dame, Ind.: University of Notre Dame Press, 1967.

Breech, James. *The Silence of Jesus: The Authentic Voice of the Historical Man.* Philadelphia: Fortress Press, 1983.

Brown, Raymond. *The Virginal Conception and Bodily Resurrection of Jesus.* New York: Paulist Press, 1973.

_____. "Who Do Men Say That I Am? A Survey of Modern Scholarship on Gospel Christology." In *Biblical Reflections on Crises Facing the Church,* 20–37. New York: Paulist Press, 1975.

_____. *The Birth of the Messiah.* Garden City, N.Y.: Doubleday and Co., 1977.

_____. *The Community of the Beloved Disciple.* New York: Paulist Press, 1979.

Burke, Edmund. *A Philosophical Enquiry into the Origin of Our Ideas of the Sublime and the Beautiful.* London: Routledge and Kegan Paul, 1958.

Burrows, Eric. "The Doctrine of the Shekinah and the Theology of the Incarnation." In *The Gospel of the Infancy and Other Biblical Essays,* 101–10. London: Burns, Oates, and Washbourne, 1940.

Bynum, Caroline Walker. *Jesus As Mother: Studies in the Spirituality of the High Middle Ages.* Berkeley, Calif.: University of California Press, 1982.

Cargas, Harry James, and Bernard Lee, eds. *Religious Experience and Process Theology.* New York: Paulist Press, 1976.

Carson, Ronald A. "The Motifs of *Kenosis* and *Imitatio* in the Work of Dietrich Bonhoeffer, with an Excursus on the *Communicatio Idiomatum." Journal of the American Academy of Religion* 43 (1975) 542–53.

Casey, Maurice. *Son of Man: The Interpretation and Influence of Daniel 7.* London: S.P.C.K., 1979.

Cassirer, Ernst. *An Essay on Man: An Introduction to a Philosophy of Human Culture.* New Haven: Yale University Press, 1944.

————. *The Philosophy of Symbolic Forms.* 3 vols. New Haven: Yale University Press, 1953–1957.

Champellion, "La place de termes 'gemeute' et 'grunt' dans le vocabulaire de Tauler." In *La mystique rhenane,* colloque de Strasbourg, 179–92. Paris: Presses Universitaires de France, 1963.

Charles, R. H. *Eschatology: The Doctrine of a Future Life.* New York: Schocken Books, 1963.

Charlesworth, James H. *Jesus within Judaism.* Garden City, N.Y.: Doubleday and Co., 1987.

Charpentier, Louis. *The Mysteries of Chartres Cathedral.* Trans. Ronald Fraser. Wellingborough, Eng.: Thorsons Publishers, 1980.

Chenu, Marie-Dominique. *La "Doctrine Sociale" de l'Église comme ideologie.* Paris: Les Editions du Cerf, 1979.

Chestnut, R. C. *Three Monophysite Christologies. Severus of Antioch, Philoxenus of Mabbug, and Jacob of Sarug.* New York: Oxford University Press, 1976.

Chilton, Bruce D. *A Galilean Rabbi and His Bible: Jesus' Use of the Interpreted Scripture of His Time.* Wilmington, Del.: Michael Glazier, 1984.

Clark, James M. *The Great German Mystics: Eckhart, Tauler, and Suso.* London: Oxford University Press, 1949.

Cobb, John B. *God and the World.* Philadelphia: The Westminster Press, 1969.

————. *Christ in a Pluralistic Age.* Philadelphia: The Westminster Press, 1975.

Cone, James H. *A Black Theology of Liberation.* Philadelphia: Lippincott, 1970.

Congar, Yves M.-J. "La deification dan la tradition spirituelle de l'Orient, d'après une étude récente." *Vie spirituelle* (1935) 91–107.

————. *The Mystery of the Temple.* Trans. Reginald F. Trevett. Westminster, Md.: The Newman Press, 1962.

————. *Jesus Christ.* Trans. L. O'Neill. New York: Herder and Herder, 1966.

_____. *I Believe in the Holy Spirit*. 3 vols. Trans. David Smith. New York: Seabury, 1981–1983.

Cook, Michael. *The Jesus of Faith: A Study in Christology*. New York: Paulist Press, 1981.

Cooke, Bernard. "Non-Patriarchal Salvation." *Horizons* 10 (1983) 22–31.

Crossan, John Dominic. *The Historical Jesus: The Life of a Mediterranean Jewish Peasant*. San Francisco: Harper Collins, 1991.

Culbertson, Diana. *The Poetics of Revelation, Recognition and the Narrative Tradition*. Studies in American Biblical Hermeneutics 4. Macon, Ga.: Mercer University Press, 1989.

Cullmann, Oscar. *The Christology of the New Testament*. Rev. ed. Trans. S. C. Guthrie and C.A.M. Hall. Philadelphia: The Westminster Press, 1963.

Dahl, Nils Alstrup. "The Crucified Messiah." In *The Crucified Messiah and Other Essays,* 10–36. Minneapolis: Augsburg Publishing House, 1974.

Daniélou, Jean. *Platonisme et théologie mystique; essai sur la doctrine spirituelle de Saint Grégoire de Nysse*. Paris: Aubier, Editions Montaigne, 1944.

_____. *The Theology of Jewish Christianity*. Vol. 1 of *The Development of Early Christian Doctrine before the Council of Nicaea*. Trans. John Austin Baker. Chicago: Henry Regnery Co., 1964.

_____. *Gospel Message and Hellenistic Culture*. Vol. 2 of *The Development of Early Christian Doctrine before the Council of Nicaea*. Trans. John A. Baker. Philadelphia: The Westminster Press, 1973.

_____. *The Origins of Latin Christianity*. Vol. 3 of *The Development of Early Christian Doctrine before the Council of Nicaea*. Trans. David Smith and John A. Baker. Philadelphia: The Westminster Press, 1977.

_____. *From Glory to Glory*. Trans. Herbert Musurillo. New York: St. Vladimir's Seminary Press, 1979.

Davis, Leo Donald. *The First Seven Ecumenical Councils (325–787): Their History and Theology*. Wilmington, Del.: Michael Glazier, 1987.

Deely, John. *Introducing Semiotic, Its History and Doctrine*. Bloomington, Ind.: Indiana University Press, 1982.

Derrett, J. Duncan M. *Jesus' Audience: The Social and Psychological Environment in Which He Worked*. New York: Seabury Press, 1974.

_____. *The Anastasis: The Resurrection of Jesus as an Historical Event*. Shipston-on-Stour, Eng.: P. Drinkwater, 1982.

Dillistone, F. W. *The Power of Symbols in Religion and Culture*. New York: Crossroad, 1986.

Dionysius the Areopagite. *The Divine Names.* Trans. Editors of the Shrine of Wisdom. Fintry Brook, Eng.: The Shrine of Wisdom, 1957.

Dodd, C. H. *The Founder of Christianity.* New York: The Macmillan Co., 1970.

Dornisch, Loretta. *Faith and Philosophy in the Writings of Paul Ricoeur.* Lewiston: The Edwin Mellen Press, 1990.

Douglas, Mary. *Natural Symbols, Explorations in Cosmology.* London: Barrie and Jenkins, 1973.

Duby, Georges. *The Age of the Cathedrals, Art and Society, 980–1420.* Trans. Eleanor Levieux and Barbara Thompson. Chicago: University of Chicago Press, 1981.

Dufrenne, Mikel. *The Phenomenology of Aesthetic Experience.* Trans. Edward Casey et al. Evanston, Ill.: Northwestern University Press, 1973.

Dulles, Avery. "Contemporary Approaches to Christology: Analysis and Reflections." *Living Light* 13 (1976) 119–44.

_____. *Models of Revelation.* Garden City, N.Y.: Doubleday and Co., 1983.

Dunn, James D. G. *Baptism in the Holy Spirit.* London: SCM Press, 1970.

_____. *Jesus and the Spirit: A Study of the Religious and Charismatic Experience of Jesus and the First Christians as Reflected in the New Testament.* London: SCM Press, 1975.

_____. *Unity and Diversity in the New Testament.* Philadelphia: The Westminster Press, 1977.

_____. *Christology in the Making: A New Testament Inquiry into the Origins of the Doctrine of the Incarnation.* Philadelphia: The Westminster Press, 1980.

_____. *The Evidence for Jesus.* Philadelphia: The Westminster Press, 1985.

_____. *The Partings of the Ways: Between Christianity and Judaism.* Philadelphia: Trinity Press International, 1991.

Durrwell, F. X. *The Resurrection.* Trans. Rosemary Sheed. New York: Sheed and Ward, 1960.

Dwyer, John C. *Son of Man and Son of God: A New Language for Faith.* New York: Paulist Press, 1983.

Echegary, Hugo. *The Practice of Jesus.* Trans. M. J. O'Connell. Maryknoll, N.Y.: Orbis Books, 1984.

Eckhart. *Meister Eckhart.* Trans. and ed. Edmund Colledge and Bernard McGinn. Classics of Western Spirituality. New York: Paulist Press, 1981.

_____. *Meister Eckhart, Sermons and Treatises.* 2 vols. Trans. and ed. M. O'C. Walshe. London: Watkins Publishing, 1979, 1981.

_____. *Meister Eckhart, Teacher and Preacher.* Trans. and ed. Edmund Colledge and Bernard McGinn. Classics of Western Spirituality. New York: Paulist Press, 1986.

Evans, C. F. *Resurrection and the New Testament.* Studies in Biblical Theology, 2nd ser., 12. London: SCM Press, 1970.

Fairweather, Eugene R. "The 'Kenotic' Christology." In F. W. Beare, *Commentary on the Epistle to the Philippians.* London: Adam and Charles Black, 1969.

Falk, Harvey. *Jesus the Pharisee: A New Look at the Jewishness of Jesus.* New York: Paulist Press, 1985.

Farrell, Walter. *Only Son.* New York: Sheed and Ward, 1953.

Farrer, Austin. "The Prior Actuality of God." In *Reflective Faith: Essays in Philosophical Theology,* 178–91. Grand Rapids, Mich.: William B. Eerdmans Publishing Co., 1972.

Fitzmyer, Joseph A. *A Christological Catechism: New Testament Answers.* New York: Paulist Press, 1982.

Fransen, Piet F. *Divine Grace and Man.* New York: Desclee Co., 1959/1962.

_____. *The New Life of Grace.* Trans. Georges Dupont. New York: Seabury Press, 1969/1973.

_____. *Hermeneutics of the Councils and Other Studies.* Collected by H. E. Mertens and F. de Graeve. Leuven: Leuven University, 1985.

Fuller, Reginald H. *The Foundations of New Testament Christology.* New York: Charles Scribner's Sons, 1965.

_____. *The Formation of the Resurrection Narratives.* New York: The Macmillan Co., 1971.

Galot, Jean. *Who Is Christ? A Theology of Incarnation.* Chicago: Franciscan Herald Press, 1981.

_____. *The Person of Christ: A Theological Insight.* Chicago: Franciscan Herald Press, 1984.

Galtier, Paul. *Saint Hilaire de Poitiers, le premier docteur de l'Église Latine.* Paris: Beauchesne et ses fils, 1960.

Galvin, John. "The Resurrection of Jesus in Contemporary Catholic Systematics." *Heythrop Journal* 20 (1979) 123–45.

Gilkey, Langdon. *Reaping the Whirlwind.* New York: Seabury Press, 1976.

Glasson, Francis T. "Two Notes on the Philippians Hymn (2:6-11)." *New Testament Studies* 21 (1975) 133–39.

Gleason, Robert. *Grace.* New York: Sheed and Ward, 1962.

Goergen, Donald J. *Personality-in-Process and Teilhard de Chardin,* unpublished doctoral dissertation, 1971, University Microfilms.

_____. *The Power of Love.* Chicago: The Thomas More Press, 1979.

_____. "Albert the Great and Thomas Aquinas on the Motive of the Incarnation." *The Thomist* 44 (1980) 523–38.

_____. "The Desert as Reality and Symbol." *Spirituality Today* 34 (1982) 70–79.

_____. *The Mission and Ministry of Jesus.* Vol. 1 of *A Theology of Jesus.* Wilmington, Del.: Michael Glazier, 1986.

_____. *The Death and Resurrection of Jesus.* Vol. 2 of *A Theology of Jesus.* Wilmington, Del.: Michael Glazier, 1988.

_____. *The Jesus of Christian History.* Vol. 3 of *A Theology of Jesus.* Collegeville, Minn.: The Liturgical Press, 1992.

_____, ed. *Process Thought in Theology and Ecumenism,* a collection of eight essays in *Listening* 14 (1979) 163–278.

_____, ed. *Being A Priest Today.* Collegeville, Minn.: The Liturgical Press, 1992.

Gogarten, Friedrich. *Christ the Crisis: Basic Questions Concerning Christology.* Trans. R. A. Wilson. Richmond: John Knox Press, 1970.

Gorodetsky, Nadejda. *The Humiliated Christ in Modern Russian Thought.* New York: AMS Press, Inc., 1973 reprint (first ed. London: S.P.C.K. and New York: The Macmillan Co., 1938).

Goulder, Michael, ed: *Incarnation and Myth. The Debate Continued.* Grand Rapids, Mich.: William. B. Eerdmans Publishing Co., 1979.

Green, Michael, ed. *The Truth of God Incarnate.* Grand Rapids, Mich.: William B. Eerdmans Publishing Co., 1977.

Grelot, Pierre. "Deux expressions difficiles de Philippiens 2:6-7." *Biblica* 53 (1973) 495–507.

Griffin, David Ray. *A Process Christology.* Philadelphia: The Westminster Press, 1973.

_____. *God, Power and Evil.* Philadelphia: The Westminster Press, 1976.

Grillmeier, Aloys. "Jesus Christ. III. Christology." In *Sacramentum Mundi. An Encyclopedia of Theology,* ed. Karl Rahner et al, 3:186–92. New York: Herder and Herder, 1969.

_____. *From the Apostolic Age to Chalcedon (AD 451).* Vol. 1 of *Christ in Christian Tradition.* Trans. John Bowden. Rev. ed. London: Mowbrays; Atlanta: John Knox Press, 1975.

_____. *From Chalcedon to Justinian I.* Vol. 2 of *Christ in Christian Tradition.* Trans. Pauline Allen and John Cowte. Atlanta: John Knox, 1987.

Guillet, Jacques. *The Consciousness of Jesus.* Trans. E. Bonin. New York: Newman Press, 1972.

Hall, Thor. *The Evolution of Christology.* Nashville, Tenn.: Abingdon, 1982.

Hardy, Richard P. *Search for Nothing: The Life of John of the Cross.* New York: Crossroad, 1982.

Harries, Karsten. *The Meaning of Modern Art.* Evanston, Ill.: Northwestern University Press, 1968.

Hart, Thomas N. *To Know and Follow Jesus: Contemporary Christology.* New York: Paulist Press, 1984.

Harvey, A. E. *Jesus and the Constraints of History.* Philadelphia: The Westminster Press, 1982.

Harvey, Van A. *The Historian and the Believer: The Morality of Historical Knowledge and Christian Belief.* Philadelphia: The Westminster Press, 1966.

Hebblethwaite, Brian. *The Incarnation.* Cambridge: Cambridge University Press, 1987.

Hellwig, Monika. *Jesus, The Compassion of God: New Perspectives on the Tradition of Christianity.* Wilmington, Del.: Michael Glazier, 1983.

Helminiak, Daniel A. *The Same Jesus: A Contemporary Christology.* Chicago: Loyola University Press, 1986.

Hengel, Martin. *The Son of God.* Trans. John Bowden. Philadelphia: Fortress Press, 1976.

_____. *The Atonement: The Origins of the Doctrine in the New Testament.* Trans. John Bowden. Philadelphia: Fortress Press, 1981.

_____. *The Charismatic Leader and His Followers.* Trans. James Greig. New York: Crossroad, 1981.

Hick, John H. "Religious Faith as 'Experiencing As.' " In *Talk of God,* ed. G.N.A. Vesey. New York: The Macmillan Co., 1964.

_____. *Death and Eternal Life.* New York: Harper and Row, 1976.

_____, ed. *The Myth of God Incarnate.* Philadelphia: The Westminster Press; London: SCM Press, 1977.

Higgins, A.J.B. *The Son of Man in the Teaching of Jesus.* London: Cambridge University Press, 1980.

Hodgson, Peter C. *Jesus—Word and Presence: An Essay in Christology.* Philadelphia: Fortress Press, 1971.

Hooker, Morna D. "Christology and Methodology." *New Testament Studies* 17 (1971) 480-87.

Hoover, Roy W. "The Harpagmos Enigma: A Philological Solution." *The Harvard Theological Review* 64 (1971) 95-119.

Horsley, Richard A., and John S. Hanson. *Bandits, Prophets, and Messiahs: Popular Movements in the Time of Jesus.* Minneapolis: Winston Press, 1985.

_____. *Jesus and the Spiral of Violence: Popular Jewish Resistance in Roman Palestine.* San Francisco, Calif.: Harper and Row, 1987.

_____. *Sociology and the Jesus Movement.* New York: Crossroad, 1989.

Howard, George. "Phil. 2:6-11 and the Human Christ." *Catholic Biblical Quarterly* 40 (1978) 368-87.

Hughes, Philip. *The Church in Crisis: A History of the General Councils, 325-1870.* Garden City, N.Y.: Doubleday Image, 1964.

Hugueney, E., G. Thery, and A. L. Corin, eds. and trans. *Sermons de Tauler.* 3 vols. Paris: Librairie Desclée, 1927-1935.

Jeremias, Joachim. *The Prayers of Jesus.* Naperville, Ill.: Alec R. Allenson, Inc., 1967.

_____. *New Testament Theology: The Proclamation of Jesus.* Trans. John Bowden. New York: Charles Scribner's Sons, 1971.

Johnson, Elizabeth A. "The Theological Relevance of the Historical Jesus: A Debate and a Thesis." *The Thomist* 48 (1984) 1-43.

_____. *Consider Jesus.* New York: Crossroad, 1990.

Johnston, William. *The Inner Eye of Love.* New York: Harper and Row, 1978.

Jossua, Jean-Pierre. *Yves Congar: Theology in the Service of God's People.* Chicago: The Priory Press, 1968.

Jüngel, Eberhard. *The Doctrine of the Trinity: God's Being Is in Becoming.* Trans. Horton Harris. Edinburgh: Scottish Academic Press, 1976.

Käsemann, Ernst. *Jesus Means Freedom.* Philadelphia: Fortress Press, 1969.

Kasper, Walter. *Jesus the Christ.* Trans. V. Green. New York: Paulist Press, 1976.

Kazantzakis, Nikos. *The Last Temptation of Christ.* Trans. P. A. Bien. New York: Simon and Schuster, 1960.

Kelber, Werner H. *The Oral and the Written Gospel.* Philadelphia: Fortress Press, 1983.

Kelley, C. F. *Meister Eckhart on Divine Knowledge.* New Haven: Yale University Press, 1977.

Kelly, J.N.D. *Early Christian Doctrines.* 2nd ed. New York: Harper and Row, 1960.

Kissinger, Warren S. *The Lives of Jesus: A History and Bibliography.* New York: Garland Publishing Co., 1985.

Kitamori, Kazo. *Theology of the Pain of God.* Richmond: John Knox Press, 1965.

Knox, John. *The Humanity and Divinity of Christ: A Study of Pattern in Christology.* Cambridge: Cambridge University Press, 1967.

Komonchak, Joseph. "The Return of Yves Congar." *Commonweal* (15 July 1983) 402-05.

Küng, Hans. *On Being a Christian.* Trans. Edward Quinn. Garden City, N.Y.: Doubleday and Co., 1976.

_____. *The Incarnation of God.* Trans. J. R. Stephenson. New York: Crossroad, 1987.

Kuenneth, Walter. *The Theology of the Resurrection*. Trans. J. W. Leitch. St. Louis: Concordia Publishing House, 1965.

Lane, Dermot. "The Incarnation of God in Jesus." *Irish Theological Quarterly* 46 (1979) 158–69.

Langer, Susanne K. *Philosophy in a New Key*. Cambridge: Harvard University Press, 1963.

Lee, Bernard J. *The Galilean Jewishness of Jesus: Retrieving the Jewish Origins of Christianity*. New York: Paulist Press, 1988.

Leinhard, J. T. "Marcellus of Ancyra in Modern Research." *Theological Studies* 43 (1982) 486–503.

Leivestad, Ragnar. "Exit the Apocalyptic Son of Man." *New Testament Studies* 18 (1971–1972) 243–67.

Leslie, Robert C. *Jesus and Logotherapy: The Ministry of Jesus Interpreted through the Psychotherapy of Viktor Frankl*. Nashville, Tenn.: Abingdon, 1965.

Lindars, Barnabas. "Re-enter the Apocalyptic Son of Man." *New Testament Studies* 22 (1975) 52–72.

Lindars, Barnabas, and Stephen S. Smalley, eds. *Christ and Spirit in the New Testament. Essays in Honor of C.F.D. Moule*. Cambridge: Cambridge University Press, 1973.

Lisle, Laurie. *Portrait of an Artist: A Biography of Georgia O'Keeffe*. New York: Washington Square Press, 1980.

Loewe, William P. "Appearances of the Risen Lord: Faith, Fact and Objectivity." *Horizons* 6 (1979) 177–92.

_____. "Encountering the Crucified God: The Soteriology of Sebastian Moore." *Horizons* 9 (1982) 216–36.

Loomer, Bernard. "Two Conceptions of Power." *Process Studies* 6 (1976) 5–32.

Lossky, Vladimir. *Théologie negative et connaissance de Dieu chez Maitre Eckhart*. Paris: J. Vrin, 1973.

_____. *In the Image and Likeness of God*. New York: St. Vladimir's Seminary Press, 1974.

Lynch, William F. *Christ and Prometheus*. Notre Dame, Ind.: University of Notre Dame Press, 1970.

MacGregor, Geddes. *He Who Lets Us Be: A Theology of Love*. New York: Paragon House Publishers, 1987.

Macquarrie, John. "True Life in Death." *Journal of Bible and Religion* 31 (1963).

_____. "A Dilemma in Christology." *The Expository Times* (1965) 207–10.

_____. *Principles of Christian Theology*. New York: Charles Scribner's Sons, 1966.

_____. *Jesus Christ in Modern Thought*. London: SCM Press, 1990.

Maloney, George A. *The Cosmic Christ: From Paul to Teilhard.* New York: Sheed & Ward, 1968.

Maritain, Jacques. *On the Grace and Humanity of Jesus.* Trans. J. W. Evans. New York: Herder and Herder, 1969.

Marsh, John. *The Gospel of Saint John.* Pelican New Testament Commentaries. London: Penguin Books, 1968.

Martin, Ralph P. *Carmen Christi: Philippians 2:5-11 in Recent Interpretation and in the Setting of Early Christian Worship.* Rev. ed. Grand Rapids, Mich.: William B. Eerdmans Publishing Co., 1967/1983.

Mascall, E. L. *Christ, The Christian and the Church: A Study of the Incarnation and Its Consequences.* London: Longmans, Green and Co., 1946.

May, Rollo. *Power and Innocence.* New York: W. W. Norton and Co., 1972.

_____. *The Courage to Create.* New York: W. W. Norton and Co., 1975.

McArthur, Harvey K. *The Quest through the Centuries.* Philadelphia: Fortress Press, 1966.

McIntyre, John. *The Shape of Christology.* Philadelphia: The Westminster Press, 1966.

McKinney, R.W.A., ed. *Creation, Christ and Culture.* Edinburgh: T. & T. Clarke Ltd., 1976.

Meier, John P. *A Marginal Jew: Rethinking the Historical Jesus.* New York: Doubleday, 1991.

Meyendorff, John. *Byzantine Theology: Historical Trends and Doctrinal Themes.* New York: Fordham University Press, 1974.

_____. *Christ in Eastern Christian Thought.* New York: St. Vladimir's Seminary Press, 1975.

_____. "New Life in Christ: Salvation in Orthodox Theology." *Theological Studies* 50 (1989) 481-99.

Meyer, Ben F. *The Aims of Jesus.* London: SCM Press, 1979.

Miguez-Bonino, Jose, ed. *Faces of Christ: Latin American Christologies.* Trans. R. R. Barr. Maryknoll, N.Y.: Orbis Books, 1984.

Moltmann, Jürgen. *The Crucified God: The Cross of Christ as the Foundation and Criticism of Christian Theology.* Trans. R. A. Wilson and John Bowden. New York: Harper and Row, 1974.

Mooney, Christopher F. *Teilhard de Chardin and the Mystery of Christ.* New York: Harper and Row, 1966.

Moore, George Foot. "Intermediaries in Jewish Theology, Memra, Schechinah, Metraton." *Harvard Theological Review* 15 (1922) 41-85.

_____. *Judaism in the First Centuries of the Christian Era.* 2 vols. New York: Schocken Books, 1971.

Moore, Sebastian. *Let This Mind Be in You: The Quest for Identity through Oedipus to Christ.* Minneapolis: Winston Press, 1985.

Moule, C.F.D. *The Origin of Christology.* Cambridge: Cambridge University Press, 1977.

Murphy-O'Connor, Jerome. "Paul's Understanding of Christ as the Personal Presence of God in the World." In *A Companion to Paul: Readings in Pauline Theology,* ed. M. J. Taylor, 1–12. New York: Alba House, 1975.

_____. "Christological Anthropology in Phil. 2:6–11." *Revue biblique 83 (1976) 25–50.*

_____. *Becoming Human Together.* 2nd rev. ed. Wilmington, Del.: Michael Glazier, 1982.

Neill, Stephen. *Jesus through Many Eyes: Introduction to the Theology of the New Testament.* Philadelphia: Fortress Press, 1976.

_____. *The Supremacy of Jesus.* Downers Grove, Ill.: InterVarsity Press, 1984.

Neuner, Josef, and Heinrich Roos. *The Teaching of the Catholic Church.* Trans. Geoffrey Stevens. New York: Alba House, 1967.

Nichols, Aidan. *The Art of God Incarnate: Theology and Image in Christian Tradition.* New York: Paulist Press, 1980.

_____. *The Shape of Catholic Theology.* Collegeville, Minn.: The Liturgical Press, 1991.

Nickelsburg, George W. E. *Resurrection, Immortality, and Eternal Life in Intertestamental Judaism.* Cambridge: Harvard University Press, 1972.

Niebuhr, H. Richard. *Christ and Culture.* New York: Harper and Row, 1951.

Niebuhr, Richard R. *Resurrection and Historical Reason: A Study of Theological Method.* New York: Charles Scribner's Sons, 1957.

Nineham, D. E., et al. *Historicity and Chronology in the New Testament.* London: S.P.C.K., 1965.

Nolan, Albert. *Jesus before Christianity.* Maryknoll, N.Y.: Orbis Books, 1978.

Norris, Christopher. *The Context of Faculties: Deconstruction, Philosophy, and Theory.* New York: Methuen, 1985.

North, Robert. *In Search of the Human Jesus.* New York: Corpus Books, 1970.

O'Collins, Gerald. *The Resurrection of Jesus Christ.* Valley Forge, Penn.: Judson Press, 1973.

_____. *Jesus Risen.* New York: Paulist Press, 1987.

_____. "Mary Magdalene as Major Witness to Jesus' Resurrection." In *Interpreting the Resurrection,* 22–38. New York: Paulist Press, 1988; originally in *Theological Studies* 48 (1987) 631–46.

O'Grady, John F. *Models of Jesus.* Garden City, N.Y.: Doubleday Image, 1982.

Otto, Rudolf. *The Idea of the Holy.* Trans. John W. Harvey. 2nd ed. London: Oxford University Press, 1958.

Ouspensky, Leonid. "The Meaning and Language of Icons." *The Meaning of Icons* by Leonid Ouspensky and Vladimir Lossky. New York: St. Vladimir's Seminary Press, 1982.

Pannenberg, Wolfhart. *Jesus—God and Man.* Trans. Duane A. Priebe and Lewis L. Wilkins. Philadelphia: The Westminster Press, 1968.

Pannikar, R. *The Unknown Christ of Hinduism.* Rev. ed. Maryknoll, N.Y.: Orbis Books, 1980.

Panofsky, Edwin. *Gothic, Architecture and Scholasticism.* New York: New American Library, 1976.

Pawlikowski, John T. *Christ in the Light of the Christian-Jewish Dialogue.* New York: Paulist Press, 1982.

Pelikan, Jaroslav. *The Emergence of the Catholic Tradition (100–600).* Vol. 1 of *The Christian Tradition: A History of the Development of Doctrine.* Chicago: University of Chicago Press, 1971.

_____. *The Spirit of Eastern Christendom (600–1700).* Vol. 2 of *The Christian Tradition: A History of the Development of Doctrine.* Chicago: University of Chicago Press, 1974.

_____. *The Growth of Medieval Theology (600–1300).* Vol. 3 of *The Christian Tradition: A History of the Development of Doctrine.* Chicago: University of Chicago Press, 1978.

_____. *Reformation of Church and Dogma (1300–1700).* Vol. 4 of *The Christian Tradition: A History of the Development of Doctrine.* Chicago: University of Chicago Press, 1984.

_____. *Jesus through the Centuries: His Place in the History of Culture.* New Haven: Yale University Press, 1985.

_____. *Christian Doctrine and Modern Culture (since 1700).* Vol. 5 of *The Christian Tradition: A History of the Development of Doctrine.* Chicago: University of Chicago Press, 1988.

Perkins, Pheme. *Resurrection, New Testament Witness and Contemporary Reflection.* Garden City, N.Y.: Doubleday and Co., Inc., 1984.

Perrin, Norman. *Rediscovering the Teaching of Jesus.* New York: Harper and Row, 1967.

_____. *A Modern Pilgrimage in New Testament Christology.* Philadelphia: Fortress Press, 1974.

Pesch, Rudolf. "Jesus Christ. II. Quest of the Historical Jesus." In *Sacramentum Mundi: An Encyclopedia of Theology,* ed. Karl Rahner et al, 3:183–86. New York: Herder and Herder, 1969.

Pittenger, W. Norman. *The Word Incarnate: A Study of the Doctrine of the Person of Christ.* New York: Harper and Brothers, 1959.
_____. *Christology Reconsidered.* London: SCM Press, 1970.
Power, David. "Representing Christ in Community and Sacrament." In *Being A Priest Today,* ed. Donald J. Goergen, 97–123. Collegeville, Minn.: The Liturgical Press, 1992.
Prestige, G. L. *Fathers and Heretics.* London: S.P.C.K., 1977.
Pujdak, Steven. "Schoonenberg's Christology in Context." *Louvain Studies* (1977) 338–53.
Rahner, Karl. "On the Theology of the Incarnation." In *Theological Investigations* 4, trans. Kevin Smyth, 105–20. Baltimore: Helicon Press, 1966.
_____. "The Theology of the Symbol." In *Theological Investigations* 4, trans. Kevin Smyth, 221–52. Baltimore: Helicon Press, 1966.
_____. "Incarnation." In *Sacramentum Mundi: An Encyclopedia of Theology,* ed. Karl Rahner et al, 3:110–18. New York: Herder and Herder, 1968.
_____. *The Trinity.* New York: Herder and Herder, 1970.
_____. "One Mediator and Many Mediations." In *Theological Investigations* 9, trans. G. Harrison, 169–84. New York: Herder and Herder, 1972.
_____. "The New Image of the Church." In *Theological Investigations* 10, trans. David Bourke, 3–29. New York: Seabury Press, 1977.
_____. *Foundations of Christian Faith: An Introduction to the Idea of Christianity.* Trans. William V. Dych. New York: Seabury Press, 1978.
_____. "Christology Today?" In *Theological Investigations* 17, trans. M. Kohl, 24–38. New York: Crossroad, 1981.
_____. "Jesus Christ in the Non-Christian Religions." In *Theological Investigations* 17, trans. M. Kohl, 39–50. New York: Crossroad, 1981.
_____. "Chalcedon—End or Beginning." In *Theological Investigations* 1, trans. Cornelius Ernst, 149–200. New York: Crossroad, 1982.
_____. "Christology in the Setting of Modern Man's Understanding of Himself and His World." In *Theological Investigations* 11, trans. David Bourke, 215–29. New York: Crossroad, 1982.
_____. "The Eternal Significance of the Humanity of Jesus for Our Relationship with God." In *Theological Investigations* 3, trans. Karl H. Kruger, 35–46. New York: Crossroad, 1982.
_____. "The Position of Christology in the Church between Exegesis and Dogmatics." In *Theological Investigations* 11, trans. David Bourke, 185–214. New York: Crossroad, 1982.

————. "Christology within an Evolutionary View of the World." In *Theological Investigations* 5, trans. Karl H. Kruger, 157–92. New York: Crossroad, 1983.

————. "The Death of Jesus and the Closure of Revelation." In *Theological Investigations* 18, trans. E. Quinn, 132–42. New York: Crossroad, 1983.

————. "Dogmatic Reflections on the Knowledge and Self-Consciousness of Christ." In *Theological Investigations* 5, trans. Karl H. Kruger, 193–215. New York: Crossroad, 1983.

————. "Following the Crucified." In *Theological Investigations* 18, trans. E. Quinn, 157–70. New York: Crossroad, 1983.

————. "Human Aspects of the Birth of Christ." In *Theological Investigations* 13, trans. David Bourke, 189–94. New York: Crossroad, 1983.

————. "The One Christ and the Universality of Salvation." In *Theological Investigations* 16, trans. D. Morland, 199–224. New York: Crossroad, 1983.

————. "Oneness and Threefoldness of God in Discussion with Islam." In *Theological Investigations* 18, trans. E. Quinn, 105–21. New York: Crossroad, 1983.

————. "The Quest for Approaches Leading to an Understanding of the Mystery of the God-Man Jesus." In *Theological Investigations* 13, trans. David Bourke, 195–200. New York: Crossroad, 1983.

————. "Remarks on the Importance of the History of Jesus for Catholic Dogmatics." In *Theological Investigations* 13, trans. David Bourke, 201–12. New York: Crossroad, 1983.

————. "The Two Basic Types of Christology." In *Theological Investigations* 13, trans. David Bourke, 213–23. New York: Crossroad, 1983.

Rahner, Karl, and William Thuesing. *A New Christology.* New York: Seabury Press, 1980.

Reumann, John. *Jesus in the Church's Gospels: Modern Scholarship and the Earliest Sources.* Philadelphia: Fortress Press, 1968.

Richard, Lucien. *A Kenotic Christology: In the Humanity of Jesus the Christ, the Compassion of our God.* New York: University Press of America, 1982.

Riggin, George A. "Two Christic Paradigms. Focuses of a Theological Revolution." In *Christological Perspectives,* ed. R. F. Berkey and S. A. Edwards, 238–60. New York: Pilgrim Press, 1982.

Rist, Martin. "Jesus and Eschatology." In *Transitions in Biblical Scholarship,* ed. J. C. Rylaarsdam, 193–215. Chicago: University of Chicago Press, 1968.

Robinson, John A. T. *Honest to God.* Philadelphia: The Westminster Press, 1963.

_____. *The Human Face of God.* Philadelphia: The Westminster Press, 1973.

Rondet, Henri. *The Grace of Christ.* Westminster, Md.: The Newman Press, 1948/1967.

Rylaarsdam, J. C. "Jewish-Christian Relationship: The Two Covenants and the Dilemma of Christology." *Journal of Ecumenical Studies* 9 (1972) 249–70.

Sanders, E. P. *Jesus and Judaism.* Philadelphia: Fortress Press, 1985.

Sanders, Jack T. *The New Testament Christological Hymns.* Cambridge: Cambridge University Press, 1971.

_____. "Biblical Criticism and the Bible as Canon." *Union Seminary Quarterly Review* 32 (1977) 157–65.

Schillebeeckx, Edward. *Christ the Sacrament of the Encounter with God.* New York: Sheed and Ward, 1963 (original Dutch edition, 1959).

_____. *Jesus: An Experiment in Christology.* Trans. Hubert Hoskins. New York: Seabury/Crossroad, 1979.

_____. *Christ: The Experience of Jesus as Lord.* Trans. John Bowden. New York: Seabury/Crossroad, 1980.

_____. *Interim Report on the Books, Jesus and Christ.* Trans. John Bowden. New York: Crossroad, 1981.

_____. *Church: The Human Story of God.* Trans. John Bowden. New York: Crossroad, 1990.

Schillebeeckx, Edward, and J.-B. Metz, eds. *Jesus, Son of God?* New York: Seabury Press, 1982.

Schillebeeckx, Edward, et al. *Who Is Jesus of Nazareth?* New York: Paulist Press, 1965.

Schoof, Mark. "Dutch Catholic Theology: A New Approach to Christology." *Cross Currents* 22 (1973) 415–27.

Schoonenberg, Piet. *God's World in the Making.* Techny, Ill.: Divine Word Publications, [1964] 1967.

_____. "He Emptied Himself—Philippians 2:7." In *Who Is Jesus of Nazareth?* trans. Theodore Westow. Concilium 11:47–66. New York: Paulist Press, 1965.

_____. *Man and Sin, a Theological View.* Trans. Joseph Donceel. Notre Dame, Ind.: University of Notre Dame Press, 1965.

_____. *Covenant and Creation.* Notre Dame, Ind.: University of Notre Dame Press, 1968.

_____. *The Christ, a Study of the God-Man Relationship in the Whole of Creation and in Jesus Christ.* Trans. Della Couling. New York: Herder and Herder, [1969] 1971.

_____. "God's Presence in Jesus: An Exchange of Viewpoints."

Theology Digest 19 (1971) 29–38. First published in *Tijdschrift voor Theologie* 9 (1969) 375–405. Schoonenberg's response to questions raised by a 1966 symposium of the theologians Ansfried Hulsbosch, Edward Schillebeeckx, and Piet Schoonenberg. For further discussion with reference to the symposium, see articles by Robert North, Steven Pudjak, Mark Schoof, and R. C. Ware, listed in this bibliography.

————. "Evolution and Theology." In *L'Origine dell'uomo,* 331–48. Roma: Academia Nazionale dei Lincei, 1973.

————. "Process or History in God?" *Louvain Studies* 4 (1973) 303–09; summarized in *Theology Digest* 23 (1975) 38–44. Schoonenberg's sympathetic and critical evaluation of process theology.

————. "Trinity—the Consummated Covenant: Theses on the Doctrine of the Trinitarian God." *Studies in Religion* 5 (1975–1976) 111–16. First published in German, in *Orientierung* (1973). A clear statement of the direction of Schoonenberg's Trinitarian thought.

————. "God as Person(al)." In *A Personal God?* Concilium 103:80–93. New York: Seabury Press, 1977.

————. "Spirit Christology and Logos Christology." *Bijdragen* 38 (1977) 350–75.

————. "God as Relating and (Be)Coming: A Meta-Thomistic Consideration." *Listening* 14 (1979) 265–78. Schoonenberg's most recent statement in English on the mutability of God.

————. "Reflections on the Prologue of John's Gospel," a lecture delivered at Aquinas Institute, Dubuque, Iowa, 25 October 1979.

————. "Genesis and Evolution." *Listening* 15 (Spring 1980) 150–58.

————. "A Sapiential Reading of John's Prologue: Some Reflections on Views of Reginald Fuller and James Dunn." *Theology Digest* 33 (Winter 1986) 403–21.

————. "The Doctrine of the Trinity: An Empty Dogma or a Fruitful Theologoumenon?" *Louvain Studies* 16 (1991) 195–206.

Schreiter, Robert, ed. *The Schillebeeckx Reader.* New York: Crossroad, 1984. Includes a Schillebeeckx bibliography.

————, ed. *Faces of Jesus in Africa.* Maryknoll, N.Y.: Orbis Books, 1991.

Schreiter, Robert, and Mary Catherine Hilkert, eds. *The Praxis of Christian Experience: An Introduction to the Theology of Edward Schillebeeckx.* San Francisco: Harper and Row, 1989.

Schurer, Emil. *The History of the Jewish People in the Age of Jesus Christ (175 B.C.–A.D. 135).* 2 vols. A new English version revised and edited by Geza Vermes, Fergus Millar, Matthew

Black, and Pamela Vermes. Edinburgh: T. and T. Clark, 1973–1979.

Schweitzer, Albert. *The Quest of the Historical Jesus: A Critical Study of its Progress from Reimarus to Wrede.* Trans. W. Montgomery. New York: The Macmillan Co., 1968.

Scroggs, Robin. *The Last Adam: A Study in Pauline Anthropology.* Philadelphia: Fortress Press, 1966.

————. "The Sociological Interpretation of the New Testament. The Present State of Research." *New Testament Studies* 26 (1979/80) 164–79.

Seesholtz, Anna Groh. *Friends of God: Practical Mystics of the Fourteenth Century.* New York: AMS Press, 1934/1970.

Sellers, R. V. *Two Ancient Christologies.* London: S.P.C.K., 1954.

————. *The Council of Chalcedon: A Historical and Doctrinal Survey.* London: S.P.C.K., 1953/1961.

Sherrard, Philip. *The Greek East and the Latin West.* London: Oxford University Press, 1959.

Sherwin-White, A. N. "The Trial of Christ." In *Historicity and Chronology in the New Testament.* Theological Collections 6:97–116. London: S.P.C.K., 1965

Sloyan, Gerard S. *Jesus on Trial: The Development of the Passion Narratives and Their Historical and Ecumenical Implications.* Philadelphia: Fortress Press, 1973.

————. *Jesus, Redeemer and Divine Word.* Wilmington, Del.: Michael Glazier, 1989.

Smith, Cyprian. *The Way of Paradox: Spiritual Life as Taught by Meister Eckhart.* New York: Paulist Press, 1987.

Smulders, Piet. *La doctrine trinitaire de S. Hilaire de Poitiers.* Rome: Analecta Gregoriana, 1944.

Sobrino, Jon. *Christology at the Crossroads.* Maryknoll, N.Y.: Orbis Books, 1978.

Soelle, Dorothee. *Christ the Representative.* Philadelphia: Fortress Press, 1967.

Sykes, S. W., and J. P. Clayton, eds. *Christ, Faith, and History.* Cambridge Studies in Christology. New York: Cambridge University Press, 1972.

Tambasco, Anthony. *In the Days of Jesus: The Jewish Background and Unique Teaching of Jesus.* New York: Paulist Press, 1983.

Tauler, Johannes. *Spiritual Conferences by Johann Tauler.* Trans. and ed. Eric Colledge and Sister M. Jane, O.P. Rockford, Ill.: Tan Books and Publishers, 1978.

————. *Sermons.* Trans. Maria Shrady. Classics of Western Spirituality. New York: Paulist Press, 1985. All the authentic sermons can be found in a French edition, *Sermons de Tauler,*

3 vols. (Paris: Librairie Desclee, 1927-1935), ed. and trans. E. Hugueney, G. Théry, and A. L. Corin.

Tavard, George H. "The Christology of the Mystics." *Theological Studies* 42 (1981) 561-79.

_____. *Images of Christ: An Enquiry into Christology.* Lanham, Md.: University Press of America, 1982.

Teilhard de Chardin, Pierre. *The Phenomenon of Man.* Trans. Bernard Wall. New York: Harper and Row, 1959.

_____. *The Divine Milieu.* New York: Harper and Row, 1960.

_____. *The Future of Man.* New York: Harper and Row, 1964.

Terrien, Samuel. *The Elusive Presence.* New York: Harper and Row, 1978.

Theissen, Gerd. *The Shadow of the Galilean.* Philadelphia: Fortress Press, 1987.

Thompson, Marianne Meye. *The Humanity of Jesus in the Fourth Gospel.* Philadelphia: Fortress Press, 1988.

Thompson, William M. "The Christic Universe of Pierre de Bérulle and the French School." *American Benedictine Review* 29 (1978) 320-47.

_____. *The Jesus Debate: A Survey and Synthesis.* New York: Paulist Press, 1985.

Tillich, Paul. *The Courage to Be.* New Haven: Yale University Press, 1952.

_____. *Existence and the Christ.* Vol. 2 of *Systematic Theology.* Chicago: University of Chicago Press, 1957.

Tolstoy, Leo. *What Is Art?* Trans. Aylmer Maude. London: Oxford University Press, 1969.

Tracy, David. *Blessed Rage for Order: The New Pluralism in Theology.* New York: The Seabury Press, 1975.

_____. *The Analogical Imagination: Christian Theology and the Culture of Pluralism.* New York: Crossroad, 1981.

Trueblood, Elton. *The Humor of Christ.* New York: Harper and Row, 1964.

Underhill, Evelyn. *Mysticism.* New York: E. P. Dutton and Co., 1961.

van Beeck, Franz Jozef. *Christ Proclaimed, Christology As Rhetoric.* New York: Paulist Press, 1979.

Vann, Gerald. *The Pain of Christ and the Sorrow of God.* Oxford: Blackfriars Publications, 1947.

von Campenhausen, Hans. *The Fathers of the Greek Church.* Trans. Stanley Godman. New York: Pantheon Books, 1959.

_____. *The Fathers of the Latin Church.* Trans. Manfred Hoffman. Stanford, Calif.: Stanford University Press, 1969.

von Simson, Otto. *The Gothic Cathedral.* New York: Harper and Row, 1962.

Ware, Robert C. "Christology in Historical Perspective." *Heythrop Journal* 15 (1974) 59–66.

Watson, Philip S. *Let God Be God: An Interpretation of the Theology of Martin Luther.* Philadelphia: Fortress Press, 1947/1970.

Weisheipl, James A. *Friar Thomas d'Aquino.* Garden City, N.Y.: Doubleday and Co., 1974.

Welch, Claude, ed. and trans. *God and Incarnation in Mid-Nineteenth Century German Theology.* New York: Oxford University Press, 1965. A translation that includes writings of Thomasius, Isaak Dorner, and Alois Biedermann.

Wheelwright, Philip. *The Burning Fountain: A Study in the Language of Symbolism.* Bloomington, Ind.: Indiana University Press, 1954.

_____. *Metaphor and Reality.* Bloomington, Ind.: Indiana University Press, 1962.

White, Leland Jennings. *Christ and the Christian Movement: Jesus in the New Testament, the Creeds and Modern Theology.* New York: Alba House, 1985.

Wilson, W. R. *The Execution of Jesus.* New York: Charles Scribner's Sons, 1970.

Woods, Richard. *Eckhart's Way.* Wilmington, Del.: Michael Glazier, 1986.

Woshienko, Nicholas. *Christ's Human Knowledge According to the Theology of St. Thomas.* Ph.D. diss. Boston University, 1979.

Yoder, John Howard. *The Politics of Jesus.* Grand Rapids, Mich.: William B. Eerdmans Publishing Co., 1972.

Young, Frances. *From Nicaea to Chalcedon: A Guide to the Literature and Its Background.* Philadelphia: Fortress Press, 1983.

Zimmerli, W. and Joachim Jeremias. *The Servant of God.* Naperville, Ill.: Alec Allenson, 1957.